Educational Facilities

Educational Facilities

Planning, Modernization, and Management

Fifth Edition

Richard Bauscher and E. Michael Poe

ROWMAN & LITTLEFIELD
Lanham • Boulder • New York • London

This book was previously published by Pearson Education, Inc.

Published by Rowman & Littlefield
A wholly owned subsidiary of The Rowman & Littlefield Publishing Group, Inc.
4501 Forbes Boulevard, Suite 200, Lanham, Maryland 20706
www.rowman.com

Unit A, Whitacre Mews, 26–34 Stannary Street, London SE11 4AB

British Library Cataloguing in Publication Information Available

Library of Congress Cataloging-in-Publication Data Is Available

ISBN 978-1-4758-3004-0 (cloth: alk. paper)
ISBN 978-1-4758-3005-7 (pbk: alk. paper)
ISBN 978-1-4758-3006-4 (electronic)

∞™ The paper used in this publication meets the minimum requirements of American National Standard for Information Sciences—Permanence of Paper for Printed Library Materials, ANSI/ NISO Z39.48–1992.

Printed in the United States of America

Contents

Acknowledgments

The authors would like to recognize Dr. Basil Castaldi for his pioneering work in school facilities. Even though Dr. Castaldi passed away in 1999, his writings still stand in regard to the important work of planning and maintaining school facilities and are the basis for our current work of this textbook.

Part I

THEORY AND PRINCIPLES
OF PLANNING

Chapter 1

The Evolution of Educational Facilities

It should be stated at the outset that this book is envisioned as a broad-based guide for a wide array of school officials, school boards of education, school administrators, school maintenance personnel, educational consultants, students of school administration, facilities directors, and school architects. The text is organized so that readers may refer only to the sections that are of high interest to them.

Part of this book deals with curriculum development—principles of learning applicable to the planning of school facilities that promise innovations in educational methodology. Another part concentrates on the process and activities related to the identification of educational needs for the foreseeable future. A third focus of this publication is on the actual planning of a specific type of school facility that has been recommended by the school board.

Such a recommendation by school officials may involve the construction of a new facility or the modernization of an existing school building. A fourth new section deals with the strategies of getting a levy committee organized and set up to pass a school bond referendum. Lastly this book includes materials on the maintenance and operation of a school building and on techniques for saving energy.

This book looks at educational facilities from both a theoretical and a practical point of view to meet the needs of both the student and the practitioner. Students preparing for positions in educational administration will be interested in the principles that underlie the suggested application of the theory. Practicing school administrators such as superintendents of schools, school principals, and deans of administration will find the variety of specific and pragmatic suggestions of immediate value. This dualism of purpose, however, should not be construed to mean that students are not interested in practice or that practitioners see little or no value in theory.

As a practical matter, the student frequently has more time to examine the "why" of the practice, while the hard-pressed practicing administrator—who often must provide an immediate solution to a problem—has little time to deal with theory.

In the first case, the objective is to arrive at a feasible ideal solution through the application of accepted principles. In the second instance, school administrators seek to find practical answers in the shortest possible time, using the theory and principles to support their recommendations to their respective school boards. Principles and concrete solutions to problems are not mutually exclusive. Each reader will place a different emphasis on theory or practice depending upon the situation.

For example, the school principal who is asked to submit a set of recommendations to the superintendent of schools within a few days as to how he/she could best use his/her present school building under a given set of circumstances would find it very helpful to focus immediately on the suggested practices that apply to his/her problem. In preparing this report, however, he/she would find it advantageous to review the principles and theory appropriate to his or her situation in order to support his/her recommendations.

Clearly theory and practice are mutually supportive. The student needs some knowledge of the practices to better understand the theory, and the practitioner can take advantage of certain basic principles to bolster his or her recommendations. Principles and practices serve both the student and the practitioner.

THE "THINGS" OF EDUCATION

For centuries, very little attention was given to the "things of education." Education was envisioned primarily as people—teachers and learners. School buildings were incidental to the learning process. Wherever the Athenian teacher could conveniently hold a discussion with a small group of learners, that was where the school was. Education was primitive and uncomplicated in those days. Parents simply selected a teacher and sent only their boys to him. Oftentimes the school was nothing more than a teacher and a few students meeting on the open stairs of an ancient temple.

Recent advances in instructional methodology, educational psychology, and learning technology have stimulated the development of a wide variety of effective teaching aids. These new instructional tools have had a profound effect on modern educational thinking about the "things of education." Today's school buildings are more sophisticated in design and function. More than just a shelter for its occupants, the school is a complete educational tool, capable of supporting a wide variety of learning experiences. The electronic revolution and the availability of sophisticated teaching aids have introduced a multitude of exciting and innovative features in the design of futuristic school buildings—from kindergarten to graduate school.

The new teaching devices are an important addition to the collection of educational hardware. Hardware alone, however, is educationally useless unless it is coupled with an ample supply of related educational software and professional development. Excellent school facilities and dedicated teachers are the basic ingredients of a good educational program. As important as "the things of education" may be, they do not produce first-rate instruction. It cannot be assumed that functionally designed school buildings containing a wide variety of modern teaching aids will automatically improve the quality of the educational programs.

The importance of skillful teachers cannot be overstated. On the other hand, a skillful teacher working in a well-designed and highly functional school building, supplied with a wide array of resources and technology, can achieve a level of instructional effectiveness that far exceeds what is possible when the necessary "things of education" are not provided.

EXTENDED USE OF EXISTING BUILDINGS

During the recent period of increasing birthrates and expanding school enrollments, the solution to overcrowded classrooms is, in most cases, a new, or addition to the school building. The major questions, under these circumstances, are what type of a new building and where should it be located? With taxes rising higher, and with a significant increase in taxpayer resistance to the construction of new school buildings, it might be extremely profitable to explore the ways and means of making existing buildings more educationally effective.

A way must be found to overcome obsolescence and to provide for a moderate increase in building capacity without overburdening the taxpayers of the school district. We must begin to look more seriously at the buildings we have. These buildings represent a sizable capital outlay, and every conceivable avenue should be explored to protect this investment without shortchanging the students.

As will be discussed in detail in chapter 13, remodeling is not always the most economical solution to the problem of obsolescence and additional capacity. On the other hand, we can no longer afford the luxury of abandoning school buildings simply because they are old, educationally obsolete, or both. No school buildings should be recommended for disposal by a school district until an in-depth study is made, and it is determined the building has no further value. Undoubtedly there are situations in which the cost of remodeling is not in the best financial interest of the school district over a fifty-year period, but would adequately meet short-range needs.

For example, a heavily bonded school district might have two options. It could remodel an existing building for $5,000,000 with an expected useful life of fifteen years, or it could construct a new one for $8,000,000 with an expected useful life of sixty years. Simple mathematics dictates that the new eight-million-dollar building is the "better buy." However, let us, for a moment, examine the financial impact of these two options on the school district. The school district is already heavily in debt and is paying for a number of recently constructed school buildings. Taxes for other services are also high. Its tax leeway is approaching an alarming level.

Under these circumstances, would it be better to consider some form of installment purchasing to provide for its educational needs? Build what is needed in the foreseeable future for the smallest capital outlay and accept the interest that must be paid, because the school district is not in a position to take full advantage of long-range financial benefits.

Admittedly, this approach is pragmatic, but more and more school districts will be confronted with a similar situation in the not-too-distant future. The recent period of rapid enrollment growth has left many school districts in precarious financial straits. For some time to come, such school districts must make the best use of existing facilities until they can recover some of their borrowing MV (market value) potential.

PROTECTING THE CAPITAL INVESTMENT
OF THE SCHOOL DISTRICT

Maintaining the educational efficiency and the aesthetic attractiveness of school buildings, concerns both educators and school boards. But new buildings do not always fare
too well in this regard. Understandably, the public often assumes that a new building
requires little or no further attention. Actually, a building is new only when the keys
are turned over to the school board. From that day forward, it starts to get old. The
mechanical equipment begins to wear, the intensity of the artificial lighting visibly
declines, metal surfaces tarnish, and painted areas accumulate a film of condensed air
pollutants. The well-known aging process has set in.

These changes are slow, subtle, natural, and cumulative. In addition, normal use accentuates the problem of maintenance. Students contribute to the soiling of floors and walls and the
expected wear and tear on surfaces. Also, there is a substantial amount of unpredictable damage, due to abuse or misuse of the building or teaching equipment. Consequently, new school
buildings may deteriorate due to lack of proper maintenance.

A long-range program of preventive and restorative maintenance that protects
the initial capital outlay is important to the school district. Maintenance should be
conceived of as an ongoing activity designed to keep the educational function and
environment of a school building at peak efficiency. This is more likely to result in
maximum educational return per maintenance dollar. Various suggestions concerning
the maintenance and operation of a school building are presented in chapter 15.

A HISTORICAL PERSPECTIVE ON EDUCATIONAL FACILITIES

Space for learning has undergone dramatic change over the past 2,000 years. In the
beginning there were no educational facilities at all. There were no classrooms, and
there were no desks and chairs. Plato and Aristotle met with students to exchange
and discuss ideas in the open air at any convenient location, perhaps in the shade of
a temple or a wall. Since then, educational facilities have become effective laboratories of learning, where teachers and students benefit from the latest advances in
educational technology and instructional methodology. The once rudimentary space
for learning is now a complex enclosure that controls the environment and supports
the learning process.

It is difficult to imagine that school architecture is a relatively recent development. In fact, prior to World War II, school buildings were not viewed as specialized
public buildings. Some of them reflected Greek or Roman architecture. Others were
simple, uncomplicated nondescript buildings housing a rather traditional curriculum.
Schools were generally utilitarian structural envelopes that simply protected teachers
and pupils from the elements. In essence, they were shelters in which teachers cited
and pupils recited, and where the "things of education consisted primarily of benches,
tables, books, pencils, paper, pens, and perhaps a slate blackboard."

At the risk of reiterating certain historical facts that are quite familiar to many
educators, it is fascinating to examine the development of educational facilities over

the centuries in relation to corresponding educational practices. Until recently, little or no attempt was made to design school buildings for specific educational functions. It may take some readers by surprise to learn that school buildings did not become architectural entities until the middle of the twentieth century!

For centuries architects envisioned architecture as an overall science of building construction without a view to school design per se. Until recent times, a school building was not considered a vehicle of architectural expression. In fact, school buildings did not attract the serious attention of architects until mass education was established in many countries about a century ago.

The development of architecture in relation to school buildings is traced through three periods of history. The first is the Hellenistic Era. Although there was some development of church grammar schools in Italy, France, Germany, and England during the fifteenth and sixteenth centuries, a review of the historical literature reveals no special interest in school facilities as a form of architecture at that time. Consequently, the second phase of this type of study jumps to the early American and post–Civil War period. The third phase is the twenty-first century.

THE TWENTIETH AND TWENTY-FIRST CENTURIES

The Consolidated School Movement

At the turn of the twentieth century, the size and shape of American schoolhouses were greatly influenced by the consolidation movement that spread rapidly throughout the country. Thousands of one-room schoolhouses were abandoned immediately following World War I, and students were transported to so-called grammar schools housing grades one through eight. Kindergartens were included in a few urban school systems.

The consolidation movement was directly responsible for the rapid development of multi-classroom school buildings. They appeared in various shapes and sizes. For the most part, they continued to serve primarily as shelters designed to protect students from the weather. The interiors remained simple and rudimentary with copious blackboards and screwed-down furniture.

The Emergence of School Architecture

According to Roth,

> Schools were either castles or palaces and their architectural style either Gothic, Renaissance, or Baroque, or a combination of styles. Whatever their shapes or forms were, they in no way resembled a school (in the functional sense). The child's own scale was not taken into consideration, either practically or emotionally. Out-sized entrances, corridors, stairways seem to be particularly selected by the architect for his/her "artistic" effects with the well-meant aim of contributing to the child's education in art.
>
> It would be wrong and unfair to blame the architect alone. The absence of unbiased pedagogical conceptions, and of a curriculum based on them were as much a cause of

mistaken evolution, as was the lack of close collaboration between the architect, educator and building authorities.[1] During this past period of time, schoolhouses were, for the most part, not architecturally exciting. The effect of European architecture was noticeable in some school buildings (figure 1.1), and a few schools built earlier in the century did reflect the classical influence, but the majority of them were structures without architectural character.

Many looked like large boxes enclosed by red brick walls and covered by a steep slanted roof. The large boxes were subdivided into four or eight smaller, uniform cubicles called classrooms. Sometimes the attic space under the slate roof was used as an assembly hall. At that time, these buildings undoubtedly represented the best conceivable answer to the school housing problem, but, as Roth points out, neither the architects nor the educators really had a clear understanding of the educational tasks to be accomplished.[2]

In the twenty-first century, many educators and architects are now becoming aware of the need for functional planning of school buildings. Unfortunately, a few school boards and school administrators still do not recognize the need for cooperative action between educators and architects. Some school districts still ask an architect to design a school on the basis of the information listed on a single sheet of paper. This information may include the grade level and number of pupils to be housed in a school and, perhaps, the number of the various types of special spaces desired.

To ask an architect to design a school without giving him/her a complete set of educational specifications requiring perhaps fifty or sixty pages of programming information is ridiculous and unfair. Until it is generally recognized that educational facility planning is a team operation involving architects, educators, and boards of education, many schools will continue to be built to meet housing, rather than instructional, needs, and many will include the shortcomings of the schools of yesterday and today. According to Roth: "The development of school buildings up to the present time must be considered faulty for, indeed, it has not achieved the standard required by sound and valid pedagogic principles."[3]

Figure 1.1.   The Classical American School

During the latter part of the twentieth century and early into the twenty-first century, the development of school buildings was rapid, innovative, and dramatic. Immediately following World War II, architects became quite excited about "bringing the outside into the building." Accordingly, large expanses of window walls and skylights were built into school buildings. Beautiful vistas and natural light in great quantities were the order of the day. This development created problems of controlling heat buildup within the buildings during certain parts of the year and glare from direct and reflected sunlight.

The 1960s ushered in the era of the "finger design." Energy losses and gains were very high due to the large expanses of outside walls. But, with a plentiful supply of inexpensive energy at that time, this design posed no significant problems. During the 1970s, air conditioning of school buildings was widely accepted. But, due to the large amounts of energy required for air conditioning, architects became greatly concerned with the heat gain of a school building during hot days when air conditioning was required. In order to solve this problem, architects introduced the controversial "windowless" school.

Finally, the enormous increase in the cost of energy following the Iranian Revolution in the 1970s introduced a multitude of changes in the design of educational facilities for the purpose of conserving energy and facilitating energy management. These and other developments are discussed in detail in various parts of this text.

The Formation of an Educational Facility Council

In 1921, three concerned educators—Samuel Challman of Minnesota, Charles McDermott of New Jersey, and Frank H. Wood of New York—met in a hotel room in Atlantic City to discuss the possible formation of an organization to deal with the problems of school plant planning. The original intent of the proposed organization was "to promote the establishment of reasonable standards for school buildings and equipment with due regard for economy of expenditure, dignity of design, utility of space, healthful conditions, and safety of human life."[4]

The above-mentioned triumvirate together with other concerned educators met a year later, in 1922, and created a national organization to develop minimum standards of school building construction and equipment from the standpoint of meeting educational needs. The members of the group agreed to meet from time to time to share ideas and to collectively prepare specifications to serve as national standards for school construction and equipment. The founders named this embryonic organization the National Council on Schoolhouse Construction (the Council).

For over a quarter of a century, the Council, as it was often called, served as an information center for anyone engaged in the planning of school buildings. Its primary function was to develop minimum standards for school building construction and make them available to school plant planners.

In 1930, however, the Council introduced a new service for school administrators throughout the United States and Canada. Instead of simply responding to requests for information, it began publishing guides for the use of anyone engaged in a school building program. These guides focused primarily on the dissemination of specific minimum standards for the planning and construction of school buildings.

The impact of these guides on the planning of school buildings was overwhelming. The influence of the Council on schoolhouse construction far exceeded the expectations of its founders. School districts began to rely more and more on the Council for technical information concerning the planning of school buildings. Under these circumstances, the Council felt that it had an obligation to reexamine the content of its guides and to reevaluate its goals and objectives.

Thus, in 1946, the Council set new policies and guidelines for material contained in its publications. Fearing that minimum standards might become maximum practice, the Council de-emphasized minimum standards and promoted basic principles of sound educational facility planning in all of its subsequent publications. The main thrust of the new policies was to encourage innovation and creativity in the planning of educational facilities. The Council also broadened the scope of educational facility planning. It changed the designation of "school building planning" to "school plant planning" by including the school site as an integral part of the planning.

Over the years, the Council has been a positive and dynamic force in the field of educational facility planning. The Council has been flexible and innovative in meeting the challenges of an unsettled society. The influence and membership of the Council has grown dramatically. The name of the National Council on Schoolhouse Construction was changed to the Council of Educational Facility Planners International (CEFPI). Its membership is no longer restricted to educators and education-related persons. It has a roster of hundreds of members, including persons from a wide variety of disciplines. Little did the three founders of the Council ever dream in 1921 that their brainchild would ultimately influence the nature of school buildings throughout the world.

DISCUSSION QUESTIONS

1   What are some of the new technological teaching devices that are being added into our schools?
2   What are some of the differences that school architects today are now making which allows for these new technological teaching devices to function properly?
3   How are our schools being utilized by outside groups (to appease the taxpayers) during non-school hours?
4   Define what the CEFPI is. Are they active in your region?

NOTES

1. Alfred Roth, *The New School* (New York: Frederick Prager, 1957), p. 26.
2. Ibid.
3. Ibid., p. 24.
4. *Guide for Planning School Plants*. National Council on Schoolhouse Construction (now Council of Educational Facility Planners International) (Nashville, TN: Peabody College, 1953). Foreword.

Chapter 2

Educational Practices and Technological Developments

Both administrative policy and classroom methodology have some bearing on the design of educational facilities. Almost without exception, planners routinely provide for those classroom practices that are already operating in the school district. But they do not always include other innovative concepts that are likely to improve the educational learning experience. A few of these neoteric concepts and practices are presented here. They and others can be examined for possible implementation during the planning stages of an educational facility.

PREVALENT EDUCATIONAL PRACTICES RELATED TO EDUCATIONAL FACILITY PLANNING

Many exciting educational practices are being introduced from time to time in various school districts. Some are the product of imaginative classroom teachers who are on a never-ending search for more effective teaching methods. Others are conceived in more theoretical settings in colleges and universities. Regardless of their origin, some new educational concepts eventually become an accepted part of the curriculum.

Innovations are proposed and applied in quick succession. Curriculum seems to be in a constant state of flux. Some concepts are terminated, some are continued, and new ones are introduced. Educators jokingly point out that, if one makes no changes for a sufficiently long time, present practices will someday be seen as promising innovations. Under this recycling concept, a traditional school system could become a pioneer in education, simply by waiting for the others to complete their cycle. Many educators compare curriculum to a pendulum: as public attitudes and values change, the curriculum changes with it. It should not come as a complete surprise, therefore, when an old concept is revived and reintroduced in the school curriculum.

It is sometimes assumed that all innovative practices and imaginative concepts are good because they are new and exciting. This position is not always tenable, however. Some innovations are readily accepted. They persist over a number of years. Some that are tried and dropped without much fanfare are considered fads. Others continue in practice in an atmosphere of uncertainty and controversy. In past years

11

"the windowless school concept" and "the open space plan" have been subjected to considerable controversy. Their popularity has come and gone as many schools have been renovated to add natural light/windows and to close in classrooms.

The design of functional futuristic school buildings requires superhuman capabilities. School plant planners should not only be superbly endowed with creative powers but they should also be able to clearly distinguish between those educational concepts and practices that will persist for a long time and those that are likely to be short-lived. Obviously, it is humanly impossible to perform this task with any degree of certainty. At best, planners can study a large number of concepts and practices and identify those that best fit into the philosophy of the parents who will have their children served in the proposed school building(s).

The concepts and practices that follow are judged to be educationally sound and administratively feasible. But educational facility planners should not limit themselves to this small list. Other ideas should be considered. On the other hand, innovations should not be incorporated simply because they appear to be new and exciting. In some instances, it might be wise not to introduce new practices upon the completion of a new or modernized school building, particularly if the community, the staff, and the students are not yet ready for such changes. In these instances, school plant planners should design the school building to be flexible so that these features could be added at a later date.

Promising Instructional Practices

Negotiated Learning

The concept of negotiated learning is not new. It is a revival of the learning methods familiarly known as "the contract method," "independent study," or "multioption instruction." The application of these concepts has much merit for those students who can profit from them. In general, their success depends upon the skill of the teacher in preparing and using well-conceived units of instruction and upon the initiative and resourcefulness of the student. When both are present, the results from this approach to individualized instruction can be gratifying to both teacher and student. Negotiated learning allows the student to participate in shaping the learning experiences that he or she will undergo in achieving certain predetermined educational outcomes that may be in harmony with personal goals.

Implications for School Plant Planning

There are no special design features associated with this concept. Obviously, it requires a faculty workroom of about 600 square feet (depending on the number of teachers that are assigned to the school). Thus, where the teachers' workroom is provided, nothing special is required to accommodate them.

To learn on an individual basis, students need space in which to study, experiment, and discuss. Classrooms need to be about 900 square feet with flexible furniture to allow group and individual instruction to take place at any time during the day.

The Laboratory Classroom Combo Concept

The laboratory concept can be applied to any learning situation requiring students to perform experiments, gain skills, or conduct demonstrations of basic principles—for example, science laboratories, food service laboratories, and engineering science laboratories. This approach is not overly complicated but the cost is higher since most of them are around 1,400 square feet. This style lets the teachers of these subjects have a part of the room to lecture in and then they can easily move to the lab work (within their same room) without having to check a lab out or share one with the adjoining teacher.

Cooperative Learning

Cooperative or collaborative learning is a version of the old practice of students learning from each other. It is a group process whereby students share information, understandings, and experiences in a small group setting. The role of individual members of the group may vary from one group to another depending upon the purpose underlying the operation of each subject area. A cooperative learning group may perform as a heterogeneous team in which each member functions as an individual interacting with other members of the team.

Or, the group may operate in a teammate mode in which the performance of each member contributes toward the achievement of the group as a whole in accordance with goals set forth by its members. Finally, the team may function as a team-interdependent group whereby each team engages in friendly competition with other teams having similar goals and objectives.

From the standpoint of educational facility planning, most classrooms can accommodate these activities associated with cooperative learning without much difficulty. The rearrangement of where the book shelves and storage cabinets are placed can often provide the necessary spatial separation for independent group activities conducted within a classroom. While the success of cooperative learning depends largely on the resourcefulness of the classroom teacher, the selection of highly mobile furniture and cabinets facilitates the implementation of this instructional activity.

Students teaching one another, however, is not a new concept. It is perhaps as old as teaching itself. It is not unusual to find students teaching concepts or skills on an informal basis to one or two of their peers. This practice is beneficial to both the teaching student and to those being taught. The teaching student strengthens his/her knowledge or skills in order to transmit them clearly to his/her peers, while the learners profit from having concepts explained in simple language that they can readily understand.

Relevant Administrative Policies and Concepts

The Variable Group Size Teaching for Secondary Schools

One intriguing concept being considered for secondary school instruction could replace the conventional instruction of students in classes or sections. Under the variable group size concept, primary attention is given to the curriculum and the individual learning experiences that it includes. The entire curriculum is analyzed to determine the most effective group size for each learning experience. Such an analysis would clearly indicate that, for some experiences, a 1:1 ratio is best: one teacher instructing a single student.

For other types of learning, the ratio might well be one teacher for three or four students, or one teacher to fifteen learners. For still others, the ratio could be one teacher to as many as 150 or 300 students. This approach treats learning in a realistic and sensible fashion, providing for tutoring where it is needed and for large-group instruction where that is effective. The overall cost of instruction to the school district is not changed materially under this plan. The increased cost of teaching groups smaller than the conventional twenty-five or thirty students is offset by the saving in instructional time when a single teacher teaches large groups of 150 or more students.

Implications for School Plant Planning

School plant planners should give serious thought to this concept in designing schools. It goes much further than the mere installation of randomly scattered, movable partitions throughout the building. Such half-measures are not justifiable. It would be wiser to include destructible partitions or garage-type doors that work electronically rather than costly movable ones that are not secure.

A school building planned for variable class size must contain spaces that can be divided and subdivided easily by the teacher at any time. The major requirement, in this instance, is a system of interlocking operable partitions having a noise reduction coefficient of about 38 decibels. Spaces should be capable of accommodating groups of 6, 15, 30, 60, 90, 150, and 300 students.

The number of spaces required for groups of a given size depends upon the nature of the educational program. It is suggested that the following formula be used to determine the requisite number of *instructional areas* (not rooms):

$$T = \frac{E}{C} \times \frac{n}{N}$$

where:
T = Number of areas needed (rounded off to the closest whole number)
E = Total number of students requiring space for a given group size
C = Number of students in a given group or class
n = Number of minutes that a given group size meets per week
N = Number of minutes in the school week

Example: Let us assume that an elementary school program calls for 275 students to meet in groups of 16 for 10 percent of the time. Suppose further that there are 1,500 minutes in the school week based on a 5-hour school day. The students would meet 150 minutes per week (10 percent of 1,500) in groups of 16.

$$T = (1.25)\frac{275}{16} \times \frac{150}{1,500} = 1.25(17.19)(0.1) = 2.15 \ teaching \ stations$$

   This means that two areas (teaching stations) will be required on a full-time basis to satisfy the needs of 275 students divided in groups of 16. The computation is repeated for all of the other groupings. The total number of areas needed is the sum of the individual computations.

The Variable Class Size Concept for Elementary and Middle Schools

Some educators agree that certain learning experiences in elementary and middle schools can be imparted just as effectively to groups of 150, 75, and 50 as they can to the conventional group of 25. On the other hand, there are some learning situations in which the traditional group of 25 is far too large. In fact, a ratio of one student to one teacher is required for transmission of certain skills in special services or therapy sessions. There may be other learning experiences where the group should consist of 2 or 3, 6 or 8, or 12 to 15 students.

Implications for School Plant Planning

In view of the growing acceptance that grouping for instruction should vary according to the character or complexity of the learning activity, educators have begun planning elementary and middle school buildings to accommodate groupings of various sizes. Teachers are being provided with small rooms (with windows in their classroom) where they can work with individual students. A few small seminar-type rooms that can be subdivided by permanent operable partitions are being included in elementary schools to meet the need for small group instruction. Conventional classrooms are being designed so that three or four of them can be joined to form a large instructional space for a single group with the use of operable garage-type doors or sliding sound proof divider walls.

Modular Scheduling

For years educators have shown a keen interest in some form of modular scheduling. Under this concept, unit modules vary in length from 15 to 20 to 22 or 30 minutes. The number of minutes is immaterial. It is the number of modules included in a time block that is significant. Time blocks vary in size, depending upon the nature of the learning. Two or more unit modules may comprise a single time block for a given teaching period on certain days of the week. Consequently, the length of time a student spends in a given class may vary from day to day.

   From time to time, educators have expressed fears that high school students would become confused under a schedule that varied from hour to hour and from day to day. In practice, however, these fears are unfounded. In one school district, for example, modular scheduling was introduced in the middle school. When asked as to how students managed to remember their schedule as it changed from day to day, the answer was simple: each student was asked to make a copy of his or her schedule and paste it inside their locker door. Thus, every morning each student was reminded of his or her schedule for the day. Electronic calendars now make this an even easier process.

Implications for School Plant Planning

Modular scheduling greatly increases the movement of students during the school day. Under traditional secondary school scheduling, students move from one location to another at intervals ranging from 45 to 60 minutes. If modular scheduling is employed, students move much more frequently. Under these conditions, special attention should be given to student circulation patterns and to the design/width of corridors that expedite student movement. The walls separating the corridors from classrooms and laboratories should be soundproofed in order to minimize disturbances for students engaged in classroom activities while other students are traveling from one room to another.

Team Teaching

The idea of team teaching goes much further than the cooperative efforts of teachers currently practiced in conventional schools, and the structure and procedures associated with the implementation of this concept are receiving greater attention. A team of teachers with talents and abilities in different fields of instruction can develop the curriculum and methodology most likely to achieve the objectives set cooperatively by the team itself and by the school administration. The school designed for team teaching should provide a small meeting space where three or four teachers can plan together, space where a single teacher can prepare materials for large-group presentation, and work space where other types of instructional materials can be produced.

Implications for School Plant Planning

A seminar/meeting room of about 300 square feet should be provided for each of the two teams. Several workrooms having an area of approximately 400 square feet should be planned, preferably in the library. Team teaching can also be effective in schools that cannot convert several traditional classrooms into a single large one. When large-group instruction is desired, such schools can use the auditorium, multi-purpose room, or cafeteria. Schools designed for convertibility of ordinary spaces into larger or smaller ones, however, possess the flexibility essential to the application of the concept of variable group size, discussed previously.

The Open Campus

Some secondary schools are implementing the open campus concept to provide greater student freedom. Under this concept, students are treated as adults. They are allowed to engage in a wide variety of activities within the building and, in some cases, may even leave school if they have no class in a given period. On the face of it, the concept has considerable merit. It should make students responsible for using their time wisely.

The open campus concept, however, could become a nightmare. In one particular secondary school, students were permitted complete freedom within the building during their free periods. While students could work in the library, go to a study area, or confer with a faculty member, most of them, in this instance, chose to socialize in the corridors. These corridors were so noisy that conducting classes in these areas was impossible.

Some of the students engaged in all sorts of pranks. It was reported that a teacher in a room adjoining a noisy corridor heard a loud pounding noise coming from the direction of the corridor. Upon investigation, the teacher discovered that two or three boys had stuffed a girl into one of the large corridor lockers reserved for faculty storage.

Vandalism became a problem because students given a greater latitude of freedom were not provided with activities in advance. This picture seems gloomy. The above describes an actual situation, and the lesson to be learned is, "Don't institute an open campus in a facility that is not designed for it." It was not the philosophy of giving students greater freedom that was faulty, but the lack of facilities that would permit students to use this freedom wisely.

When a school facility is in the planning stages, consideration of movement and circulation should be considered if the open campus concept is to be adopted. In existing school buildings, the introduction of the open campus concept should be delayed until proper facilities can be provided. Without such spaces, the open campus concept can become a real disappointment.

Implications for School Plant Planning

The open campus concept requires spaces for a wide variety of activities. These spaces can provide educationally enriching experiences for many students enrolled in a secondary school. A secondary school housing the open campus concept should:

1   provide two or three classrooms where instructional videos are shown throughout the school day. Any student who has a free period can choose one of these videos to watch.
2   include two or three video-reviewing rooms. Each room's video should be set to one of the major network stations.
3   provide a student lounge where students can socialize. This space should be planned for some form of passive supervision.
4   include a snack bar meeting nutritional guidelines.
5   feature a recreation room with Ping-Pong tables and other equipment.
6   be designed so that noisy spaces do not interfere with the instructional process in other parts of the building.
7   be planned to minimize vandalism. There should be no isolated, out-of-the-way alcoves, rooms, or corridors where students could loiter.
8   take full advantage of glass walls. These isolate noise but maintain visual contact among students.

The Open Space Plan

Despite the great deal of national interest in the design of school buildings without partitions, some educators are beginning to have second thoughts. There are many strong arguments favoring the open space plan and an equal number of good reasons against it. Most objective planners have mixed feelings and usually compromise in designing school buildings. The single large space is interrupted only by supporting columns, including a number of partial walls—floor to ceiling—supplemented by folding partitions. Both sides of this issue will be discussed in detail next.

For the Open Space Plan

The large expanse of space is psychologically liberating. One feels free in both movement and thought. Since partitions are often light, movable visual screens, the spaces for instruction *can* be changed in size and shape at will and at once. The omission of solid walls allegedly reduces the cost of the building substantially. The open space plan lends a feeling of informality to the learning process. Students feel less regimented. There is likely to be a greater intermingling of both students and teachers. The open space plan facilitates the grouping and regrouping of students and tends to encourage change, experimentation, and innovation.

Against the Open Space Plan

Confusion and a laissez-faire attitude are often present in the "school without walls." Since there are no corridors under the open space plan, students simply roam from area to area, passing from one teaching space to and through another. Although there are as yet no validated research findings on the quantity and quality of learning in the open space plan, it can be hypothesized that the amount of learning is open to question. From a first-hand qualitative study of the open plan school, one may find oneself straining to hear the teacher from a position in the rear of the room. After two or three hours, fatigue would set in.

In discussing the open space plan with students, all seemed to like it, but two major shortcomings were identified by students. Subjects that require concentration are more difficult for students to master. Students complained particularly of mathematics. The subject matter was not usually very exciting, while the topic on the other side of the screen seemed more interesting. Also, sufficient whiteboards for student work was lacking.

The other serious drawback concerned audiovisual materials that are clearly incompatible with the open space plan. One school administrator had a ready-made solution: construct three audiovisual rooms. The open "classroom" is not used while the class is in the audiovisual room, so any savings in walls are spent in constructing audiovisual rooms to supplement the open space plan. Many teachers liked the "liberated" feeling of the open space plan but stated that constant background noise forced them to concentrate so much on hearing that they were physically fatigued by the end of the day.

Implications for School Plant Planning

The open space plan is a mixed blessing. Ideally, it would be desirable to plan space in such a way that the open plan atmosphere and informality could be produced whenever it was desired, and effective teaching spaces could be created through the single operation of garage-type doors when it was educationally advantageous to do so. Imaginative school planners may wish to face the challenge of designing a school facility that contains the advantages of the open space plan without its deficiencies. Training for teachers in how to appropriately utilize an open concept space is a must.

Flexibility in Space

The proponents of the open space plan also extol the virtues of flexibility in space. While this is theoretically possible, faculty members using the open space plan indicated that the space allocated to a given class activity is rarely changed in actual practice. From a practical point of view, the "flexible" space becomes almost inflexible. In a given high school, the open space plan consisted of the space normally occupied by twenty-nine conventional classrooms plus space for corridors. Spaces for classes were loosely related to patches of colored tile on the floor. The colored patches also served an aesthetic function. Classes were located randomly within the open space.

A mathematics class, for example, could adjoin an English class, a social studies class, and a foreign language class. Under these conditions, increasing the space in one class could not be done without encroaching on the space occupied by another group of students. Thus, the potential flexibility that was built into the open space plan could not be realized under normal operating conditions. In fairness to the open space plan, however, if a comprehensive team teaching approach were employed in the instructional program, flexibility of space could be achieved. On the other hand, the degree of flexibility in a conventional building is limited by the number, length, and arrangement of permanent folding partitions or garage-type doors and the configuration of the walls in a given area.

The School-within-a-School Concept

Under the school-within-a-school concept, a large secondary school is envisioned as two or more secondary schools operating independently on the same school site. Each school has students randomly assigned to it at all grade levels. Each school has its own administrative guidance and teaching personnel, and each is planned to operate as though it were located separately in another part of the school district.

For at least a decade, the school-within-a-school idea has been gaining considerable support. In areas where the population is so concentrated that enrollments in excess of 1,500 students must be educated at one location, this concept, sometimes called the "house plan," should be seriously explored. A word of caution is in order, however. Some school districts resort to the school-within-a-school concept, not because of high population density, but because they may want a single football or basketball team—an indefensible rationale for planning any kind of high school.

After all, some students must be transported over fairly long distances if 2,500 students are to be enrolled in one school. The money spent in transporting pupils from home to this larger school represents a necessary but noneducational expenditure, and such funds, whether they are from state or local sources, might be better utilized in direct support of the educational program.

Implications for School Plant Planning

When a secondary school is likely to have an enrollment of more than 1,500 students, school boards and school planners should seek to provide multiple school plants in two or more parts of the school district. A superintendent of schools once defended the planning of a single large high school in a sparsely settled school district by pointing out that students were bussed anyway. So "What difference does it make?"

Actually, it makes a considerable difference in cost, much more than the superintendent implied. In this situation, two secondary schools would have cut the bus mileage almost in half, not to mention the time students spent on the buses. Unless there is a compelling reason for building secondary schools with capacities greater than 1,500, the planning of one or more 1,200-student secondary schools should be given serious consideration.

FUTURISTIC TECHNO-EDUCATIONAL SYSTEMS

It can be assumed, a priori, that the design of educational facilities reflects the educational thinking and architectural philosophy at the time when school facilities are proposed, planned, conceived, and constructed. The end product at any given time represents a blending of prevailing architectural concepts, dominant educational practices, and promising curricular innovations. The well-planned educational facility not only provides for the accepted and conventional educational practices that are widespread at that time but also includes features that can accommodate a few of the more promising foreseeable educational concepts. There are many well-designed and educationally effective technological teaching devices on the market. They range from a simple laptop computer to a smart board to interactive LCDs.

The next generation of technology marks the beginning of the widespread use of supplementary instructional devices. The development of high-intensity LED light bulbs inaugurated a new era in projection techniques. Most schools are aiming for a 1:1 ratio of computer devices (laptops, desktops, iPads, etc.) to students.

Today, electronic teaching devices have become extremely sophisticated and highly specialized. A few of them are programmable and many are completely automated. Once they are started, the equipment requires no further attention.

New exciting technological devices, however, have yet to be fully exploited. To be sure, educators are aware of their capabilities and potential, but their future use depends upon the adaptability of the teachers and upon the ingenuity of school administrators to provide staffing, equipment, necessary software, and in-service on its usage. These electronic devices are becoming rapidly attuned to the specific instructional techniques underlying the educational process. According to Van Horn, "New instructional delivery systems will generate a new sense of hope in our schools, because (now) we have a way to increase the useful work of schools exponentially."[1]

The computers are well recognized as invaluable educational tools. In addition to their ability for communicating information to students, those devices are perfectly suited for assisting in a wide variety of teaching techniques currently available in many school systems. Curriculum planners now have the challenge to capitalize on these new devices and sophisticated software.

Emerging Instructional Delivery Systems

Software, also known as courseware, is being developed to cover an entire curriculum in many fields of education. Some of the developers of such courseware work directly with school districts in creating programs that are tailor-made for their needs. These learning systems are referred to as Integrated Learning Systems (ILS) or Integrated Instructional Systems (IIS).

Schools have the use of satellites, cable, and fiber-optic transmission lines in providing educational capabilities that were only a dream years ago. These technologies made it possible to disseminate ILS programs, for example, over large geographical areas. They provide a practical and affordable vehicle for the enrichment of instructional programs in small school districts and in isolated one-room schools. Also, instructional programs are being transmitted via satellite or over fiber-optic lines received by microcomputers in homes, as well as in schools. Thus, homebound students can continue learning during periods of recuperation.

Social Media

School districts need to encourage collaboration with teachers, students, staff, parents, patrons, news media, and other community members through social networking. This can include (but is not limited to these sources):

1 Twitter
2 MySpace
3 Facebook
4 YouTube
5 Wiki
6 Flickr
7 Blogs
8 Web pages
9 Other means

Electronic communication and entertainment devices to communicate via the aforementioned sources should include (but are not limited to): smartphones, iPods, PDAs, pagers, MP3 players, media players, and other Bluetooth devices.

Electronic media applies to a broad category of technology that is constantly evolving. It includes all forms of social media, including (but again not limited to) text messaging (SMS), instant messaging (IM), electronic mail (e-mail), web logs (blog), electronic forums (chat rooms), video sharing (i.e., YouTube), comments on Twitter, and electronic media discussions.

School levies and voter-approved elections should utilize these sources as a way to connect and share informational content pertaining to the need for improved facilities. More information will be covered in chapter 14 on bond passage strategies.

School Design for Tomorrow's Technology

School districts need to recognize that access to technology in schools gives students and teachers greater opportunities to learn, engage, communicate, and develop skills that will prepare them for work, life, and citizenship.

School design in the twenty-first century must include the following (but not limited to these items):

- Broadband access to all schools
- Fiber-optic connections between the schools
- A secure network for storing, accessing, and online communication
- Dedicated power sources to run desktop computers, laptops, iPads, mobile devices, videoconferencing capabilities, online collaboration capabilities, message boards, e-mail, security cameras, and all other desired technology equipment

School district facilities/schools will need to provide their users with access to the: Internet, including websites, resources, content, and online tools. Additional square footage will need to be included in order to provide adequate room for switching, WiFi equipment, technology help desk, and for various work areas for the technology specialists.

DISCUSSION QUESTIONS

1 Define "modular scheduling." Is it currently being utilized in your school(s)?
2 Define the "school within a school" concept. How would that concept help a large high school with 2,500 students?
3 Is social media incorporated within your school(s)? If so, how and what is being utilized?
4 How will the design of a new school need to be defined to accommodate social media?

NOTE

1. Royal Van Horn, "Educational Power Tools: New Instructional Delivery Systems," *Phi Delta Kappan* (March 1991), p. 527.

Part II

PROCEDURES AND CRITERIA FOR LONG-RANGE PLANNING

Chapter 3

School Surveys

Education is a product of the dynamic culture in which we live. Like the changing society in which it thrives, education must continually change in response to the demands of our patrons. School districts are confronted periodically with the question of whether or not their schools are satisfying the current needs of society, a question that is often difficult to answer. The school survey method offers educators a promising technique for determining the extent to which our schools are meeting our nation's needs.

School surveys vary in profundity, in subject matter, and in method of execution, but they all have a number of elements in common. All surveys require relevant information about the school district, gathered and assembled in an orderly manner. School surveys usually include an interpretation and analysis of all pertinent data. They all contain a number of conclusions and a set of suggestions for the consideration of the school board, and some suggest a step-by-step plan of action.

THE NATURE AND CHARACTER OF SCHOOL SURVEYS

A school survey is the sine qua non of educational planning. No school district can plan intelligently for its future without first making a survey of its school system. A school district cannot be assured that it is spending public funds wisely, nor can it really know with certainty whether or not its students are being properly educated, without implementing a school survey. No school district can know whether it is receiving a reasonable educational return for the tax dollars it expends without some form of professional study. In fact, a school district that fails periodically to review its educational program, operating procedures, and future needs never really knows whether or not the educational goals set forth by the school board are being achieved.

Enlightened school administrators and forward-looking members of school boards are beginning to recognize that the school survey represents an intelligent and sound approach to educational planning. In fact, the school survey could be viewed as an essential element of the decision-making process in education. Long-range planning that stems from a school survey is more likely to be soundly based than are decisions made without the benefit of a systematic study of the school district and the education it offers.

According to Huxley, "Irrationally held truths may be more harmful than reasoned errors."[1] The survey technique provides a powerful means of removing many irrational notions from consideration in the development of a long-range plan. Yet it does not restrict action on matters that seem reasonable and logical, although some of these actions will inevitably fall into the category of "reasoned errors."

The school survey is not uniformly perceived by all educators. Some view it as an in-depth study of any or all matters related to education. Some regard it simply as an educational inventory of the school district. Others may use it to evaluate present practices within the school district for the purpose of effecting educational improvement. Some educators utilize the school survey as an objective and systematic approach to future planning, indeed as an application of the scientific method to the development of long-range educational plans. To still others it is a public relations device whereby the attention of members of boards, citizens, faculty, and staff becomes focused upon the goals of the school and the degree to which they are being attained by the school district. Educators generally agree, however, that a well-designed school survey reveals as objectively as possible the educational status of the school district and specifies the action required if the educational objectives of the school district are to be realized.

The principal purpose of most school surveys is to develop a long-range plan of action based upon an objective and systematic study of needs, resources, and educational goals of the school district. The findings, conclusions, and recommendations resulting from a school survey are presented in a written report to the school board. A realistic plan of action should be part of this report. According to Moser, "The purpose of many surveys is simply to provide someone with information."[2] In a school survey, that someone may be a school official, a school board member, or a citizen.

Distinctive Features of School Surveys

There are a number of compelling arguments for designing and running of a school survey. Many of the benefits of school studies are not immediately apparent to school officials or members of school boards. Nevertheless, the case for the school survey is quite impressive from the standpoint of improved education and the more efficient use of tax dollars. The survey method is a logical approach to the ever-present task of devising a well-reasoned plan of action that serves the best interest of the students, the public, and the taxpayers of a school district. A few of the fundamental considerations related to school surveys are as follows.

1   *The school survey creates a favorable psychological climate for making an objective study of the educational affairs of a school district.* A school study is generally perceived as a scientific and impartial approach to the examination and evaluation of matters related to education. Such studies should contain objective, professional judgments and a well-reasoned analysis of the educational operation. The psychological climate for educational progress is most favorable during a school survey. Local school officials and members of the board of education

usually maintain an open mind during a school survey. Action on major educational issues is often postponed pending the outcome of a survey, and decisions are more likely to be made on the basis of fact than emotion in school districts where school surveys have been conducted by competent people.

2   *The school survey offers an effective process for systematically assembling and analyzing data.* The survey process demands that meticulous attention be given to the gathering and analysis of all data. The validity and soundness of the survey recommendations are directly related to the care with which all of the basic data are assembled, compiled, analyzed, and evaluated. This methodical approach is an important aspect of the survey process.

3   *The school survey is an application of the scientific method of inquiry to educational problems.* In most school surveys, the data are gathered, analyzed, and evaluated. Then conclusions are drawn, and recommendations are formulated on the basis of these conclusions. Purposes and goals of the school system are clearly specified. In the school survey, existing educational practices in a school district are compared with those considered acceptable and desirable nationally. Recommendations developed in the survey are designed to correct any differences between observed and desired educational performance and to provide for any special educational needs of the community.

4   *The recommended long-range program resulting from a school survey is built almost entirely upon facts and logic.* In a school survey emotional forces are kept to a minimum. Expert-type surveys can be conducted without being unduly influenced by emotional attitudes related to local issues. Consultants working on expert-type surveys usually treat emotionally oriented information simply as one factor that must be taken into account in formulating a logical and realistic long-range plan for the school district.

5   *The school survey looks toward the future.* All too often, school districts live in a glory of their past. Some are interested in the present, and a few focus their attention on the immediate future, but only rarely do school districts plan, in detail; five to ten years in advance. Though the survey relies heavily on past experience and performance in the school district, it is concerned with both immediate and long-range needs. Through the process of extrapolation, it is possible to identify the educational needs five or ten years hence. The school survey rests solidly on the past, is shaped by the present, and projects logically into the future.

6   *The school survey puts all parts of the educational enterprise into proper perspective.* A school survey looks at all pertinent aspects of the educational undertaking. It includes an analysis and evaluation of all relevant information. A school study can disclose the status and quality of the educational program at the elementary, middle school, and senior high school levels at a given time. It can also reveal the articulation and relationships existing among these schools. Since a survey examines all facts that shape the overall effectiveness of the school system, each part of the educational enterprise may be viewed by itself and in relation to other parts of the school operation.

7   *The school survey may reveal inequalities of educational opportunity within a school district.* The comprehensive school survey, described later, includes an

examination of every classroom, every subject, and every course in the school district. In such a study, the differences between similar activities in different parts of the school district are readily apparent. For example, there may be two second-grade classrooms in two different buildings. One class may be taught in a small, poorly ventilated classroom in the basement, while the other is housed in a well-designed classroom that provides a wide variety of student experiences. The differences in the quality of educational opportunity are quickly revealed when such facts are presented in a survey report.

8 *The school survey enables school boards to plan on the basis of facts.* As mentioned earlier, the recommendations contained in school surveys stem from a professional analysis of the facts, not from opinions, hearsay, or public perceptions.

9 *The school survey represents a sound, businesslike approach to school operation.* Because of the decentralization of education in the United States, however, the enormity of school business is not always recognized. Although not a profit-making enterprise, school business does, indeed, represent a large investment of our national resources.

The School Survey Process

The school survey process has been significantly improved in recent years. The rapid increase in pupil population has created a substantial disparity between building capacity and anticipated enrollments. Local school boards are confronted with overwhelming problems caused by obsolescence of school plants, increased enrollments, and rising costs.

State departments of education and state universities responded to this need by establishing service divisions within their administrative structures. By and large, the state universities, where service bureaus were instituted, made the greatest contribution to the development of a sound school survey process. The various offices of field services in the state universities have contributed significantly to the development of the school survey techniques that are in use today.

For example, the percentage of survival technique, which is discussed further on in this chapter, is frequently called "The Ohio State Method." This technique is commonly used in making enrollment projections. Merle Sumption and Basil Castaldi concentrated mainly on the development of citizens' school surveys at the University of Illinois. Some of the private schools of education have also played an important role in furthering the knowledge and application of survey techniques.

Cyril Sargent and Donald Mitchell, formerly of the Center of Field Studies at Harvard University, developed noteworthy techniques in projecting pupil enrollments, in assessing community characteristics and growth, and in viewing school problems from the standpoint of the community planner and the sociologist. At Stanford University, James McConnell made a great contribution to the survey process, before he began a promising program in school research under the sponsorship of the Ford Foundation.

The survey process can be divided into four distinct sequential operations. (1) The initial step of the survey method involves the systematic gathering and organization of *basic data*. (2) All pertinent information is then subjected to *professional interpretation and evaluation.* (3) The analysis, synthesis, and evaluation of the basic data lead to the *development of professionally sound conclusions.* (4) Finally, the conclusions form the basis for the *preparation of recommendations* designed to chart the future course of the school district. Each phase of the survey process is discussed in the order that it would normally appear in any school survey.

The Data-Gathering Phase

The validity, quality, and usefulness of any school survey depend entirely upon the sufficiency, accuracy, and appropriateness of the basic data assembled during the study. No survey recommendations can be considered valid if the data upon which they are based are faulty in any way. A few simple guides for the data-gathering process should be kept in mind.

Selection of Necessary Data

Survey data should be relevant, necessary, and sufficient. The selection of appropriate data for a school survey is crucial to the success of the study. Before embarking on the data-gathering phase of the survey, each member of the study group should spend some time determining exactly what information is needed. Experienced school survey consultants often begin by mentally reviewing every detail associated with the purpose, content, and scope of the school survey to be undertaken.

They carefully analyze the objectives of the survey and list the nature of the basic data required for the study. They imagine, as accurately as possible, the field of inquiry that must be pursued in view of the topics that may be included in the recommendations, which are related in turn to the concerns expressed by the school board and the nature of the problem itself. They also envision the *topical* aspects of the conclusions likely to be included in the survey report.

At this point, the surveyors are not concerned at all about the content or specific nature of the possible conclusions and recommendations. They are interested only in the subjects or topics about which recommendations are likely to be developed. This plan of action enables the consultants to prepare a list of the kind of specific data required for the study before they actually begin the data-compiling process.

It should be emphasized that school surveyors do *not* begin a school study by setting forth the desired theoretical solutions for which they later develop the rationale to substantiate their biases. Rather, they should anticipate the *topics* that may be included in the recommendations but *should* not concern themselves with specific answers to problems at this stage of the survey process.

To illustrate this point, let us cite a typical situation. A superintendent has requested a building survey of a school district. The surveyors review the topics that might be included in such a study. In so doing, they would probably ask themselves a number of questions:

- Which buildings should be abandoned immediately?
- Which schools should be expanded?

- Which buildings should be remodeled?
- Which structures should be modernized?
- What is the maximum amount of money that should be spent in each school being remodeled?
- How much capacity should be added to the expanded schools?
- Where will new schools be located?
- What should be their capacity?
- What safety hazards should be avoided in locating new schools?
- What grade organization is best for the school district, in view of the desired educational program and the adequacy of the present buildings?
- What special facilities will be needed for handicapped and special education students? Where should the central administration be located?
- Should there be centralized warehousing and centralized kitchens?

These and many other questions could be raised. As can easily be seen, these questions are not recommendations or answers to problems. They are simply topics that might be included in the recommendations. By studying questions such as those listed above, the school surveyors can begin to list the specific types of information that should be gathered.

This preliminary overview of the study will enable the surveyors to prepare forms and checklists that will assist them in gathering the data systematically and efficiently, and help them to avoid gathering superfluous and irrelevant information. Superintendents need to realize that if a survey is run and comes back with recommended changes, then they and the school board have to agree that recommended changes and adjustments will be made in their original plans. If that is not true, then a survey should not be run.

Information about Community Mores and Attitudes

Survey data should include information on local attitudes and underlying community forces. Some educators and professional persons conducting surveys would argue that the mores of a community and the way people of a school district feel about educational matters may be ignored in a school survey, but such forces, though intangible, are real and must be taken into account.

This point of view, however, does not suggest that the emotional forces within the school district should be allowed to dominate survey recommendations. Instead, it views the emotional forces and the mores of a community as the setting within which sound educational action may be planned. With knowledge of these intangible forces, a new dimension is added to long-range planning strategy and timing.

Organized Data-Gathering Procedure

The data-gathering process should be efficient and well structured. After a list of needed data is prepared, the logical source of information for each item should be determined. Efficiency in data gathering demands that the number of visits to the same source be kept at a minimum, not only to conserve time, but also to promote goodwill. Persons in a position to dispense information may become annoyed if they are subjected to repeated visits. Also, when surveys are made by a group of citizens, the goodwill of those supplying information often is shattered when different survey people repeatedly ask them for the same data. Not only do such practices adversely affect human relations but they also reveal inefficiency in the data-gathering process.

Data Analysis, Interpretation, and Evaluation

The second phase of the survey process involves analyzing, interpreting, and evaluating the data. It is critical in any type of study of this nature.

Data Organization and Analysis

Accurate data must be organized logically and set forth in a meaningful and useful form. Figures should be arranged in tables. Material related to the educational program should be organized around subject matter, courses, or activities. All ideas and explanations of the facts should be clearly stated. There should be a well-substantiated *descriptive* analysis of all matters related to the educational aspects of the school district. In a sense, this phase of the study consists of a detailed description of the present status of the school facilities, the educational program, and the operational aspects of the school districts.

Data Evaluation

Once the data are organized into a logical pattern, they must be evaluated and interpreted before they can contribute to the conclusions derived from a study. The process of evaluation involves judgment; judgment that depends upon the values, experience, knowledge, and background of the person making the judgment.

The appraisal and interpretation of data should be made only by persons competent to do so. While this statement may seem superfluous, educators often allow technical decisions to be made by citizens in the name of democratic action, on the assumption that everyone has a right to express an opinion. This overlooks the fact that there is a vast difference in validity between an opinion and a professional judgment.

All data related to *operational* and *instructional* aspects of education should be analyzed and evaluated by professionally trained persons. The strengths and weaknesses of the educational program and of the administrative organization should be identified and lucidly stated. The educational adequacy of all facilities should be covered in detail. All matters that work a hardship on the teacher-learning situation should be clearly noted.

Any feature of the school that endangers the safety and health of those occupying the building should be strongly emphasized. In view of the wide array of topics that may be covered in a school survey, it is often necessary to contract with a professional team whose members are capable of rendering professional judgments on matters related to structural engineering, community planning, fire safety, educational program, school plants, educational finance, school operation, and architecture.

Types of School Surveys

Although there appears to be a wide variety of school surveys, each is a specialized version of the comprehensive school survey. Specialized school surveys are generally conducted within a specified area of study for two main reasons:

- The first is related to cost. Specialized surveys are less costly and usually require less time for completion.
- The second reason for selecting a specialized survey is need. Often, the greatest need for a survey lies in one area of investigation only.

For example, a school district confronted with a declining enrollment may wish to make a study of community growth and pupil population in order to plan its personnel needs for the future. It may have a lesser need for studying the educational program at such time. Each type of survey will be discussed in some detail in the subsequent sections of this text.

Specialized School Surveys

Although a wide variety of specialized school surveys are available, four major categories include practically all types of surveys likely to be conducted in a school district. There may be instances where a school survey includes more than one type of the specialized surveys described in this section. Regardless of the scope of the survey, the same general principles apply to all types of school studies.

The Community and Pupil Population Survey

Studies in this category are concerned primarily with changes in pupil population and with the growth potential of the school district. This type of survey includes an examination of the geographical growth potential of the school district, a study of the population growth pattern of the community, a careful analysis of past pupil enrollments, and the computation of a statistically sound, grade-by-grade, year-by-year enrollment projections.

Projection of Anticipated Pupil Population

The preparation of an enrollment projection is indispensable to long-range educational planning. Although several techniques for making enrollment projections are currently in use, the perfect method for accurately predicting future enrollments has not yet been invented. Nevertheless, current methods are extremely helpful in planning for the future, even though the results are only reasonable approximations of anticipated future enrollments. As crude as our present methods seem to be, however, it can be reasonably expected that deviations from actual enrollments later should not exceed plus or minus 10 percent under normal circumstances.

The most widely used technique for projecting pupil population is the percentage of survival technique. The basic concept of this method is very simple. For each year and each grade in the past five to ten years, the percent of retention is computed. (The number of years selected, which is based upon the type of growth pattern, requires professional judgment.)

For example, what percent of the number of pupils in the first grade this year will appear in the second grade next year? The average percent for each grade, properly adjusted for factors foreseeable in the future, becomes the percent figure used in computing future enrollments. If, on the average, 98 pupils appear in the second grade in any given year for each 100 pupils in the first grade during the previous year, then this 98 percent plus an adjustment for foreseeable factors will determine the enrollment in each second grade if we know the enrollment of the first grade in the preceding year.

This procedure is followed for each grade. A more detailed version of this method is described in *The Road to Better Schools*.[3] Worksheets and instructions are provided for the numerical computations associated with this type of enrollment projection.

The Finance Survey

The finance survey includes a study of the business practices of the school district, a review of the disbursements and income, and a determination of the expenditure trends of the school district. The finance survey analyzes in detail the cost of operating the school district, using nationally accepted classifications of expenditures such as administration, instruction, operation of plant, attendance and health services, pupil transportation, maintenance of plant, and fixed charges.

Financial figures should also be presented on a cost or income per student basis, so that it is possible not only to compare the cost or income per student with that in other school districts but also to make comparisons among the various educational centers within the school district.

Survey experts also probe other aspects of school finance. They conduct an intensive search for all possible sources of school revenue and try to determine whether or not the school district is receiving all of the revenue to which it is legally entitled from local, county, state, federal, and private sources. The finance survey also contains an analysis of present indebtedness and bonding potential, as well as a projection of the bonding capacity of a school district for the foreseeable future. Such a survey includes future trends of wealth, pupil load, and financial ability of the school district, as well as a look at assessment procedures and their effect on school revenue.

The finance survey may also contain a study in depth of the school business affairs of the district. The organization of the business services and the efficient use of all nonacademic personnel in the school district are scrutinized. The planning and procedures related to budget-making are evaluated in terms of educational soundness and financial efficiency. The accounting system and record-keeping functions are examined and studied.

Purchasing procedures are judged in relation to sound business practices. The existence of adequate safeguards in the school system is also explored—safeguards to protect honest people from being falsely accused for malfeasance of duty and safeguards for the school district to protect it from being deceived or defrauded by persons or groups who are not acting in the public interest.

Educational Program Survey

Ideally, every school survey should include a comprehensive expert study of the educational program offered by the school district. The educational program of a district, after all, is the heart of the educational system in the United States. Unfortunately, school surveys often do not include an expert study in depth of the educational program. Perhaps the two principal reasons for the frequent omission of such studies are: (1) the cost of the program study is often higher than the school district is willing to pay, and (2) the need to employ outside experts for such a study is not readily acknowledged.

The belief that a local staff survey of equal value can be conducted without outside assistance and at no additional cost to the school district tends to neutralize the desire of the school boards to have experts make a study of the educational program.

Regardless of who conducts the study, the educational program survey examines a wide variety of instructional materials and techniques. The program study also reviews and analyzes the specific educational goals of the school district and appraises the extent to which these goals are being met. The survey is designed to discover and identify shortcomings in the educational program and to include suggestions that will overcome such deficiencies. Properly conducted, a program study is a systematic and penetrating study of each element of the existing program in relation to the most advanced and effective instructional practices.

The program survey covers all of the instructional experiences that pupils undergo in a school. The course content, its sequence, and its depth are closely examined. The methodology and instructional techniques are scrutinized and the textbooks and instructional materials used in the schools are examined from the standpoint of appropriateness and educational effectiveness. Finally, the overall program and related activities in each area of learning are judged in terms of the practices of today and the probable techniques of tomorrow.

It should be pointed out that the degree of excellence of an educational program is difficult to determine objectively. Most of our evaluations are subjective, and many of our judgments must, of necessity, be inferential. For example, if we observe a practice that appears to be outstanding, we infer, often without proof, that good learning is taking place as a result of this practice. This conclusion is not necessarily valid in all situations.

Ideally, outside experts from the various areas of instruction should be employed to work with teachers and school staff in making a program study, but for financial reasons this cooperative venture is not always possible. Consequently, the success of the teacher-staff study must rely heavily upon the competence of the school administrators and the resourcefulness of the teachers involved. With vision, cooperation, and mutual respect between the teachers and members of the administrative staff, it is possible to conduct a staff school program survey that can result in modernization of the curriculum in any school district.

The School Building Survey

One of the school surveys that is most often demanded and conducted is the building study. In many school districts, the need for a building survey often supplies the required spark that results in a much broader study. The building survey, in such cases, starts a sort of chain reaction in the thinking of members of school boards regarding the educational areas that should be covered in a survey of the school district.

While a program study, a community study, and a finance study can be made independently, since the facts needed are self-contained in the study, a building study cannot be made intelligently without a knowledge of future enrollments (community study), educational program (program study), and the financial ability of the school district (finance study). Consequently, whenever a valid building survey is made for a school district, the surveyors must take into account the findings resulting from other types of school surveys. The school building evaluation is discussed in detail in chapter 4.

Product Outcome

In pursuing the scientific method of inquiry, no recommendations are possible unless they are preceded by the development of well-founded conclusions. Although the process of forming conclusions from data assembled in school surveys is complex and sometimes difficult, by examining many small pieces of related educational information it is often possible to arrive at valid conclusions. This approach demands logic, common sense, and professional judgments, together with objectivity and understanding of the situation. Admittedly, conclusions in school surveys cannot always be derived from completely objective information and from a precise mathematical analysis of the available data. But there is no justification for substituting clichés or biases, opinions, and hearsay for logic and sound reasoning. To ignore well-considered professional judgments in arriving at conclusions in school surveys in the absence of more exact information is to destroy the very foundation of the survey process.

Conclusions

Conclusions Supported by Facts and Sound Professional Judgment

Conclusions included in a school survey must be substantiated by irrefutable evidence or sound professional judgment. It is extremely important that the relationship between the conclusions and the facts or judgments be clearly established and easily recognized by the reader of the survey report.

The care with which conclusions are formulated can also have an impact on school-community relations. Citizens are less likely to disagree with professional conclusions when such conclusions stem directly from valid professional judgments, objective data, and intelligent reasoning. If school officials can present conclusions that many citizens can understand on the basis of information included in the survey, the superintendent of schools and the board of education will encounter less opposition to the implementation of recommendations.

Conclusions in a school survey suggest a plan of action. Any study that leaves the reader with the feeling of "so what" defeats its purpose and represents a waste of both effort and money on the part of the school district. On the other hand, a survey containing sound recommendations can be invaluable to the educational growth and development of the school district. The essential characteristics of survey conclusions and recommendations are discussed in the following paragraphs.

Conclusions Must Avoid Educational Clichés

Again, if a conclusion cannot be made on the basis of the evaluation and interpretation of the facts or professional judgments, it might better not be made at all. One weak conclusion that is questioned by citizens can cast doubt on other conclusions that are perfectly sound. The use of educational jargon to substantiate a conclusion does not impress the citizens of a school district.

Analogies may be introduced to emphasize a conclusion, but they should not be used to substitute for the factual basis supporting it. Citizens may get the impression that educators must resort to analogies because the facts of the situation are not strong enough to support the conclusions.

Conclusions Focused on Strengths and Weaknesses of a School District

Many school officials and school board members have the erroneous impression that the purpose of a survey is solely to find out what is wrong with a school district. This version of a school survey is correct as far as it goes, but it is too limited. The survey should also recognize and give due credit for the strengths and superior characteristics of the school program.

No school district is all bad or all good. It has been found without exception that several positive statements can always be truthfully made about any school district. The positive approach to school surveys demands that evidence of excellence be given the same emphasis as evidence of inadequacy, inefficiency, and inferiority. Obviously, very little, if any, improvement can be expected from a survey report that accentuates the positive and eliminates a discussion of the negative.

On the other hand, the shotgun approach that tears mercilessly into the negative aspects of the school district is also damaging. It tends to build up resentment among those affected by the study and often places school officials and boards of education on the defensive. What in reality is needed, of course, is a well-reasoned, factual, and firm presentation of the shortcomings discovered during the study, which, if possible, implicates neither individuals nor groups. In any effective school survey, it is essential that both praiseworthy and uncomplimentary features be given equal consideration.

Conclusions Tactfully Stated

Conclusions that reflect unfavorably on the people of a school district are always unpopular. Many citizens may already recognize the deficiencies of their school district, but for some reason no one dares to raise questions about them. In this respect, the school survey can serve a most useful function by bringing the truth out into the open for wide discussion. Without distorting the truth or minimizing the shortcomings of a school district, conclusions can be carefully prepared to make the needed impact in language that does not arouse readers in the immediate defense of personal pride or the school district.

There is sometimes a tendency for school officials and school surveyors to deemphasize the deficiencies observed in a school district. This is not justifiable, because boards of education pay substantial fees for school studies, from which they hope to gain a complete picture of their districts so that improvements can be effected. It is a disservice to the boards of education to withhold or minimize the negative aspects of a school district. On the other hand, there is no point in antagonizing members of boards of education, school officials, and citizens by stating conclusions in an offensive or tactless manner. A judicious choice of words is appropriate in expressing conclusions that are not complimentary.

Conclusions and Recommendations Clear and Concise

Conclusions, as well as recommendations, should be clear, concise, and to the point. Conclusions may reflect a positive, negative, or neutral position. It is not uncommon to encounter conclusions that tend to confuse the reader. In their attempt to be fair, educators sometimes present more than one position related to a single point in one concluding statement. This technique should be avoided, if possible, since it only bewilders the citizens. If no definite conclusion can be drawn from the facts on a point of interest to the citizens, it should be stated in the conclusions.

It should be emphasized, in this connection, that every conclusion will not necessarily include a positive or negative statement on the issue. A neutral conclusion is possible and sometimes desirable. While a neutral conclusion does not usually lead to recommended action, other than perhaps suggesting further study on the issue in question, the inclusion or exclusion of a neutral conclusion in a survey depends upon the importance and nature of the issue under consideration.

Complex recommendations frequently confuse the readers and are likely to result in misunderstanding. It is true that many recommendations are inherently complex, but these can often be broken down in such a manner that two or three simple recommendations can replace a single complex statement.

Recommendations

Recommendations consist of a series of statements designed to achieve the goals and purposes of the school survey. Recommendations serve many purposes. They are instrumental in correcting deficiencies uncovered during the study. They promote improvements in the educational program. They focus on economic efficiency, and they suggest viable solutions to educational problems confronting the school district.

Regardless of the intent of a recommendation, it should not be proposed unless it is the direct outcome of a well-documented conclusion. A valid recommendation, therefore, is one that can be traced back to one or more conclusions that can, in turn, be substantiated by the facts stated in the respective report. As indicated previously, recommendations should be unambiguous, concise, and clear-cut. They should be expressed in tactful language. On the other hand, recommendations should not be worded so evasively or so conditionally that they lose their effectiveness. Each recommendation should focus on a specific type of action and each set of recommendations should apply to one option.

It is possible for a survey report to include several options, but each option should be educationally sound. If the team conducting the survey believes that the alternative recommendations, though educationally sound, vary in quality from one another, it is within the prerogative of the survey team to list the alternatives in priority order and to give reasons for its choice of priority. This information is helpful to the school officials and school boards who will be making final decisions after they have had an opportunity to study the survey report.

Recommendations—Realistic, Educationally Practicable, and Financially Feasible

Unless a recommendation appears logical, reasonable, practicable, and feasible to those responsible for taking action, it is doomed to failure. Educational soundness and financial feasibility are two fundamental considerations in the formulation of recommendations in school surveys.

Recommendations: Evolutionary in Nature

The application of the principle of gradualism is essential in recommendations that involve changes or the introduction of innovations. Fundamental changes often demand changes within and outside of people. When recommendations provide for evolutionary changes, the desired results are more likely to be achieved because gradual change seems to be more acceptable to most people.

Recommendations—Sensitive to the Values and Attitudes of the Community

In school surveys, recommendations are designed to correct educational deficiencies, to effect essential improvements, and to provide for future needs. But any recommendation that contains ideas contrary to the feelings and attitudes of the people responsible for taking action will probably receive little, if any, consideration. The school surveyor thus finds herself or himself in a dilemma.

Should recommendations be designed to improve the educational ills of the school district or to please those empowered to act on the recommendations? It would be ideal if all recommendations could accomplish both purposes, but with regard to recommendations dealing with highly controversial educational topics, it is unlikely. In such instances, only knowledge and understanding of the values and attitudes of the people enable the school surveyor to express sensitive recommendations tactfully.

DISCUSSION QUESTIONS

1   What are the fundamental purposes of school surveys?
2   Define the "sine qua non" concept. How would this planning help a school district?
3   Discuss the pros and cons of a school district running a survey. If one is run what guidelines should be followed?
4   How is a school survey conducted? Who are the parties that should be involved in creating a survey?

NOTES

1. Thomas Huxley, "The Coming of Age of the Origin of the Species," *Science and Culture*, 1880, V. 12.

2. C. A. Moser, *Survey Methods in Social Investigations* (Toronto: Heinemann, 1958), p. 2.

3. Basil Castaldi, *The Road to Better Schools* (Cambridge, MA: New England School Development Council, 1955).

Chapter 4

The Building Condition Evaluation Form and Long-Range Planning

The Building Condition Evaluation Form (BCEF) is currently used in seventeen states. Some legislatures currently require that school districts throughout their state utilize this or a similar form to assess current building maintenance needs. Each of the four components of the BCEF plan will be briefly discussed with examples shown on the forms.

PRINCIPLES OF THE BUILDING CONDITION EVALUATION FORM

The BCEF has four components:

1 Exterior of the building,
2 Interior of the building,
3 Mechanical systems of the building, and
4 Safety of the building.

Each one of these four components is rated on a numerical scale that represents good, fair, poor, and unsatisfactory. In addition, this form also includes a scale of an unadjusted and adjusted score, handicap accessibility, functional adaptability, and space suitability.

Exterior of Building

The exterior of the building falls under component one of the BCEF. The exterior of the building includes: outside walls, roofs, foundations, windows, and doors and is the most expensive part of the building. When scoring the exterior of the building, the evaluator needs to look for evidence of cracks in the foundation and if there is any proof of a sinking foundation. Other areas of inspection include the roof, windows, doors, and exterior trim (see Table 4.1).

Interior of Building

The interior of the building falls under component two of the BCEF. Interior elements of the building includes: floors, interior walls, ceilings, and fixed equipment. Many school districts are moving from carpet to tile in the hallways, classrooms, and other areas of the building. Ceiling tiles need to be inspected to make sure water stains, scratches, and holes are not present. If water stains, scratches, and holes appear in the ceiling tiles, there is a good possibility that a moisture leak caused them.

Mechanical Systems

Mechanical systems of the building fall under component three. These include: the electrical, plumbing, and heating and cooling systems. Checking the breaker box to make sure an inspection has recently taken place will help ensure proper electrical functioning. Talking with school staff members about recent breaker trips will also provide valuable information when scoring the electrical components of the building.

Plumbing elements include inspection of hot and cold water outlets, inspection around toilets and sinks for possible leaks. Determining the accessibility for handicapped individuals, and if the number of units is sufficient for the student population is very important. The architects will need to provide this unit number, as it is required under the UBC (Unified Building Code) which is not readily accessible to educators.

Heating, cooling, and lighting elements are essential for appropriate student learning. For example, the lighting needs to be bright enough for student learning and still be energy efficient. The heating and cooling systems need to provide an environment that is comfortable for students, although some colder weather states don't always recognize the importance of cooling systems. However, many school staff and officials believe air conditioning is essential, even in many of these colder states. Air conditioning is essential in buildings with internal classrooms. As more buildings are constructed with sealed window systems, full heating/cooling systems become even more important.

Safety

Safety elements of a building include: the illumination and placement of exit signs, enough exits to be evacuated in an appropriate time, and fire alarm stations easily accessible for use in case of a fire.

Fire controllability can save a building from extensive damage and costs. For example, buildings should have fire-rated sheet rock that prevents the spread of fire. School administrators are responsible to ensure that alarm systems are working, emergency lighting is operational, and the paper walls and blinds that could enhance a fire are eliminated. School buildings are moving toward cinder brick walls to help prevent a fire. Lastly, many school districts are currently moving away from exterior doors in each of the classrooms due to security issues.

Table 4.1. Building Condition Evaluation Form (BCEF)

BUILDING CONDITION EVALUATION FORM (BCEF)

School District:

School Name:

Building Number:

COMPONENTS	SYSTEMS	GOOD (1)	FAIR (2)	POOR (3)	UNSAT. (4)	Comments
			RATINGS			
1.0 Exterior Building Condition	1.1 Foundation/Structure	+12	+8	+6	+4	
	1.2 Walls	+8	+5	+3	+1	
	1.3 Roof	+7	+5	+3	+1	
	1.4 Windows/Doors	+2	+1	0	0	
	1.5 Trim	+2	+1	0	0	
Component Score:						
2.0 Interior Building Condition	2.1 Floors	+8	+5	+2	0	
	2.2 Walls	+8	+5	+1	0	
	2.3 Ceilings	+5	+3	+1	0	
	2.4 Fixed Equipment	+2	+1	0	0	
Component Score:						
3.0 Mechanical Systems Condition	3.1 Electrical	+6	+4	+2	0	
	3.2 Plumbing	+4	92	91	0	
Component Score:						
	3.3 Heating	+6	+4	+2	+1	
	3.4 Cooling	+6	+4	+2	+1	
	3.5 Lighting	+4	+3	+2	0	
4.0 Safety/Building Code	4.1 Means of Exit	+6	+4	+2	0	
	4.2 Fire Control Capability	+4	+3	+2	+1	
Component Score:						
	4.3 Fire Alarm System	+4	+3	+2	+1	
	4.4 Emergency Lighting	+2	+1	0	0	
	4.5 Fire Resistance	+4	+3	+2	+1	
TOTAL CONDITION SCORES						Unadjusted Score Adjusted Score
5.0 Provisions for Handicap Accessibility		YES	FAIR	NO	UNSAT.	
6.0 Functional Adaptability	EXCEL	GOOD	FAIR	POOR	UNSAT.	
7.0 Suitability of Space		GOOD	FAIR	POOR		
Evaluator Name:	Date:		Yr. Built:			Total Sq.Ft.

CALCULATION OF THE BCEF FORMULA

The correct and accurate calculations using the BCEF formula can allow a school district to appropriately design their five- to ten-year building maintenance plans. The formula demonstrated below includes the following four mathematical steps:

Step one 100–92 = 8 or 0.08%
Step two 100,500 square footage × 0.08% = 8,040 sq.ft.
Step three 8,040 × $150/sq.ft. = $1,206,000
Step four $1,206,000 rounded up = $1.21 million

One hundred represents the maximum total points any school building can earn on an inspection. In this example, you calculate each of the four component areas using the BCEF rubric and points system (see Table 4.2). This representative school building earned ninety-two points.

- In *step one* subtract the earned score [92] from the maximum total score of [100] and find the difference to be [8]. This point score equates to a point zero eight (0.08)

Table 4.2.   BCEF Calculations Sheet

BCEF Calculations Sheet

Calculations for _____ School

• Square footage of building	_____ sq.ft.
• Conversion on BCEF	100 – ____ = ____%
• Cost per sq.ft.	$150
• Mathematical calculation	____ * × ____% = ____ sq.ft.
• Total upgrade cost	$_____
• Total upgrade (*rounded up*)	$_____ million

Suitability of Space Problems for _____ School Include the Following Items:

(1) Narrow hallways Yes____ No____
(2) Insufficient science labs Yes____ No____
(3) Insufficient band room Yes____ No____
(4) No choir room in building Yes____ No____
(5) No auditorium Yes____ No____
(6) No art room in building Yes____ No____
(7) Small library Yes____ No____
(8) No kitchen in building Yes____ No____
(9) No central air in building Yes____ No____
(10) Core areas too small for an Yes____ No____
expansion to educate 1,500
students (which would need
35 additional classrooms)

Comments: _____
_____
_____

representing the percent of upgrade that needs to take place to bring the school building up to "good condition."

- In *step two* record the total square footage (sq.ft.) of the school building. Then multiply the sq.ft. [100,500] by the percent of upgrade earned [0.08%] to give you the total amount of square footage [8,040] that will need to be improved to bring the school building up to "*good condition.*"
- In *step three* use the calculated number from step two [8,040] and multiply it by the average cost per square foot to renovate a school in your locality [$150], which is only an example for this sample calculation cost. This total amount [$1,206,000] is the amount needed to bring the school building up to "good condition."
- In *step four* the total cost calculated in step three is then rounded up to three digits [$1.21 million] for the sake of getting a total dollar amount that can be used in a creating a bond issue question place holder amount.

This four-step process provides you with the estimated upgrade costs for the school building that you have just evaluated and scored in the four component parts.

Annual evaluation of school buildings is critical to the district and their overall budget for the funding of needed building maintenance issues. Improper scoring of the BCEF system (resulting in a higher score) could cost taxpayers significant amounts of money and the possibility of school buildings not receiving the proper maintenance care needed to advance educational opportunities for students.

DEVELOPMENT OF THE LONG-RANGE BUILDING PROGRAM

Long-range planning is the process whereby the actions of the past and present are logically and sensibly related to those planned for the future. Because of the permanent and fixed nature of both school buildings and instructional equipment, it is essential that future planning be based upon sound reasoning and desirable educational objectives.

Before a sound long-range plan can be developed, the conclusions related to educational program, existing buildings, student population, and finance must be examined and carefully considered. A valid long-range building program is the product of many factors. Logically, conclusions pertaining to the desired educational program and anticipated student enrollments establish the overall housing need of a school district. Conclusions about the adequacy of present facilities indicate the extent to which present buildings can meet the overall need.

Conclusions concerning finance (BCEF figures can assist in this area) and rate of population growth determine the rate at which new facilities will be needed and the extent to which construction of new buildings can be financed.

Principles of Long-Range Planning

Sometimes, of course, a superintendent must deviate from a well-conceived long-range plan because of public sentiment or the necessity for gaining public support.

However, before yielding to a less-desirable solution, the school board should do all within its power to raise the educational expectation level of the citizens. A sound long-range building program should address each of the following thirteen areas:

1   *It is based on fact and sound professional judgments. A* good long-range plan of action should stem from conclusions derived from facts and professional judgments, not hearsay, unsubstantiated opinions, personal biases, and superficial explanations. Facts, together with common sense and practicality, are likely to produce a plan that is financially prudent, educationally defensible, and logically justifiable to the public.

2   *It makes the most effective use of serviceable facilities.* Present school buildings represent a substantial amount of capital outlay and should not be cast away lightly. Obviously, any building that is hopelessly obsolete should not be continued in operation, but every bit of useful life should be extracted from a school, even though it may mean that some compromises must be made temporarily. Furthermore, no school should be abandoned simply because it is old, if it is still structurally and educationally sound.

3   *It does not freeze the action of future school boards.* Any building program that commits future boards to a single plan is not desirable. A "one-way street" feature of a long-range plan ignores the unforeseeable changes that may take place in the future and may prevent future boards from making choices advantageous to the students and the school district at a later date.

    For example, a school board and superintendent may decide to add to an existing high school instead of constructing the nucleus of a new one on a separate site. Adding to an existing building may well mean that it is committed to further additions to that school because the amount of space needed might not justify building the nucleus of a new high school at a later date. The one-way street action is quite insidious, because it has every appearance of an ideal solution at the time it is taken. It is important, therefore, that the school board be constantly on the alert to recognize the one-way street approach and avoid it.

4   *It avoids the "tack-on" policy.* The practice of adding space to a school a little at a time, or of planning a series of small additions to existing buildings, is very costly and may provide capacity where it is not needed a few years hence. A sound long-range plan, therefore, can best satisfy the principles of economy and efficiency when construction consists of sizeable units on adequate sites *where schools will be needed in the foreseeable future.*

5   *It specifies the most suitable grade/class organization.* There may be several solutions regarding grade organization and attendance areas in a school district, depending upon the character of the educational program; distribution of homes; and the capacity, location, and use of existing schools. Any grade organization should be carefully considered in terms of educational, psychological, and operational factors. The fact that a given grade organization works well in one school district is no guarantee that it will work in or even be applicable to any other.

    To some degree, the capacity, location, and type of available facilities will favor one grade organization over another, but the focus should be primarily on the educational soundness of the plan, rather than simply on providing space for desks. The recommended grade organization should help to provide high quality of education and effective utilization of present buildings with a minimum of pupil inconvenience.

6   *It is educationally effective.* A good, long-range plan should produce the maximum educational impact upon the students enrolled in the schools by promoting high staff utilization in schools that are designed for efficient instructional practices. Spatial adequacy and suitability are of paramount importance in providing meaningful learning experiences. Thus, the use of school buildings possessing these two characteristics should be maximized.

7   *It is economical.* A good long-range plan is geared to long-term economy in capital outlay, maintenance, and operation. Such a plan provides for maximum space utilization and keeps costs of operation, maintenance, transportation, supervision, and administration to a minimum. Buildings with a high maintenance cost per pupil should be scheduled for abandonment. Schools that are too small to offer a broad program of modern education should not be continued in operation except on an emergency basis.

8   *It is flexible.* Any long-range plan must provide for the foreseeable and make allowances for the unforeseeable. The plan should be devised to leave open as many alternatives as possible to future boards of education. For example, if a board of education has a choice of providing two high school buildings or one, it would be far more advantageous, from the standpoint of future planning and community growth, to include two high schools in the long-range plan.

   The flexibility of such a plan is quite clear. Any future school board could add to one or both schools, or in the event of a large growth in a given area, could simply plan a third unit and still retain a balance in the size of the high schools in the district.

9   *It takes into account the accepted minimum and maximum range in the size of enrollment.* Current educational practice in the United States suggests certain limits in the size of the various types of schools. Table 4.3 indicates the generally accepted minimum and maximum capacities for elementary, middle, and high schools.

Admittedly, there are a few high schools in the nation exceeding the limits stated in table 4.3, but such large enrollments in a single school are due primarily to circumstances, such as an extremely high student population density, which is fairly common only in major cities. It can be demonstrated mathematically that there is no significant

Table 4.3.   Generally Accepted Range of Enrollment of Various Types of Schools

Type of School	Minimum Enrollment	Maximum Enrollment
Elementary	200	600–650
Middle School (7–8 or 7–9)	500–600	900–1,000
High School (9–12 or 10–12)	600–700	1,200–1,500
High School (9–12 or 10–12) using school-within-a-school concept	2,000	5,000–6,000

economic advantage in increasing the size of a secondary school beyond a capacity of about 1,400 students.

While no validated research findings exist on the relationship between school size and educational effectiveness, advanced educational programs can be found both in schools whose enrollments are within the accepted range and in those exceeding it. It can be concluded, therefore, that size beyond a certain minimum enrollment does not, per se, contribute to improved education. In considering the size of a school, it is also necessary to take into account the added cost of transportation often associated with large schools.

Many educators maintain that very large high schools have no significant advantage over schools with a capacity of about 1,200, and that there is an appreciable loss psychologically and instructionally in such schools owing to their size.

10 *It takes into account the size of the school site needed.* Table 4.4 indicates minimum standards for size of school sites. Within the past decade, the trend has been toward acquiring the largest possible school site. Many school districts have acquired large tracts of land only to discover that neither the architect nor school personnel could devise ways of using so much space. Excessively large sites cannot be justified in urban and suburban areas where land costs are exceedingly high. On the other hand, we cannot be satisfied with the "postage-stamp" sites prevalent during the Depression years. It can be demonstrated through the use of a scaled drawing of the site layout that the size of the sites suggested in table 4.4 will provide sufficient space for all of the activities and outdoor instructional programs *normally* associated with the respective schools.

Ideally, school sites should be located at the center of the attendance area served by a given school building. Thus, a properly situated school site is logically found in the middle of a relatively well-developed residential area. Unless the school site is already owned by the school district, however, school boards often learn—to their regret—that the price of the land has skyrocketed. They find themselves in a dilemma. Land is scarce at locations where school sites are needed and the price of the land is frightening. For this reason, many educators are rethinking the old cliché that "the cost of a school site is negligible compared to the cost of the building" and are beginning to explore more precise methods of determining the proper size of a school site.

One way to overcome the problem of skyrocketing land prices, of course, is to develop a sound long-range plan well in advance of the need for school sites, when undeveloped land can still be purchased at reasonable prices at locations where

Table 4.4. Reasonable Minimum Standards for School Sites

Type of School	Basic Number of Acres		Additional Acres per 100 Students
Elementary (PK-6)	5	+	1
Middle School (7–8 or 7–9)	25	+	1
High School (9–12 or 10–12)	40	+	1

schools will likely be needed. This goal sounds simple and straightforward but often requires clairvoyance far beyond the power of the human mind.

In some situations, of course, the center of future population growth in a community is foreseeable well ahead of the need. But, in many others, school sites are often purchased after a significant portion of the residential development has occurred, simply because the location of the residential development was unforeseeable. Consequently, in these instances, it can no longer be assumed that the cost of a school site is negligible compared to the cost of the building itself.

A more rational, pragmatic approach is needed in determining the size of a school site. Some states have adopted a new method. In these states, the size of a school site is no longer specified in terms of school enrollment and acres required. The new approach requires that the total area be determined on the basis of the educational functions to be accommodated on the site, with proper allowances for future expansion and potential changes in the educational program. This is a much more practical approach in determining the size of a school site, especially at a time when taxpayers are more sensitive to capital outlay expenditures.

For the purpose of making a judgment relative to the adequacy of an existing school site during the survey process, however, it is suggested that the figures in table 4.2 only be used as a point of reference. Generally, it is not economically feasible to expand an existing school site located in a densely populated area. Nevertheless, it is important to give some indication in a survey report as to the degree of deficiency of a school site in a given situation.

11 *It is related to the financial ability of the district.* A long-range building program should be geared within the financial ability of the school district. It should be realistic and practical from the standpoint of public acceptance but should not compromise desirable goals and sound principles. Fortunately, most citizens are willing to support good education if they are fully informed of current needs and the soundness of proposed methods of meeting these needs.

12 *It provides for safety, welfare, and convenience.* Schools should be located so that students do not have to cross principal highways when walking to school. Other barriers such as railroads and rivers should be taken into account. Elementary-grade students should not have to walk more than three-fourths of a mile to school, and it is preferable that the walking distance from home to school does not exceed one-half mile "as the student walks." The use of half-mile radius circles is not realistic in areas such as the Midwest where the grid system is used in laying out streets. It is suggested that a square, three-fourths of a mile on each side, be used as the unit for the placement of schools in urban or suburban areas where the layout of streets forms a grid pattern.

13 *It provides new facilities in strategic locations.* The long-range building program relates the location of new schools to those that are to be continued in operation indefinitely. Also, the location of new schools should take into account the ultimate abandonment of some of the existing buildings, insofar as possible. This goal is sometimes difficult to attain when school sites are not available at a reasonable cost where they are needed. Nevertheless, every effort should be made

to locate new schools so that they can absorb the capacity of schools scheduled for abandonment, without causing unnecessary inconvenience or hardship for the students involved.

THE EDUCATIONAL PROGRAM AND
THE LONG-RANGE PLAN

School buildings should be regarded as educational tools designed to facilitate, promote, and stimulate the educational programs. Unfortunately, some school buildings sometimes possess physical characteristics that impose severe restrictions on the educational program. Inadequate or unsuitable instructional facilities can reshape, limit, or modify the school curriculum beyond tolerable limits. Consequently, the school surveyor should clearly envision the complete educational task to be accomplished *before* making any attempt to devise a long-range building program.

Future Uses of Present School Buildings

Before a long-range building program can be developed, the most effective use or uses of existing facilities must be determined. To do this, the school surveyor should review the evaluation of each building discussed in the survey report, study carefully all of the conclusions derived from the basic data, and examine the preliminary estimate of the overall housing needs of the school district. With this knowledge clearly in mind, he or she is prepared to make an intelligent decision regarding the future use of each building. Any of four fundamental decisions may be made in regard to each school.

The use of the building for instructional purposes may be recommended for discontinuation. It may continue to be used on a temporary or emergency basis. It may be remodeled and used for an indefinite period of time. Or it may be continued in use indefinitely "as is." Also, serviceable buildings may be utilized in the future to house the same or different grade-level groupings. Once the specific future use of an existing school is determined, the student capacity should be computed.

While citizens seem to take the continued use of existing school buildings almost for granted, the experienced school building surveyor insists that under certain conditions school buildings should not be continued in operation. A few of these conditions are as follows. The continuing use of a school building is considered questionable if;

1   The building is educationally obsolete and cannot be modernized at a reasonable cost.
2   The building is structurally unsound and endangers its occupants.
3   The building is no longer needed at its present location, and it is financially unwise to transport students to it.
4   The building is unsafe from the standpoint of fire hazards and cannot be renovated to be safe and sound at a reasonable cost.

Schools to Be Abandoned

When a school is no longer suitable or desired for instructional purposes, it can either be relinquished by the school district and utilized for other purposes or disposed of by the school board according to law. In the event that a building is scheduled for abandonment, the survey should indicate the method of its disposition. It may be advantageous for a school district to sell its obsolete school buildings.

Thus, a school district receives a monetary return from the sale of capital items and simultaneously increases the value of the taxable property from which, in turn, the district may derive additional annual income. Sometimes, obsolete school buildings may still be of service to the school district as maintenance, supply, or administrative centers. It may be argued that if a school is inadequate for instructional purposes, it should not be used for other educational activities such as administration.

What is erroneously assumed in this viewpoint is that the spatial requirements of, let us say, administrative functions are the same as those demanded by the educational program. A building may be definitely unsuitable for instructional uses, and still be utilized to the advantage of the school district for other purposes. When a building is retained for other purposes, however, the survey report should indicate the manner in which it will be utilized in the long-range plan.

Schools to Continue in Use on an Emergency Basis

Sometimes it is financially impossible to replace obsolete and inadequate schoolhouses with new facilities. In these instances, such schools should be operated on an emergency basis. The long-range plans should provide for their ultimate and speedy abandonment. As long as they are in service, however, these schools should be kept safe and healthful. No major expenses for capital outlay should be warranted for buildings in this category.

Schools to Be Remodeled and Continue in Use

Expansion or remodeling may be justified in some schools because the building has high educational potential or because a change in use is contemplated. Not all schools with educational potential should be remodeled. Several important considerations should be carefully weighed before major remodeling is planned. The urge to remodel is often stronger than the will to rebuild. Consequently, long-range planners should resist the temptation to remodel when rebuilding might represent a wiser expenditure of public funds. The cost to renovate versus build new should be studied and a local building contractor's expertise is recommended.

The expansion of existing schools is often more readily accepted by the public than other solutions, but additions are sometimes difficult to justify from the standpoint of economy, student convenience, and need for additional capacity in that area. The question of making additions to existing schools should be considered very carefully.

Schools to Continue in Use as Is

Except in rare cases, most schools that are less than ten years old fall into this category. In these instances, the buildings would be utilized in the future in the same
manner as in the past. Only buildings or parts of buildings that are structurally safe,
educationally sound, and operationally efficient should be continued without some
type of upgrade or alteration.

COMMUNITY GROWTH AND THE LOCATION
OF NEW CONSTRUCTION

The overall need for school facilities depends on two distinct variables—the educational program and future enrollments. In the preceding section, it was pointed out
that, before a long-range building program is developed, a well-defined educational
program must be specified. While the nature of the educational program strongly
influences the type, design, and function of school buildings, a study of community
growth and student population provides the facts that determine the future number,
size, and location of school facilities within the school district.

In formulating a long-range building program, it is desirable to select a key year for
planning purposes. In general, the key year is determined by adding two years to the
estimated date of completion of the first stage of the recommended building program.
For example, if anticipated enrollments indicate that additional facilities for a given
capacity are needed by year "X," the planning capacity should be geared to the enrollments expected in year "X + 2." This suggestion stems from practical considerations
with respect to public relations.

It is advisable to allow about two years to elapse between the time that one building
project is completed and the time at which citizens are asked to vote on another school
building referendum. Admittedly, this leeway cannot always be provided in school
districts where the bonding capacity is not increasing at the same rate as the school
enrollment. All too common is the situation in which a new school is overcrowded
on the day it opens. Adding extra classrooms for future growth is much more economical at the time of building the school rather than adding a small addition on later.
Consequently, a two-year leeway between project completion and referendum on a
subsequent project should be built into a long-range building program, if possible.

In selecting the key year in the building program, it is important to estimate the time
required for planning and construction. About two years should be allowed for the
planning and construction of schools having a floor area of less than roughly 50,000
square feet, and about three years for the planning and construction of schools not
exceeding about 200,000 square feet in usable floor area.

For example, if the survey findings indicate that a 1,000-student high school is
needed immediately, at least one year would be required for the educational and architectural planning of the school and the passage of a bond referendum. If the planning
and construction of this urgently needed school proceeded with dispatch, the building
would probably be ready for occupancy at the end of the third year. If two years are to

be allowed for leeway purposes, the key year in this instance is five years beyond the time at which the planning process for the proposed school is initiated.

Relationship of New Construction to Obsolete Schools

In determining the precise location of new schools, it is extremely important to take into account existing buildings with a limited educational life. New schools should be located so that they can absorb all or some of the load from existing schools that are likely to be abandoned because of obsolescence. The future configuration of school buildings should facilitate the abandonment of schools that are unsafe, unhealthful, or educationally unsound without causing undue hardships or unnecessary inconvenience to the displaced students.

Additions to Existing Buildings

The expansion of existing schools often appears to be an attractive solution to the inexperienced long-range planner. Oftentimes, an addition that makes good sense in the short-range view would be a serious mistake in a long-range building program. Planners should not adopt this solution to building needs without careful study.

The following guidelines should be observed in making decisions regarding school additions. An addition to an existing school is financially or educationally questionable if any of these seven conditions exist:

1   The school under consideration is no longer needed in its present location.
2   The building has structural defects that cannot be corrected at a reasonable cost.
3   The school is educationally obsolete and cannot be modernized at a reasonable cost.
4   The building is unsafe or unhealthful and cannot be made safe and sound at a reasonable cost.
5   The site is inadequate and cannot be expanded or improved at a reasonable cost.
6   The addition would not be part of *both* a short- and a long-range building program.
7   The cost of adding to the school is unreasonable in relation to the probable useful life of the existing building.

School Site Acquisition

The selection of school sites that will be required in the foreseeable future is an important aspect of long-range planning. Ideally, new schools should be located where they provide maximum convenience for traffic flow and safety for the students. New schools should be located in areas that are free from excessive noise, obnoxious gases, fumes, and approaches to businesses (i.e., airports, manufacturing, etc.). Simply stated, a school district should provide proper facilities with sufficient capacity at locations where they are needed at the time when they are needed. To achieve these objectives, a well-conceived site acquisition plan should be included in the long-range building program.

The characteristics of school sites depend upon many factors, including the type of school proposed for the site, the initial and projected ultimate enrollment, the breadth of educational program, the cost and availability of sites, the grade levels to be housed, and the aesthetic values possessed by the community. The specific characteristics and general location of the school sites needed in the future should be clearly stated and discussed in the rationale supporting the site program.

For several reasons, school sites should be acquired several years before a building is actually needed at a given location. Cost usually rises when land is converted from farming or general purposes to residential use. The availability of school sites at locations where they will be needed later is substantially reduced if the selection of a site does not precede the population growth in any part of the school district. And finally, the desired acreage for the site may have to be sacrificed if school sites are not acquired very early, sometimes as much as five years before the actual need arises.

School site acquisition may be handled in at least three ways:

1   The desired site may be acquired outright as soon as the future need for it is established.
2   The desired site may be selected but not purchased immediately. The school district may take an option on a parcel of land.
3   The desired school site may be carefully watched by the superintendent. Oftentimes, when it is not known exactly in which direction the population growth in a school district will occur, a site or sites should be watched and no action taken until homes are platted and it feels that it would be wise to acquire the needed land.

FINANCE

No long-range building program would be complete without some thorough discussions of financial matters relating to capital outlay for new construction, remodeling, and modernization. In most states, the bonding potential or capacity of a school district is set by a state finance commission or by statute. In any case, the fiscal agent for the school district must ascertain from state sources the maximum bonding capacity of a given school district before he or she can develop a realistic long-range building program. Where finances are limited, the long-range plan must be organized in stages or phases. As the school district recovers bonding potential, it can construct additional facilities that may be required.

As soon as the total need for additional facilities has been specified, cost estimates can be made to determine the magnitude of the building program required. If the total amount of capital outlay is within the bonding capacity of the school district, the long-range building program can proceed without restrictions. On the other hand, if there is a deficiency in bonding capacity, the school surveyor and superintendent must plan the long-range program as a series of steps based upon priorities of need and upon future rate of recovery of bonding capacity.

The impact of the recommended building program on the tax rate is of paramount importance in the minds of taxpayers who are, in most cases, also voters. Once the magnitude of the required capital outlay is determined and a bonding period and repayment plan are established, it is possible to compute the tax rate for the foreseeable future, provided a projection of assessed valuations has been made in the basic finance study of the school survey.

It would not be realistic, in a growing community, to base future tax rates on present assessed valuations. On the other hand, future assessed valuations can fluctuate within wide limits, depending upon assessment procedures and policies. The rate of increase of assessed valuation due to new construction in the school district is also subject to considerable fluctuation. Nevertheless, it is desirable to make a conservative estimate of future increases in assessed valuation in order to give voters as a realistic picture of the future possible tax rates.

MULTISTAGE PLANNING

The long-range building program is often organized in sequential phases. Each stage of the plan is determined largely by the rate of increase of needed capacity or by financial limitations. In school districts where the rate of growth of student population is not rapid, the various stages of the long-range building program are influenced primarily by the rate at which additional capacity is needed.

In rapidly growing school districts, however, financial ability often lags behind the demand for additional capacity. In these districts the solution to the building problem must be ingeniously contrived in order to extract the maximum capacity and educational return per dollar of capital expended. Each stage in the building program will be determined literally by dollars and cents, and the facilities provided under these circumstances require buildings that are designed with extraordinary educational vision. They must possess design features that will satisfy temporary needs without requiring costly remodeling later when their ultimate purposes are to be fulfilled.

The Long-Range Building Program: Plan of Action

A well-conceived long-range plan contains several essential elements. In the preceding paragraphs, it was suggested that the long-range school planner assembles facts, conclusions, and inferences from conclusions. He/she was urged to initiate the task of long-range planning *only* after all the salient facts were written down or carefully noted. In the process of formulating the recommended long-range building program, it might be helpful to view the entire school facility problem, first in relation to its component parts and then as a whole.

The long-range plan may include the acquisition of school site(s), construction of new facilities, abandonment of existing school(s), the remodeling and expansion of present building(s), a multistage plan of action based upon priority of need or financial limitation, financial implications of the recommended plan, and a rationale supporting the proposed long-range plan. It is realized, of course, that not all of these elements are necessarily included in all long-range building programs, but certainly each of them should be seriously considered in the formulation of any sound long-range building program.

Rationale for the Long-Range Building Program

Every long-range plan should contain a detailed rationale supporting the recommendations. It is unrealistic to expect the public or school board to accept a plan without a clear understanding of the reasoning that underlies it. The rationale should convince the readers that the recommended plan possesses most of the characteristics described in the following paragraphs:

1 *The rationale should demonstrate that the recommended plan is logical.* The rationale should deal at length with each major recommendation, tracing its evolution from facts through well-reasoned conclusions. Clichés should be avoided insofar as possible, and the voice of school administrators should be used sparingly. Facts, professional judgments, reasoning, and common sense are often more convincing to citizens than opinions uttered by some national authority.

2 *The rationale should emphasize the flexibility of the recommended plan.* School boards are often quite impressed by the variety of possibilities that the recommended plan offers to them. It is worthwhile, therefore, to accentuate all characteristics of the plan that make provision for unforeseeable developments.

3 *The rationale should stress the educational soundness of the recommended plan.* Citizens, by and large, desire the best educational program their school district can provide. School districts that are recognized statewide or nationally for excellence of educational program generate a deep sense of civic pride among citizens. In preparing the rationale, every effort should be made to point out exactly how the various recommendations contribute to high-quality education for the school district.

4 *The rationale should clearly explain the economic and financial advantages of the recommended plan.* People seek the assurance that they are getting a high return for their money. A sound and well-conceived building program is usually designed for maximum financial efficiency and its economic advantages should be stressed.

   Citizens are usually more willing to support education when they are convinced of receiving reasonably good value for their hard earned tax dollars.

5 *The rationale should emphasize any part of the recommended plan that reflects the feelings and attitudes of the people in the school district.* Any recommendation or any part of the long-range plan that is in harmony with the thinking and attitudes of the community should be highlighted in the rationale, because citizens are more likely to accept a plan they feel is designed with them in mind.

6 *The rationale should stress that the recommended plan is advanced in character but conservative in action.* People are interested in the new and yet often loyal to the old. The rationale should assure the citizens that the recommended plan is solidly based on the best practices of the past, but firmly oriented toward the promising instructional patterns of the future. It might also be desirable to explain

the evolutionary nature of the plan and to indicate the manner in which a series of gradual changes provide a smooth transition from the good practices of today to the improved teaching techniques of tomorrow. The rationale should convince the citizens that a well-reasoned and properly controlled dynamism for educational improvement is incorporated in the recommended long-range building program.

DISCUSSION QUESTIONS

1 How can a BCEF assist in school district facilities planning?
2 Define the "BCEF" concept. Explain how the instrument is weighted in terms of scores.
3 Discuss the pros and cons of a school district remodeling versus building new. How should the cost factor into this decision?
4 How is a long-range plan developed? Who are the parties that should be involved in creating it?

Chapter 5

Foundations and Principles of Education Facility Planning

A great deal of preliminary work must be completed before an architect can begin to design an educational facility. The school board must develop and publicize its plan of action. Local school officials must be ready to execute these plans. The professional expertise of the staff must be mobilized. Faculty groups must be organized so they can systematically convey their thoughts to educational planners.

Outside professional experts must be interviewed and hired. And a sound public information program must be developed and activated. The end product of all these activities is a set of educational specifications that will guide the architect in designing the proposed facility. All are rather time-consuming. The completion of these pre-architectural tasks can take as little as six months and as long as a year from the day the school board announces the need for new or additional educational facilities.

Once the architect is ready to begin the conceptual process, he or she should have a complete list of the concepts to be embodied in the design of the building. In this connection, it might be helpful to the planners to review the principles and concepts of educational facility planning presented in this chapter, as well as others that are brought to their attention. It is important to bear in mind that the school buildings of today must be adequate to house the educational program of tomorrow. It should also include design features that will facilitate the incorporation of future changes not yet clearly defined.

PREARCHITECTURAL PLANNING: THE EDUCATIONAL PROGRAM

The educational program should strongly influence the design of any school building. No educational facility that imposes unwanted restrictions upon the educational program is well planned. Faulty design or overcrowding adversely affects the function of a school. Overcrowding is sometimes unavoidable because of limited financial resources or unexpectedly rapid population growth in the school district. In designing educationally effective school buildings, it is essential that the curriculum be clearly defined before architectural planning is initiated.

Statement of the Educational Program

No architect can design a functional school building for a given educational need without a lucid description of the educational programs. The term "educational program" is often used loosely to signify curriculum and vice versa. It is not enough to inform an architect that history, physics, and music are parts of the program. What the architect must know is exactly what the students do in a physics laboratory or in a music room. He/she must know all of the desired equipment and how much physical space the educators feel a student needs in order to perform each type of educational experience.

Considerable time should be spent by the faculty in developing the curriculum before an architect is asked to put a single line on the CAD drawings. If possible, the architect should be invited to attend some of these meetings, particularly during the last stages.

It is not within the scope of this textbook to discuss effective practices and procedures in curriculum development. However, as suggested earlier, the group process should be employed in working out clearly specified educational goals and the means of attaining them. The means can then be translated into a logical and pedagogically sound series of student experiences.

As noted previously, the architect must be familiar with each different student activity, the number of students participating in it, and the nature of the activity itself. For example, he or she must know that senior English is taught to groups of 250 students who may subdivide into smaller groups of 10 or 15 or work individually or in pairs, part of the time. The architect should be informed that students are also involved in individual and group conferences with the teacher and that they may use technology devices for the purpose of program enrichment about 70+ percent of the time (if they are a one-on-one technology school).

It is essential that the school designer be aware of the use of any new technology equipment that may not yet be in our schools. Briefly, every type of student experience should be described for the architect, including the space and equipment required as well as the approximate proportion of time devoted to a given type of activity. This latter information may become quite important if compromises in a school must be made because of circumstances beyond the control of school planners, especially when it is either impossible or impractical to provide for every type of student experience within a given school building.

Curriculum development is a crucial aspect of school facility planning. Without it, an architect is deprived of the basic knowledge needed to design an educational facility that truly meets the needs of the school district client. Lacking such information, he or she must look elsewhere. This places an unfair burden upon the architect that will most likely result in a design that is inappropriate.

Many educators are pressured by architects and school boards to get the building in electronic format before the curriculum is developed. There is often a dire need to erect a new school building without delay. Under such circumstances, both the architect and the superintendent are acting expediently and in good faith. But the fact remains that a functional school building meeting the needs of a given educational program cannot be planned until such needs are clearly identified through curriculum development. School buildings have a useful life exceeding half a century and therefore should be planned to meet both immediate and long-range needs.

In developing the curriculum, faculty members should explore the possibility of introducing new practices that seem to hold promise for educational advancement. Certainly, the faculty should strive to improve existing practices as well. Faculty members can learn about other developments by attending conferences and national conventions.

A propitious time to consider incorporation of new educational practices into the curriculum is prior to the planning of a new school building(s). At this time architectural changes can be made with ease and often without additional cost.

Planning for Community Uses

Public school facilities belong to the people of the school district. They are provided primarily for the education of the children, youth, and adults of the school district. Unfortunately, these facilities are often used for this purpose less than 50 percent of the available time during the week and less than 60 percent during the year. Many school districts use school facilities for continuing education programs for adults, evenings and weekends, and offer summer courses for the children and youth of the district.

Obviously, this supplementary use of public school facilities improves their utilization to some extent, but more could be done to better serve the community that supports the public schools. Due consideration should be given to the use of school facilities for recreational and cultural community functions. It is therefore important for school planners to actively explore a wide variety of community uses for possible inclusion in the design of educational facilities.

Consequently, every effort should be made to design school facilities for both existing and anticipated community uses. Such uses can be identified through some form of citizen participation. Often, with only minor changes in the plans, play fields, gymnasiums, swimming pools, and large-group spaces can be functionally designed for numerous community activities. The benefits are quite diverse. The pool, gymnasium, and play fields contribute to better health. The auditorium serves to enrich the cultural activities of the school district. The cafeteria can be utilized for civic activities designed to improve the community through collective action.

The learning resources center is ideal for taxpayers interested in individual self-improvement and the classrooms can become meeting places for small groups engaged in constructive community activities. It is important, therefore, that the facility planners consider all of the supplementary community uses of a proposed school facility when it is in the "educational specification" stages of the planning. The architect should know as early as possible what special needs the building is to house and what specific features should be incorporated into the design of the building.

Educational facilities planned for community use are often viewed by taxpayers as a school building with a plus feature. This positive public attitude may have an important bearing on the outcome of a school bond issue. Planning school facilities for community use is, per se, a sound and wise investment of public funds, regardless of other considerations. But when it is coupled with the positive impact that such planning may have on the passage of a bond issue, the case for planning school buildings for wide community use is significantly strengthened.

If school buildings are to be used for educational and community-oriented functions, they should be planned specifically for this dual purpose. Facility planners should also take into account whether or not the community will use the building while classes are in session. At the present time, for example, there is an ever-increasing demand by community groups to establish daytime child-care centers in school buildings. With more and more mothers joining/remaining in the workforce, this trend will increase dramatically in the near future.

A crucial consideration in school planning is the potential conflict between the educational function and the community use. When school facilities are used during the school day for day-care centers, programs for the elderly, and special community health services, there may be conflict with the educational functions. Community-oriented school facilities are also used by the public after school hours during the academic year and/or during the summer months. The need for this use is quite pronounced and will grow substantially in the future as parents' working hours are shortened or positions reduced to part-time and recreational time is increased.

Under these conditions, facility planners are presented with a real challenge in designing multipurpose educational facilities. Ideally, there should be no interference whatsoever between educational and community uses of a school building. There should be no noise pollution attributable to community functions conducted in a school building. Such public use should not pose any safety hazards to the students in the building or on the school site. The community use of the school building should not restrict or impede the normal flow of student traffic within the building.

There are other design characteristics that must be given high priority in the planning of school-community centers. Facility planners should provide effective solutions to several questions:

(1) Does the design of the building provide adequate safeguards against vandalism or pilferage when the facility is used after school or during the summer?
(2) Are the spaces that are designed for community use self-contained from the standpoint of exits, zoned heating, toilet facilities, and storage spaces needed for each public use?
(3) Are the spaces planned for community use judiciously clustered in one segment of the school building in order to facilitate control over areas open to the public?
(4) Does the plan of the building minimize conflicts between public and school use and does the layout promote harmonious school-community relations?
(5) Is the site plan designed for the safety of both students and members of the community who are authorized to use the facility?
(6) Is the public access to educational spaces effectively restricted by appropriate barriers with proper traffic flow and separations of the bikes, cars, busses, delivery trucks, and emergency vehicles?

Types of School Facilities and Planned Enrollment

Although the long-range plan describes in general terms the type of facility needed, its approximate size, and the general area in which it should be located, the school survey or campus master plan should be reviewed carefully when the building is actually being planned. There are two reasons for this review. First, if the facts on which the recommendations were based have changed appreciably since the study was completed, corresponding changes would be needed in the original recommendations. And second, the school survey report or campus plan contains vital information that is directly related to the planning of school facilities.

Common Types of Educational Buildings

Educational facilities may be classified in many ways. For the purpose of this discussion, school facilities are classified according to primary function, that is, according to the grade groupings to be housed in them or the level of education they will serve. A few types of school facilities are described below:

1   An elementary school is an educational facility that usually accommodates students from preschool or kindergarten to grades 4, 5, or 6. Buildings housing students from kindergarten to grade 3 are sometimes also called primary schools.
2   The middle school is a building that serves students from grades 4, 5, or 6 through grade 8.
3   The junior high school usually serves students in grades 7–8 (the two-year junior high school) or in grades 7–9 (the three-year junior high school).
4   The high school houses students in grades 9 or 10–12.
5   The community or junior college offers two years of post–high school education in technical and semiprofessional curricula and programs that approximate the courses found in the first two years of four-year colleges.
6   A college is a four-year post–high school institution of higher education offering students a bachelor's degree upon the completion of a prescribed course of study. Technological institutes are included in this category.
7   The university is an institution that consists of two or more colleges offering degrees that range from the baccalaureate to the doctorate.

In the pre-K-12 educational domain, facilities are usually conceived in terms of the grade groupings described previously. Some of the smaller school districts may operate junior-senior high schools housing students in grades 7–12. Many eloquent arguments have been posed for and against each type of school listed. There is at present no validated research proving that one grade grouping is educationally superior to another.

To be sure, there are many opinions on the matter and a sound rationale is often presented to favor one type of school over another. But, unfortunately, there are no tested and proven guides to indicate just what type of school should be planned under any given circumstances. There is, however, a rule of thumb that might be helpful.

The type of school selected should be that which provides the greatest educational efficiency in a given school district.

Whether or not, for example, the ninth grade is included in the high school or in the junior high school is of little consequence. The important question is, "Under what organization does the ninth-grade student receive the highest level of education per tax dollar expended?" In other words, it is not what one *calls* a school that matters. What really counts is *what the student gets educationally* when he or she attends such a school. Altogether too much emphasis has been placed upon peripheral notions about the various types of schools.

In one citizen's school survey, several patrons became disturbed when a junior-senior high school was recommended. Some maintained that senior boys would be able to make dates with seventh-grade girls, and that this situation was highly undesirable. The hypothesis posed by the citizens had not been tested. In fact, this particular school district transported students at all grade levels on the same buses. Boy-girl relationships had not been a problem in unsupervised buses in the past, but suddenly it assumed great proportions in a junior-senior high school where the supervision was far greater than in the school bus.

Such are the extraneous arguments that are sometimes posed when innovations are proposed. Again, it should be emphasized that there is no best type of school or grade grouping. The type of school that makes the best sense in terms of educational efficiency is the one that should be selected.

Planned Enrollment for a Given Facility

What should be the size or capacity of a proposed educational facility? There is a dearth of research on optimum sizes of educational facilities. Obviously, the lower limit is determined by the lowest number of learners needed to justify a broad educational program at a reasonable cost per learner. The upper limit is reached when the facilities required by fields of learning enrolling the lowest number of students can no longer be accommodated in a single teaching station.

For example, if a special laboratory is required to house advanced programs in physics and chemistry, and if these two courses have the smallest enrollments, then the total school enrollment at which a second laboratory would be needed for these advanced courses would represent the upper level of the enrollment range. According to this concept, the lower and upper limits of the capacity of a school would depend upon the desired educational programs.

Elementary school capacities should range between 300 and 500 students. At the secondary level, the minimum size is set at about 300 students and the maximum at about 1,500. These enrollment ranges reflect the views of many educators.

Of course, it is sometimes necessary to deviate from desirable enrollment ranges. At the elementary level, every effort should be made to provide at least one room per grade, and therefore the minimum size for an elementary school (PK-6) should be eight classrooms or seven classrooms, if a pre-kindergarten program is not provided. In the judgment of the authors, elementary schools (K-6) should not exceed three rooms per grade or twenty-one classrooms. At the secondary level, the enrollment should not fall below 500 or about 150 students in the freshman class of a four-year high school. The upper limit should not exceed 1,500 (see table 4.1).

Contrary to popular opinion, large secondary schools are no less costly to operate, nor are they free of duplication. A study of any 4,000-student high school quickly reveals not only duplication but the multiplication of similar spaces including those in the library, which is not duplicated in the ordinary sense. It is simply made larger and more complex and must contain several copies of numerous books because of the great demand for them. In other situations, the single large high school simply channels tax dollars into transportation costs that do not directly contribute to the education of the students. In a sense, unnecessary transportation costs tend to represent a waste of public funds.

Preparation of Educational Specifications

No architect should be asked to plan a school before a complete set of educational specifications or a program has been developed by the educational planners. It is unfair and unwise to ask architects to do both the educational and the architectural planning. An architect is not an educator nor pretends to be one. While an architect may have planned many schools already, he or she should not be forced to produce plans that are pure carbon copies of buildings designed for other school districts, simply because educators have failed to prepare educational specifications as a guide.

Purpose of Educational Specifications

Educational specifications serve as the link between the educational programs and school facilities. They consist of a series of interrelated statements that translate the physical requirements of the educational program into educational facilities.

The basic purpose of educational specifications is to describe clearly and concisely the various learning activities to be housed in the school, their spatial requirements, and special features. The statements should not be couched in general terms such as "appropriate size," "sufficiently large," or "properly related." These terms are meaningless to an architect. On the other hand, educators should not submit drawings showing dimensions, shape, and relationships to an architect.

The primary purpose of preparing educational specifications (word documents) is to enable the architect to clearly imagine every detail of educational activity to be conducted in a proposed educational facility. From a study of such specifications, he or she should be able to develop a number of architectural concepts that fit the situation.

Organization of Educational Specifications

There is no best way to organize a set of educational specifications. In practice, facility planners often find it convenient to develop educational specifications in three distinct sections. The *first* is usually devoted to matters related to the educational program, including a detailed description of instructional and learning activities. Expressions of educational philosophy are of little consequence to the architect, for they do not say much about the form or design that a proposed school building should assume.

The *second* group of educational specifications deals with the numerical aspects of the architectural problem. How many students must be housed? How many of the various types of instructional spaces are needed for the desired educational program? Approximately how large should each type of space be, and where should it be located in relation (adjacencies) to other spaces?

The *third* section of the specifications describes in detail all special features that should be incorporated in the school building. These statements deal with matters such as special shapes, ceiling heights, temperature and humidity control, acoustical treatment, electrical outlets, technology equipment, and unusual lighting requirements.

Content of Educational Specifications

Some of the broader topics included in a set of educational specifications have already been mentioned. A more detailed account of such topics is presented here.

The greater the detail and clarity of the educational instructions prepared, the greater the likelihood that a school district will acquire the school building it really needs. Architects frequently refer to educational specifications as the "program" or "educational program." They often speak of "programming a building." The architectural expressions for educational specifications are quite proper, but they have not been adopted in educational terminology because the word "program" has a distinct meaning of its own in pedagogy, and the expression "educational program" conveys a meaning to some architects that is completely different from that intended when it is used in educational specifications.

Part I: Description of the Educational Function

The architect must fully understand the function of a proposed school before he or she can design it. Unless a clear description of specific student and teacher activities is provided, the architect will be forced to design a structure that reflects his or her own educational concepts or past school designs rather than those desired by the school district. Broad general statements should be kept at a minimum but included when they may give the architect valuable background information.

Perhaps the best approach in preparing Part I of the educational specifications is to describe the educational function of each space, activity by activity. For example;

- What tasks are performed by teachers and students in a room used for instruction in physics?
- How will the lobby be used?
- What specific equipment (technology equipment is changing rapidly) will be located or used in a certain space?
- What are the weight and dimensions of such equipment?
- How will it be used?

The architect must also be given a clear description of each type of teacher and student activity for each space. How large a group of students does what, with which equipment, and for what percent of the time in a semester? At first glance, the amount of time that a particular activity occupies in a semester may seem irrelevant. Actually, at some point in the planning, the architect may find that for some reason provisions cannot be made for every single activity in a given space. If compromises must be made, the architect will try to eliminate special features for those activities that students undergo for the least amount of time.

The description of the operational and educational function to be housed in every part of the building should be so detailed that the architect will be able to visualize the entire school in operation before making a single sketch. For example, if the large group-small group concept is envisioned for the school, the architect should be able to imagine exactly what takes place instructionally under each circumstance and what special features, if any, are involved.

For instance, the architect should be told about the processes involved in handling and using materials, tools, and fixed equipment. Details must also be furnished regarding the work of administrators, technology staff, secretarial personnel, health officials, custodians, and maintenance crews.

Sample Description of Educational Function

The program to be housed initially in the proposed building will probably be traditional in many respects. Class size will vary between twenty-five and thirty students in science, social studies, English, foreign languages, and mathematics. Home economics and industrial arts class sizes will range between twenty and twenty-four students. It is also expected that classes will be instructed more or less conventionally at the time the school building is first occupied after its completion.

It is believed, however, that the existing traditional instructional practices will be short-lived. As teachers and administrators become more involved in developing new and promising teaching techniques, the building will be utilized more effectively as a modem educational tool.

The educational practices envisioned for school buildings within the next decade will be quite different from those that are housed in it initially. It is postulated that within the next eight to ten years, one teacher will instruct one student in his or her office. He or she will work with six or eight students in a small room, meet fifteen students in a seminar situation, work with a few groups of twenty-five or thirty students in a class, and conduct large online instruction to groups of 150 students.

Within the next decade it is also anticipated that approximately three-quarters of the total enrollment will spend about 20 percent of its time in groups of 150–300, about 40 percent of its time in groups of 15–20, about 20 percent of its time in seminar sessions, 10 percent in groups of 5–6, and 10 percent in a 1:1 ratio in the teacher's office. The remaining 25 percent of the student body will be taught in classes of 25 students using computer technology delivery.

Part II: Physical Specifics of the Desired School Facility

From the standpoint of the architect, the data included in this section are the sine qua non of school planning.

Number and Types of Spaces

The architect must know exactly how many of the various types of spaces are desired. Such spaces include classrooms, laboratories, offices, storage spaces, libraries, cafeterias, gymnasiums, custodial closets, lobbies, and so on.

Suggested Size of Each Space

The architect should not be expected to do the research required to determine the proper size for each type of space. Educators should supply the approximate square footages needed for such spaces. In general, such information can be determined with relative ease by school officials or with the assistance of an educational consultant in an ongoing relationship with the school system. New concepts can be "tried for size" in existing structures and the approximate area needed for each type of space can be specified. If the architect fully understands the educational program, he or she can often raise the questions about sizes that seem to be too large or too small.

Space Relationships

The efficient operation of an educational institution depends partly upon the proper location of related spaces. Perhaps no one knows more than the school administrator about the relationship that needs to exist between one type of space and another. It is obvious, for example, that a storage room for chemicals should be adjacent to the chemistry laboratory, but it is not quite so apparent that the entrance to the guidance reception area should be removed from the entrance to the general office, or that the office of the guidance counselor should be adjacent to those of the principal and school nurse. A few architects, incidentally, have satisfied these relationships quite ingeniously.

Circles or ellipses could be drawn to represent each type of space. The larger spaces could be indicated by large circles or ellipses. One, two, or three straight lines could be drawn between them to indicate a weak, close, or very close relationship, respectively. The use of straight lines to indicate spaces should be avoided whenever possible, because by using them educators would be entering into the province of the architect.

Table 5.1. Sample Statement of Physical Specifics

Teaching Stations Required		Proposed Area of Each Space (ft²)	Storage Space (Area ft²)	Relationship to Other Teaching Stations
General Art				
Art	3	1,500	150	
General Typing—Business	1	900	50	Near Homemaking or Shop
Homemaking	1			
General	1	1,200		
Clothing	1	1,100	150	
Foods	1	1,200	150	
Office	1	150		Near Multipurpose Room
Multipurpose Area	1	400	50	Between Foods and Clothing

Furthermore, educational specifications should allow the architect as much freedom in their design as possible.

Part III: Description of Special Physical Features

In some instances, the educational program demands the incorporation of certain special features in the design of the school. These special features may be dictated by the need for technological equipment or by the requirements of certain teaching or learning activities.

It is essential that all exceptional or special features of a school building be clearly set forth space by space. Special features are most often concerned with shape, ceiling height, intensity of lighting, acoustical conditioning or insulation from other spaces, humidity and temperature control, orientation, color, ability of the floor to support more than average weight, type of flooring covers, arrangement of built-in equipment, and utilities.

Sample Descriptions of Several Special Features

The **Art** Room. The spaces should possess the following features:

1 Long dowels resting on built-in racks should be provided to hold rolls of paper at least 36″ wide.
2 Two work sinks and work counters should be installed in the art room. Long gooseneck spigots should be provided.
3 A northern exposure with as much natural lighting as possible.
4 About 200 square feet of the art room should be planned for ceramics and a wet area. The floor should be durable and capable of being easily cleaned in this area where water, clay, paints, and abrasive materials are used.
5 Electrical power (220 V) for a kiln should be available in the ceramic art area.
6 Artificial lighting should simulate the daylight spectrum as closely as possible.
7 About 12 linear feet of tack board from floor to ceiling should be provided.
8 This room should be capable of being blacked out in order that all details can be seen on color slides and films.
9 If this room has a beautiful vista at a second-floor location, window sills should be dropped as close to the floor as possible to facilitate painting of landscapes.
10 The room should convey the feeling of being an art studio where creative activity is stimulated.

The Home Economics Spaces. This category also includes the clothing laboratory:

1 Provide a three-way mirror in the fitting area.
2 Include about 20 linear feet of shelving for reference books.
3 Include cabinets with at least 150 tote trays for sewing supplies and equipment.
4 At least two cabinets to be used as wardrobes should be provided. Each cabinet should be about 4 feet in length. Unfinished garments are stored in such cabinets while work is in progress.

5 A work sink and counter should be provided in the clothing laboratory near the grooming center.
6 In addition to high-intensity general lighting, provision should be made for local lighting.
7 At least twenty-four to thirty-six double electrical outlets should be provided, two for each student.
8 About four outlets should be located in the demonstration area used by the teacher.
9 At least two ironing boards should be provided in the clothing laboratory. Provision for storage of irons and other small equipment should be made in the storage space specified for the clothing lab.
10 At least two cutting tables, 32 inches wide and 6 feet long, should be provided in addition to tables holding sewing machines.
11 At least twelve electric sewing machines should be provided in the clothing laboratory.

The inclusion of specialized spaces will be determined by the educational specifications provided by the district.

EDUCATIONAL FACILITIES PLANNERS

Many people participate in the planning of a school building in one capacity or another. The planning process should tap the creative potential of the faculty, professional persons, administrators, nonprofessional personnel, and students. To realize this potential, these people must be organized. Two basic planning groups are needed, one group to serve as the executive planning team and the other to act in an advisory capacity to the executive planning team. A former superintendent (with this type of facilities experience) could be a nice asset to a school district to hire and add to their team.

The Executive Planning Team

The executive planning team assumes the primary responsibility for planning an educational facility. It has full authority to develop plans of a proposed school building, subject to the review and approval of a higher board, such as the school board.

The executive planning team should consist of the chief school administrator, one of his or her assistants, the architect, the educational consultant, and a faculty member who is also a member of the institutional planning team discussed below.

The executive planning team reviews educational specifications prepared by the educational consultant and works closely with the architect in the development of architectural plans. While the architect has the primary responsibility for designing the building, the team as a whole continually reviews the plans and educational specifications in terms of educational adequacy. The chief school administrator is the representative of the school and, therefore, assumes the role of the client in dealing with the architect. In planning school buildings, however, the final approval of plans and specifications generally rests with the superintendent and school board.

The Institutional Planning Team

The institutional planning team is not a new concept in school planning, but its role has not been clearly defined, and its unlimited creative potential has not been fully utilized by school planners. The value of planning teams is well known. Properly organized in an administrative climate that is conducive to creative thinking, the institutional planning team can make a major contribution to the final drawings of educational facilities.

The institutional planning team is viewed as a central advisory committee. It is usually composed of a cross-sectional representation of faculty and nonprofessional persons employed by the institution. The group may also include one or two students whenever it is felt that their thinking will contribute to imaginative planning.

The team should include about fifteen persons, a group that is large enough to stimulate the creative process but small enough to avoid awkwardness and loss of group cohesion and informality. The subgroups send representatives to the institutional planning team. Provision should be made in the organizational structure of these groups for ideas and feedback to move from the executive planning team through the institutional planning team to the subgroups and vice versa. Perhaps nothing kills initiative and creativity more quickly than the lack of assurance that an idea will be given full consideration. Feedback may be used to provide this needed assurance.

The institutional planning team is essentially the stimulator and clearinghouse for all ideas regarding the educational planning of a school building. The group may make studies of educational matters or recommend that such studies be made. They serve as a coordinating council for the various subgroups developing concepts, innovations, and ideas to be considered in planning of the new facility.

While the authority to implement or reject ideas, suggestions, or recommendations rests with the executive planning team, the institutional planning team is entitled to a full explanation when ideas are rejected by the executive planning team. Arbitrary action by the executive planning team would destroy the climate that fosters creativity and encourages participation by both the faculty and nonprofessional personnel. The institutional planning team reviews educational specifications and all architectural plans. It submits reactions and recommendations to the executive planning team and serves as a liaison group between the executive planning team and faculty, students, and interested parents.

The Educational Consultant

The educational consultant is another key member of the executive planning team. The services of a qualified educational consultant are invaluable in planning an economical and functional school building. A competent educational consultant (again looking for a retired superintendent with facilities experience or background) can usually offer suggestions that may result in savings amounting to several times their fee, coupled with improvements in educational efficiency that cannot be readily converted into dollars and cents.

Since, unfortunately, there is no state certification or board of registration for educational consultants, school officials must exercise great care in selecting one. School boards must be sure that the qualifications of the educational consultant are higher than those of persons already employed by the board. Otherwise money expended for a consultant would be a waste of public funds.

The Qualifications of the Educational Consultant

The educational consultant should be a person of wide and varied experience. He or she should have:

1 An advanced degree in general educational administration (the superintendency), preferably at the doctoral level, from an accredited university.
2 Formal training in school plant planning at the graduate level.
3 Broad experience. Work over a wide geographical area, including several states, is an indication that the consultant is unhampered by provincial or regional thinking.
4 Teaching experience in the public schools and, preferably, also at the college level.
5 Experience in at least two levels of educational government, such as local, state, or federal.
6 Evidence of competence confirmed through reports, studies, and services rendered to other school districts.

The Role of the Educational Consultant

The educational consultant has the prime responsibility for the educational planning of a proposed school building. As a member of the executive planning team, he or she is in an excellent position to assist and guide the architects in converting educational concepts into school facilities.

The consultant can be of assistance to school officials in a number of ways:

1 Advise school officials in the selection of an architect.
2 Be of assistance in the selection of a school site.
3 Review any existing long-range educational plan and make recommendations in the light of new developments.
4 Assist in the preparation of the educational specifications that reflect the thinking of the institutional planning team and the concepts expressed by school officials and the board of higher authority.
5 Review architectural plans and judge them in terms of their ability to satisfy educational needs and following the education specifications.
6 Evaluate all ideas submitted by the institutional planning team and make recommendations regarding the disposition of each suggestion.
7 Assist in finalizing of the bond budget, making sure the amount run is adequate to cover the scope and all equipment and furnishings.

The Selection of the Educational Consultant

Since the supply of competent educational consultants is very limited, school boards would be well advised to ask the school building authority in the state for suggestions. Schools of education sometimes have competent school facilities consultants. Care should be exercised, however, not to confuse the prestige of the school with which a person is associated with professional competence. Only professors of education who have had training in school planning and educational administration and who possess the qualifications listed above should be considered.

The Architect

As mentioned earlier, the architects are key members of the executive planning team. The lead architect has the primary responsibility for translating educational concepts and functions into educational facilities that are conducive to effective learning.

Qualifications of the Architect

In most states, minimum qualifications for school architects are prescribed by law. In and of itself, however, the employment of an architect does not automatically assure a school board authority that the school design will satisfy their institutional needs. The architect should be creative, competent, flexible, understanding, perceptive of educational needs, open-minded, aesthetically oriented but cost-conscious, imaginative, practical, and cooperative in spirit. The architect should:

1 Possess a thorough knowledge of school building design, economical construction methods, and efficient use of building materials.
2 Be endowed with creative ability and artistic talent. This characteristic can be judged by reviewing past works, which need not have been school buildings.
3 Work harmoniously with individuals or groups of people.
4 Be open-minded and willing to explore new ideas. The architect should refrain from imposing his or her will upon the executive planning team with respect to educational matters or architectural design that may adversely affect the educational program.
5 Be willing and able to follow detailed educational specifications for the design of a school by working closely with the educational consultant.
6 Be capable of producing final working drawings that are clear and precise.
7 Conduct himself or herself professionally with dignity, integrity, and honesty.
8 Demonstrate an ability to provide for aesthetics in school design without sacrificing function or ignoring cost.
9 Have past experience in the design of schools that are similar in size and cost to what the school district is proposing. Also check on past school district satisfaction with each of the architects being considered for that role.

Procedure for Selecting an Architect

As soon as funds are available for the employment of an architect, the school board should widely publicize its intention to employ an architect for a given project through the means of sending out a request for qualifications (RFQ). Architects may also learn of the potential projects through the news media and through the local chapter of American Institute of Architects (AIA.). The group entrusted with the planning of a school should seek names of architects (for other school districts) whom they may wish to consider.

In this age of rapid travel and electronic drawings, no special preference may be necessary to only hire the local architects. They should, indeed, be considered, but deserve no favored treatment simply because they live in the community and pay local taxes. The most important considerations in the selection of an architect are competence, creativity, and willingness to design a school that can accommodate the desired educational program *not* the place of business.

A number of clichés are often used in support of the employment of a local architect, such as "he is easy to contact," or "she can supervise the job more thoroughly," or "he is more conscious of our problems," and "as a local taxpayer, she will be more eager to save us money." Obviously, these arguments can be nullified one by one. Any architect is as close as their phone.

As far as supervision is concerned, on large projects, an architectural firm employs a lead or project architect, and the location of the office of the principal architect really does not matter. On small projects, most architects can afford to provide only the supervision called for in the contract, perhaps an afternoon per week. Therefore, the location of the architectural firm is of little consequence from the standpoint of supervision.

In one case, a local architectural firm admitted publicly that the reason for the collapse of an entire 200-feet-long ceiling in a school ten months after occupancy was due to the use of improper clips by the contractor during construction. This statement was not an indictment of the architect. Under the usual contract, the architect is not required to supervise the construction on a full construction-time basis.

And finally, the argument is frequently voiced that, as a local taxpayer, the architect is more likely to try to save money through efficient design. The local architect does not possess a magic cost formula. All competent architects can design inexpensive buildings if they so desire. Reputable architects differentiate between cheap buildings and inexpensive ones. If the local architect favors the cheap concept, the local school board can expect just one thing—a cheap, short-last building.

The employment of an architect by a school board is one of the most important duties performed by such a board in the construction of educational facilities. Steps to be followed in selecting and employing an architect are listed here:

1 Widespread publicity should be given to the board's intention to plan and construct educational facilities.
2 A list of architects should be prepared by the board of higher authority. All available sources of names should be consulted, including other school boards who have recently built new schools.
3 A brochure explaining the project in detail and a questionnaire requesting pertinent information should be mailed to those on the RFQ list.
4 Returns should be screened as objectively as possible and then ranked. Some form of rating sheet should be used in the screening process.
6 The ten highest-ranking architects should then be mailed questionnaires requesting additional information (beyond the RFQ documents).

7 The ten remaining architects should be re-ranked on the basis of data contained in the second questionnaire and information gathered from direct contacts with their former clients. The number of firms under consideration should be reduced to three to five at this point.

8 The architects under final consideration should be invited to appear before the superintendent and school board (1) to make presentations, (2) to answer specific questions prepared in advance and placed on a rating sheet, and (3) to exchange design ideas with the school board.

9 Visits should be made by superintendent and school board members to some of the buildings designed by the architects, and discussions should be held with other school administrators and school boards for whom each architect worked in the past.

10 A selection can be made after all ratings and scores applying to each architectural firm have been recorded on a rating sheet by each of the committee members.

The Contract with the Architect

Because school officials frequently have certain misconceptions regarding the responsibilities and duties of an architect, it may be helpful to list what is and is not within the area of scope of responsibilities of the architect in a normal contract. Some of these areas are as follows:

1 The architect *is* responsible for architectural programming. He or she is *not* responsible for creating the educational specifications.

2 He or she *is* responsible for preplanning studies. He or she is *not* responsible for making the final choices among the alternatives presented as possible solutions to the educational problems.

3 He or she *is* responsible for preliminary plans, large-scale drawings, and final plans and specifications to be approved by school officials. He are she is *not* responsible for making architectural changes, at his or her expense, after final working drawings have been approved by the school board.

4 He or she *is* responsible for working with the construction manager (CM) or bidding and contracting awards if a general contractor (GC) is utilized. He or she is *not* responsible for the legality of the contracts as to form or content.

5 He or she *is* responsible for the periodic supervision of the construction. They *are not* responsible for continuous "on-the-job" supervision, unless it is so specified in the contract.

6 He or she *is* responsible for all architectural matters related to the acceptance and occupancy of a school.

7 He or she *is* responsible for overseeing the correction of defects (punch list items) in construction during the warranty period and acts in the interest of the owner.

8 He or she *is* responsible for the selection and installation of all fixed equipment. He or she is *not* responsible for the selection and purchase of movable equipment when paid only the normal architect's fee.

9 He or she *is* responsible for certifying the amount of monthly payments due to contractors, but he or she is *not* responsible for the availability of funds at the time when payments are due.

School Officials as Members of the Executive Planning Team

The remainder of the executive planning team consists of a legal adviser/bond attorney and a financial adviser. Most institutions employ a legal counselor on a full- or part-time basis. As a member of the school planning team, he or she makes certain that all actions, contracts, and procedures comply with the law. The adviser assists in the bonding and business aspects of school planning. The fiscal adviser prepares all of the financial documents, tax rates, bonding capacity, and so on and handles the bond sales upon passage of the levy (if one is needed).

The role of the superintendent of schools is crucial. As the chief school officer, he or she is the status leader of the school district. The chief school officer represents the school board and is the client whom the architect serves. The final decision in the executive planning team rests with the superintendent.

He or she has the power to reject or veto any idea or concept proposed by the executive planning team or any member thereof or by the institutional planning team or by the architect. As a practical matter, however, the chief school officer should consider each rejection carefully before exercising veto power. On the other hand, he or she should not hesitate to reject any suggestion that is felt to be detrimental to the school district, and should explain the reason for this action to the individual or group submitting it.

THE SITE

The school site is, of course, an essential part of any new educational plans. In addition to providing the space and setting for the school building, the site must include space for a large number of essential educational functions and supporting services.

> *The size of a school site should be sufficient to accommodate all educational functions and supporting services plus an additional 25 percent in area for unforeseeable future needs.*

The Rule-of-Thumb Approach

Several approaches may be used to determine the required size of a school site. The simplest method, by far, is to apply one of the many rules of thumb that are in vogue. Applicable rules of thumb (table 4.2) are detailed for each type of school sequence under the chapters dealing with elementary and secondary institutions (chapters 10 and 11).

The Functional Approach

The approach of determining the desired size of a school site is based on an estimate of the amount of area required for each type of outdoor function demanded by modern educational facilities and contemporary educational programs. The sum of the individual areas needed plus 10 percent for unforeseeable needs represents the total size of the required site. A number of the functions served by the site are listed here.

The school site must contain space for the following:

1 The proposed educational school building. A high school building for 1,000 students, for example, requires about three acres of land just for the building footprint. An elementary school building serving 600 students occupies about one and a half acres of land again just for the building footprint.
2 Future additions to the building and increases in the other functions of the site will need additional acreage to be purchased at the time that the original site is bought by the school district.
3 Main driveways and sidewalks.
4 Lawn, trees, and landscaping.
5 Parking of automobiles (300 sq.ft. per vehicle).
6 Service drives and unloading zones.
7 Bus loading and unloading, including covered areas and turnaround drives.
8 Secondary access(es) to the school site or central campus.
9 Practice fields and stadiums for organized athletics (football, baseball, soccer, softball, etc.).
10 Hard-surfaced areas for tennis, handball, and the like.
11 Informal games.
12 Gardens and other instructional areas.
13 Social activities and large-group programs, perhaps an outdoor amphitheater.
14 Bus garages and physical plant equipment sheds.
15 Landscaping accents, such as pools, fountains, and shrubbery.
16 Football, softball, baseball, soccer bleachers, and other athletics.
17 Public and student picnic areas.
18 Walking paths, running tracks, batting buildings, greenhouses, and so on.
19 The school site should be safe, healthful, attractive, and properly located with respect to student homes.

Location

The general location of an educational facility is usually set forth in the long-range plan (chapter 4). Before a specific educational building can be planned, however, it is necessary that a definite site be selected. A well-selected school site, therefore, could conveniently absorb some of the remaining load from schools scheduled for abandonment. The school or campus site should also be located in an area that is free from air pollution/noxious gases, and far from sources of noise or danger, such as heavily traveled highways, airports, and heavy industry.

Topography and Soil Conditions

A good site possesses several physical characteristics. Its topography should be slightly convex and its level somewhat higher than the area immediately surrounding it. It is not necessary that the entire area be flat, provided there is sufficient space in which play areas may be developed at a reasonable cost for grading. In fact, buildings are sometimes built into the natural topography of the site in ingenious ways.

Boring of test holes must be done in prospective school or campus sites to determine the adequacy of the drainage and bearing of the soil. The presence of ledge cropping through the surface at a few isolated spots should not eliminate an otherwise desirable site from consideration. Modern buildings are generally constructed without basements, and therefore ledge does not generally constitute a major problem.

Aesthetics

Aesthetic considerations should be stressed in the selection of a site. The building and the site should provide an environment conducive to effective learning. Trees, brooks, parks, or golf courses, on or near a potential school site, do much to beautify the area surrounding an educational facility. Such features can be used to produce dramatic results by an imaginative landscape architect.

Safety

Finally, it is imperative that matters related to safety be given high priority in the selection of a school site. If possible, it should not border a heavily traveled highway, railroad, or high-tension electric wires. Drives and walks approaching the buildings should be designed to keep the crossing of pedestrians and vehicular traffic to a minimum. Special care should be exercised in the design of a bus-loading area. Driveways should not be located between the unloading zone and an educational facility. Neither should it be necessary for buses to travel in reverse in order to turn around on a school site.

Placement of the Buildings on the Site

Educational facilities should be located about 160 feet from any well-traveled thoroughfare in order to minimize the interference from traffic noise. Instructional facilities should be strategically situated on the site with respect to convenience and function. The gymnasium, for example, should be located near the play fields and away from quiet areas, such as the library and classrooms. On the other hand, the auditorium and recreational facilities should be convenient to the parking areas. Aesthetic considerations should also figure in determining placement and orientation of each building on the school site, but not at the expense of function.

The Development of the School Site

It is strongly suggested that a landscape architect be engaged to prepare a master plan of the site development. All too frequently, the area immediately surrounding school buildings is carefully planned and developed while the development of the remainder of the site is left to chance. When school planners recommend school and campus sites of the size mentioned in this text, they envision a site that is carefully developed and laid out to accommodate the outdoor functions associated with a modern educational program.

The layout of a school site should be geared to both safety and function. Driveways, for example, should not encircle a building. Such a plan endangers students using the building. Walks should be located along *natural* paths. One school district delayed the installation of sidewalks until after the school had been occupied for a few months. Sidewalks were then placed where foot paths had been made by students attending the school. While this is a practical approach to sidewalk location, aesthetics should also be considered in laying out the many sidewalks.

Landscaping is an extremely important part of site development. Trees, shrubs, flower beds, and the arrangement of walks and drives contribute to the general environment of a school building. The design of the building and the layout and development of the site are important ingredients in the creation of an atmosphere that is educationally stimulating. The building should blend pleasingly into the terrain and the site should accentuate the beauty of the structure. Trees should not be planted in front of reader boards, main entrance areas, or the parking lot where security cameras cannot get a full view of the site.

BROADLY BASED CONCEPTS RELATED TO EDUCATIONAL FACILITY PLANNING

1 *The concept of balance.* Educational planners should place each educational goal of the institution in proper perspective. The curriculum should reflect a well-balanced array of student learning experiences that further the basic purposes of the institution. There should be balance among the courses offered and in the depth of penetration required in each course. There should be a balance of focus on different types of student experiences. Not all courses should receive equal attention, but at the same time, emphasis in one area of learning should not be accomplished at the exclusion or expense of another area that is equally important in the attainment of the goals of the school.

   For example, school planners should guard against emphasizing the physical sciences at the expense of the humanities or emphasizing the gymnasium and competitive athletics at the expense of the library. School planners should test the proposed curriculum for balance before translating it into building specifications. They might ask: Is there a direct relationship between the emphasis to be given a learning experience and the goal it is intended to achieve? If the goals of school are well balanced, then this test leads to a balanced curriculum.

2 *The concept of educational efficiency.* Curriculum planners are deeply concerned with the type, sequence, and effectiveness of the multitude of learning experiences necessary to achieve educational goals. In selecting the experiences that should be included in the curriculum, priority should be given to those that are more likely to produce effective, high-quality learning. The type, organization, and sequence of the learning experiences, therefore, should be educationally efficient; that is,

they should produce maximum learning for the minimum expenditure of energy, time, and money.

Admittedly, it is extremely difficult to measure educational return. In this application of the principle of educational efficiency, however, it is intended that the educational planner simply recognize the objectives underlying the concept without becoming too concerned about its mathematical implications.

At some point in the process of developing the curriculum, educational planners should test the various learning experiences under consideration against the principle of educational efficiency. In applying this concept, they should select those learning experiences and educational practices that are more likely to yield more effective and desirable educational results and reject those that tend to produce limited or questionable educational outcomes.

3 *The concept of gradualism.* Evolutionary changes in educational methodology are more likely to be effected than revolutionary revisions in school practices. Since the readiness principle applies to teachers as well as to students, it cannot be assumed that all teachers will be ready for proposed changes in instructional methods simultaneously. School buildings must be designed, therefore, for a smooth and gradual progression from existing teaching methods to those that may be proposed.

Furthermore, it should be possible to vary the rate of such changes within the same area of instruction in accordance with the readiness of the teachers and students for proposed modifications in teaching methods. The application of the principle of gradualism in school plant planning has many implications for school design which transcend those of the well-established principle of flexibility.

The need for gradualism, however, should not in any way interfere with or interrupt the introduction of promising innovations into the school program. On the contrary, the concept of gradualism is viewed as an accelerator of desired change. Recognizing the existence of at least one major deterrent for change, it provides for it in a constructive and positive manner.

Thus, the architect should plan a given school facility as though a desired new practice or practices were to be instituted on the day on which it is occupied, but designed so that the contemplated innovations may be introduced slowly over a period of time. Accordingly, a school board and superintendent of schools should plan a school bond issue that can accommodate many bold and promising educational innovations without disturbing the security of its occupants or the serenity of the taxpayers who are financing the school.

4 *The concept of reversibility.* The principle of reversibility is another new dimension in school facility planning. Educational practices that seem to hold much promise when a school is designed may prove to be ineffective or inappropriate later. There must be ample provision to move gradually in a desired direction, as mentioned in the previous paragraph, but there must also be an equally efficient procedure for reversing the direction of the change at any time. Although no school can be planned for reversibility of every change, the principle of reversibility should be applied in planning school buildings whenever possible.

5 *The concept of contractibility.* In the late 1960s, contractibility was given little or no consideration in the planning of school facilities. The emphasis was mostly on expansibility since school enrollments were increasing from year to year. The enrollment trends have reversed since that time and some school districts are confronted with excess building capacity.

In other school districts where new or expanded school facilities are needed, serious consideration should be given to contractibility of educational use. Under this principle, a school building should be designed so that a predetermined part of the facility could be used for other things than strictly educational purposes.

In the event of a substantial decrease in school enrollment, the school district would be in a position to allow part of the school facility to be used by other public agencies or nonpublic enterprises whose activities are compatible with the educational function conducted in the remainder of the building. Thus, when planning new construction, school planners should ask the question, "How can this proposed school facility be used, if only about one-half of the capacity is needed at some future time?" (examples include YMCAs, public libraries, public swimming pools).

6 *The concept of equity of educational opportunity within a school district.* In formulating a long-range educational facility plan, special care must be exercised to make certain that there is equality of educational opportunity within all of the school buildings of the school district. In some situations, for example, new elementary schools are built in the growing sections of a school district while the older school buildings, often with substandard educational facilities, remain unchanged. It is realized, of course, that parity cannot usually be achieved when large capital outlay expenditures are being made to satisfy the demands of increased enrollments. It is important, however, that the long-range plan provide for the modernization of existing school buildings within the period covered by the long-range plan.

7 *Conceptual school planning.* It is difficult to express the full meaning of conceptual school planning. It is an intellectual activity that scans the universe of human thought in order to retrieve groups of related ideas for further study. It may be viewed, at times, as the end product of a search into the depths of knowledge for new and promising concepts related to the educative process.

Conceptual planning is perhaps one of the most important ingredients in the design of *educationally imaginative* school buildings. Conceptual school planning may be defined, in this connection, as the creative intellectual activity that precedes and contributes to the preparation of the educational specifications. It is the process whereby fundamental educational concepts are formulated, developed, expressed, evaluated, and incorporated in the design of the school. The steps associated with conceptual school planning lead from the intellectual to physical.

Once the concept is developed to the point at which it can be verbalized, it must be carefully evaluated in relation to psychological principles of learning, principles of administration, and local and state educational policies before it can then be included in the educational specifications.

8 *Planning functional school buildings.* In 1880 Louis Sullivan, an eminent American architect, enunciated a fundamental principle of modern architecture: "Form follows function." This principle, coupled with the influence of Richard Morris Hunt and Henry Hobson Richardson, men thoroughly trained by European study in architecture, hastened the revival of an architectural style that was destined to have a significant impact on the design of school buildings in the United States.

The future holds much promise for the planning of educationally creative and functional schools. A number of emerging educational concepts seem destined to make radical changes in the design of schools in the United States.

9 *Image-building through education.* Little thought has been given to the image-building aspect of education. The image that the community projects to the world is important to the social and economic growth of that community. Although "Good schools build better communities," many local school districts make little effort to improve their overall image through education. A high-quality educational program is a vital feature of a favorable community image, and so are well-planned school buildings that contribute to the attainment of that program.

The school building enhances the community image in two ways: (1) through its contribution to the educational program and (2) through its visual appeal. Architects are very conscious of this feature of school design, but unfortunately school boards sometimes override their judgment.

Silently, but forcefully, school buildings create favorable or unfavorable impressions upon those who view them. To someone exploring the community as a prospective industrial site, an attractive building on a well-landscaped site may speak more eloquently than thousands of words spoken by the local chamber of commerce.

10 *Curriculum-oriented school planning.* If educationally effective school buildings are to be planned in the near future, educators must explore and develop school planning in an entirely new dimension—curriculum development utilizing technology. To be sure, curriculum development is neither new nor unfamiliar to educators. Before an architect designs a school building, the local school officials should acquaint themselves with specific information related to the curriculum, the actual experiences that students undergo under the guidance of the school. For example, it means very little to an architect to say that a space is desired for general science. However, an education specification can list out the following to make these spaces customized:

- Thirty percent of the time twenty-five students watch demonstrations by the teacher,
- Twenty percent of the time a group of twenty-five perform simple experiments using water, gas, and electricity at work benches,
- Forty percent of the time a group of fourteen work on their laptops
- Ten percent of the time the instructor lectures and discusses material with twenty-five students and that special projects are done in a separate room by about five talented students.

The architect can begin to relate student activities or experiences to spatial requirements if these educational specifications are provided to him or her.

Information about the curriculum is indispensable to the architect. It might be helpful to place ourselves in the position of the architect. What would we do, as architects, if we were asked to design a general science room? We might think back twenty years to the one we used in junior high school and design one like it. We might read about the desired features of a general science room listed by the National Association of Science Teachers. We might travel to many schools and look at their science rooms in order to design one that contains what we think are the best features of all of them. If we were architects, we would be forced to design a science room of some kind, but we would never know whether or not we had designed the type of room our client needed unless we had a detailed description of the curriculum for general science.

11 *Planning schools for people.* The human aspects of school planning, known as ergonomics, is beginning to receive attention from educators and architects alike. Currently, primary emphasis is on functional planning of schools, that is, on designing the building to serve its intended functions effectively. Admittedly, functional planning is important, but it is equally important to plan for the needs of people. These needs transcend those that are met when a proper thermal, visual, and acoustical environment is created.

   The concept of planning schools for people introduces a new dimension in school planning. This concept calls for design of a school that meets the physical, psychological, and social needs of people, and protects their health, safety, and well-being. Basically, of course, the school must be planned to accommodate and facilitate the activities of students, teachers, clerical workers, custodians, and administrators. Naturally, these matters are consciously or subconsciously considered in the design of some of our most advanced schools, but little effort has been made to conceptualize these needs in a systematic and logical fashion.

12 *Planning schools for effective learning.* No competent school planner of today would, in good conscience, permit the design of a school that would not promote effective learning. But Roth, an international authority on schools, felt prompted to say that the development of school buildings up to 1957 had been "faulty" because the design had not been based upon "sound and valid pedagogic principles."[1] According to some architects currently engaged in planning schools, the situation has not significantly changed since Roth made this statement.

A survey of the literature on school buildings published during the past few years seems to support this view. Many educators are planning schools for team teaching, for variable grouping, and for the use of technology, but relatively few are consciously concerned with the direct application of accepted learning principles that should affect the design of the entire buildings. The new shift of educational technology seems to change the fundamental principles of learning that should underlie the planning of every instructional element of a new school building.

DISCUSSION QUESTIONS

1   What are the various grade-level groupings of schools?
2   Define the term "educational specification." How would this planning help the architect design the school?
3   Discuss the pros and cons of a school district hiring an educational consultant. If one is to be hired, what qualifications would be desired of this consultant?
4   How is the size of the school site determined? What are five areas that must be contained in the school site?

NOTE

1. Alfred Roth, *The New School* (New York: Frederick Prager, 1957), p. 26.

Part III

FUNDAMENTAL ELEMENTS OF EDUCATIONAL PLANNING

Chapter 6

Leeway for Change

Education reflects the world in which we are living. Our civilization is in the midst of a technological and scientific revolution. The world has shrunk as the time needed to traverse the globe has dwindled. The boundaries of our world itself are rapidly expanding into the outer limits of earth space. We are engaged in the conquest of the universe and in the discovery of the secrets of life itself.

As part of this wave of change, it is natural to anticipate changes in thought, in attitude, in modes of living, in occupations, and in education. Thus, the plans of any educational facility for tomorrow (on the drawing board) must provide not only for the instructional practices of today but for those that will be conceived by and for generations yet unborn.

The world is continually changing—climatically, economically, and sociologically. It is in a state of confused equilibrium. Cultural values remain fluid and are poised for unpredictable change. The economic structure supporting the several societies of the world is uncertain. Under these circumstances, Rogers was truly prophetic when he predicted, "that the changes of the past 20 years will seem insignificant compared to the changes in the next 20 years."[1] And his prophecy is as true today as it was then.

PREPARING FOR THE UNFORESEEABLE

Planning a school building for educational practices still unknown seems an impossible assignment. Of all the aspects of school planning, designing a school for not-yet-apparent instructional needs requires the highest level of thought from educational planners. The brainstorming technique might be quite fruitful in achieving this objective. The task is extremely difficult, however. Rogers states the problem quite concisely. "We know there will be change, but our crystal ball becomes murky when we try to anticipate exactly what those changes will be."[2] Thus, our most fruitful approach is to plan a school building that is so flexible and adaptable that it can accommodate the unanticipated needs of future educational practices.

Projection of Present Trends

Obviously, we cannot plan for the future in a vacuum. We must grasp certain clues in the concepts and practices of today in order to imagine those of tomorrow. It should be remembered, furthermore, that the ridiculous notion of today may be the accepted and desired practice of tomorrow. To plan for the unforeseeable, school planners must answer the question, "How can this seemingly fantastic innovation be accommodated in this building in the event that the citizens fifty years hence desire it?"

A word of caution is in order, however. Cost limits the extent to which a building can be planned for the unforeseeable. Obviously, design features that do not add substantially to the cost of a school should be incorporated, but those that require appreciable additional capital outlay should be adopted only after careful study.

Social Media Sites

We have to provide the infrastructure and WiFi access to allow these newer technological sites. Several of these are as follows:

- Facebook, to engage with a community of school leaders.
- iTunes, a site of free podcasts.
- LinkedIn Group, a professional networking resource.
- Radio, a program hosted by many media agencies.
- Twitter, a "microblogging" service where you can exchange short, text-based messages.
- Blogs, sites that allow information to be shared electronically.

School planners can prepare themselves for the task of planning for the unforeseeable future by carefully analyzing present trends in educational innovations, their types, and objectives. For example, do current trends seem to indicate greater or less attention to the individual learner? Do they seem to give greater emphasis to program enrichment? To self-instruction? To supervised study? To reorganization of learning experiences? To new forms of administrative and instructional organization? To increased student services? To increased or decreased student participation in learning experiences? To new and improved technology?

These are only a few of the questions that might be raised in a faculty brainstorming session. Indeed, school planners should consider both national and international developments in their review of existing and newer educational trends.

Once the trends have been identified and clearly stated, school planners should try to project them. As a bonus, projecting trends tend to bring to light many practices that can be incorporated into the plans of a building. It is important, however, that the thinking of the planning team not stop at this point. It must proceed further, much further into the future, into the realm of the unknown. Clues gleaned from a study of the present trends should be amplified and imaginatively projected, so that the school building of today can be designed with special features that will facilitate the incorporation of unforeseeable educational practices sometime in the distant future.

Clearly, it makes no sense to plan for ideas or concepts that are unlikely to be realized during the life of the proposed school building. On the other hand, there are numerous design features that can simplify future modifications. The revision of plans of conventional buildings to accommodate future innovations is a matter for considerable study in terms of long-range economy. As noted previously, the type and magnitude of such revisions depend upon the nature of the future practices inferred or suggested by a systematic study of current trends. For example, if one-on-one instruction were envisioned for the near future, present classrooms could be planned for easy conversion to teacher-offices by introducing a system of bolt-type prefabricated partitions into the plans.

As central classroom displays have evolved from whiteboards to dry erase boards to interactive whiteboards (IWBs), white boarding has grown more interactive and technologically sophisticated over time. More than a decade after their first appearance in classrooms, it's clear that IWBs and panels can engage students. However, the bigger obstacle may be the cost, need for training, and concurrent use by many students. These are barriers that could prevent schools and teachers from getting started with these potentially effective instructional technologies.

It is realized, of course, that new and improved construction materials and methods are now appearing and will continue to improve with time. But it must also be remembered that, while new products will be developed, the building constructed today may not change substantially in material or products being incorporated for at least half a century. Consequently, the architect(s) must ingeniously utilize the building materials of today in meeting the educational needs of tomorrow.

Enrollment Growth

Increases in enrollment are not always predictable. The problem in large communities is complicated by changes in population density. For example, a zoning change from single to multiple-dwelling units may mean a substantial increase in student enrollment in an area once thought to be stable.

In view of the unpredictability of enrollment growth, it would be prudent and reasonable to assume that any school should be designed with a potential increase in capacity of about 25 percent in mind. Planning for this hypothetical growth is easy when plans are in the pencil stage. Buildings can be designed so that a given space can be changed from one function to another without difficulty and without unreasonable cost.

The principle of expansibility is not new. In fact, it has been foremost in the minds of architects and educators for many decades in planning functional school buildings. It is now generally accepted that the expansion principle can be employed in planning for both the foreseeable and the unforeseeable aspects of educational change.

Flexibility for unforeseeable enrollment growth can be gained by incorporating in the initial plans features that tend to facilitate expansion at a later date. The size of the school site needs to be sufficient, and utilities and other services should accommodate the additional student load. Obviously, there are sometimes circumstances under which these conditions cannot be met, but such situations should be compelling before the planning team accepts a school site that cannot accommodate even a modest hypothetical increase of 25 percent in enrollment.

It would be ideal if the exact nature of the hypothetical addition to the building were known, but such is not often the case. Ideally, educators should assess all educational trends and extrapolate their implications for the future. But it is not practical to expect this from the superintendent of schools, and their staff, who, generally speaking, are already overworked in the day-to-day operation of schools. They have neither the time nor the funds, except in rare situations, to divert human resources for the research necessary to discover trends in the exact nature of the school of the future. In time, some state departments of education might perform this type of research service.

Planning for an enrollment growth of about 25 percent should be made on a space-by-space basis. For example, if four science rooms are required now, how could one or two more be added if they were needed? Would they be functionally related to the existing spaces? How could spaces for the fine arts be expanded by 25 percent? The answers to these questions should be more detailed than, "We think that we have the space along this corridor or at the end of this wing." (The figure of 25 percent was selected arbitrarily. Any other percent could be used. In some instances the figure might be zero if it were almost a certainty that no expansion could occur.)

In planning schools for enrollment growth, it is imperative that proper functional *space relationships* be preserved. The importance of maintaining good space relationships is well recognized among educators and school planners. Expansion does not mean numerous open-ended corridors. The ultimate student circulation pattern is a vital concern in planning. The architect should demonstrate not only the physical expansion but also the operational relationships of spaces.

For example, it is not enough to footnote that a wing can be expanded to accommodate a given number of rooms. The architect should also be able to show a school board that the unified clustering of the science spaces, shops, art rooms, and the like can still be maintained in the expanded building. He/she should prepare a simple line drawing of the expanded school for the appraisal of school officials.

Enrollment Decline

School enrollments are subject to many sociological and economic forces. There are periods of large increases in school enrollments in certain school districts followed by smaller periods of decline. Some communities mature while others age. Some are created and some are on the wane. In the preceding section, the focus was on unforeseeable enrollment increases. It is equally important for educational planners to provide plans and a road map for possible enrollment decreases.

School planners would be well advised to ask themselves the question, "How could the proposed building be utilized fully if the enrollment were to drop by 25–50 percent?" For many school districts, this question has become a reality. Unfortunately, the school buildings of the past were never designed for this eventuality.

During the design stages, school officials should make every effort to identify as many noneducational uses for a proposed school as possible and, with the architect, incorporate special features that would facilitate such uses. Examples are clustering of related spaces, isolation of one part of the building from the other, and separation of utility lines into zones so that heat, light, and power distribution can be controlled for certain segments of the building.

Educational facilities that are not used to capacity for their planned grade groupings may sometimes be used by different grade levels. For example, a middle school designed for grades 6, 7, and 8 could also accommodate students in grades 4–5, if designed with this possibility in mind. Oftentimes, when school enrollments in a school district drop drastically, it may be possible to abandon obsolete school buildings and transfer students from these schools to those that are more functional.

This practice is widespread and well justified. But the school facility to which students are transferred is not always properly planned for these students. For example, if first-grade students are transferred to a relatively new middle school, the chalk trays may be too high, the locker combination locks difficult to operate, and the urinals too high from the floor. All could have been easily designed for, if this potential use had been envisioned when the middle school was in the design stages.

Educational Practices

It seems hopeless—and yet fascinating—to try to design a structure for functions yet unknown. Our school buildings will far outlast most present educational practices and must, therefore, be designed with this in mind.

School planners should design buildings that are easily adaptable to future practices. This concept is not new, by any means, but it needs to be taken more seriously by school designers. To be sure, a small number of outstanding school architects are already designing truly adaptable school buildings. Unfortunately, a large number are still planning traditional school buildings, in accordance with the dictates of conventional school boards which want to avoid antagonizing or arousing citizens by introducing radical changes in their school design. This is, of course, understandable. But such boards ought to realize that adhering strictly to conventional design can lead only to mediocrity. Designing *adaptable* school buildings requires boldness and imagination. This adventurous spirit is contagious, and can be transmitted from the board to the electorate through a good community public relations program.

A few general principles of modifiability have been discussed in this section. Specific examples of their application are presented in the latter part of this chapter. In general:

1   All instructional spaces should be capable of being altered in size and shape at a reasonable cost.
2   All utilities should be easily accessible to all parts of the school building.
3   Mechanical and electrical elements should be installed so as not to impede the relocation of interior partitions.
4   Ceilings should be designed so as to facilitate changes within a school building.
5   The type of luminaries employed should not restrict the placement of interior walls within the building to any major extent.
6   The design of the building should facilitate the expansion of technology in all parts of the structure.

Economic Considerations

As mentioned earlier, preparing for unpredictable instructional practices should be done judiciously. Obviously, when design features do not add appreciably to the cost, they should be incorporated. On the other hand, if they increase the cost by more than 10 percent, the individual features should be studied and evaluated very carefully and reintroduced into the plans one at a time. Oftentimes, the original capital outlay can be significantly reduced by simply making a provision for later construction. In general, whenever it is less costly to provide for future change during construction than at a later date, it should be done, provided it does not increase the overall cost by more than 10 percent.

It has not been substantiated whether or not the 10 percent figure is exact. It is reasonable to assume, however, that an investment greater than 10 percent of the cost of a building might be difficult to justify. Many features that promote adaptability and flexibility can be incorporated without appreciably increasing the cost of a school building. Therefore, the 10 percent figure seems as reasonable and sufficient as possible.

Fads versus Functions

Fads often impede leeway for change. A school administrator or a faculty group can impose certain features on the design of a school that make it difficult to make sensible changes in the curriculum at a later date. Fads come and go, but the teaching function persists. Whenever the planning team is confronted by a technique or student grouping whose value is not validated or widely recognized, it should analyze the educational needs on a functional basis and design the school accordingly. It is not sound planning to design a school building around the wishes of the principal or faculty committee unless their wishes are based on educationally functional concepts.

In one case involving the design of a middle school, the middle school principal had grouped students in four rooms under four teachers for instruction in language arts, social sciences, mathematics, and science. The students moved from room to room and attended centrally located classes for physical education, music, art, and shop or home economics. In designing the middle school, the principal simply grouped the basic four rooms in a cluster with two clusters on the first floor and two on the second.

When it was pointed out that all of his science rooms were decentralized, thus necessitating a quadrupling of equipment, he simply shrugged his shoulders and insisted that the group of four rooms be kept together at all cost. The science teachers objected to the decentralization of their science rooms on at least three scores. (1) They pointed out the demonstration concept was quite important at the seventh- and eighth-grade levels. (2) They stated it was not likely that the school district would be able to afford to purchase four units of every piece of science equipment, even though the principal insisted it was theoretically possible to do so. (3) They felt the inconvenience of moving equipment daily up and downstairs was great enough to deter the use of a single piece of equipment in all science rooms.

The teachers, in this case, were not allowed to plead their case before the planning team, and so the principal succeeded in locating two science rooms on the first floor, two on the second, and, incidentally, a fifth science room at the opposite end of the building. The short-sightedness of this kind of planning is clear. Long after the principal retires, the building will remain functionally restricted for their teaching of science.

Practical Considerations

It would be almost impossible to list, even in simple fashion, the many ways to provide for the unforeseeable in planning of a school. A few examples of flexibility and adaptability of school buildings are presented in the hope that they may generate many others.

Sumption and Landes properly refer to "modifiability" in the planning of school buildings.[3] They discuss the principles of adaptability, flexibility, expansibility, and contractibility. Schools designed with these features in mind can provide amply for unforeseeable changes in methodology, student grouping, course offerings, type of instructional technology and equipment, teaching aids and materials, size of enrollment, and the like. It can be seen, therefore, that planning for the unforeseeable future could involve much more than the ability to change the size and shapes of spaces within the exterior walls of the structure and to expand it in one or more directions.

Ideally, a school building should be capable of modifications in many forms. It should be planned for both horizontal and vertical expansion. It should contain some non-loadbearing walls and supporting columns that facilitate the reshaping and resizing of interior spaces without functional limitations. It should be designed so that electrical power, utilities, communication cables, and other technological devices yet to be designed can be brought to or utilized in any part of the building. Obviously, it would be far more expensive to attain this ideal than to adopt a more realistic approach to the problem.

Expansion

The continued trend toward urbanization, with its rapid increase in population densities in metropolitan areas, means that land will be at a premium in the future. As a result, school buildings should be conceived for vertical expansion in order to conserve expensive urban land. The structure and footings of a single-story building should be designed so that additional supports could be incorporated for the addition of a second or third floor.

Horizontal expansibility has long been recognized as a desirable feature in a school building. When the function of the expanded building has been determined, the architect customarily plans the ultimate structure and then cuts it back to the spaces needed for the first stage of construction. When future need has not been determined, the building should still be planned for expansion, but in a more general fashion.

Circulation areas should not hinder future expansion. Utility lines should be designed with future expansion in mind. The planning team should always ask itself the question, "Where and what would we be likely to add to this building if we were asked to increase its capacity by 25 percent?" even when the likelihood of expansion appeared remote.

Attention should be focused on the general layout and circulation patterns of a building, as well as on specific design features. Ideally, a school building should be designed so that it is capable of being expanded sensibly and functionally in five directions, on all four sides and upward. Minimally school buildings should be able to expand in at least three directions.

Contraction

In past years in a number of school districts, total school enrollments dropped by as much as 30 percent. Consequently, a fairly large number of school districts throughout the country found themselves with a surplus of educational facilities. Under these circumstances, many school officials and school boards were caught unprepared. They had to face difficult and sensitive decisions on what to do with superfluous and unneeded classrooms or an entire school building(s).

Planning for an unforeseeable decline in school enrollment is much more difficult than planning for expansibility, but can be accomplished in two ways. (1) The simplest is to devise a long-range plan so obsolete buildings can be easily phased out if school enrollments drop. In this connection, location of new facilities is a major consideration. This approach is particularly adaptable for school facilities over fifty or sixty years old. In a relatively newer school district, however, planning for contractibility is much more complicated. If all the existing school buildings are relatively modern and highly functional, the need for less space cannot be solved easily by simply closing some excellent buildings. (2) A more realistic approach would be to continue using a school facility for educational purposes but allow part of it to be used for noneducational activities. A good example of this is a rural school district that rents out part of a no longer needed building to house city services. However, this solution is not always practical or feasible because the building may not have been designed with contractibility in mind.

Reversible Contractibility

Enrollment trends across the United States are currently in a constant state of flux. They respond to a number of concurrent influences, such as changes in economic conditions, variations in quality of life, charter schools, open enrollment districts, private schools, and changes in societal attitudes to family size. The principle of reversible contractibility is designed to assist school officials in coping with problems of capacity, particularly when school enrollments are declining. When excess capacity develops, school officials would be well advised to examine birth rates and enrollment projections along with other pertinent information.

It would be prudent for school officials and school boards to look twice at future enrollment projections and birth rate patterns when contemplating closing or reducing educational space. If a decline in enrollment is anticipated, special attention should be paid to the principle of reversible contractibility. This principle stipulates that surplus educational spaces assigned to noneducational functions should be capable of being readily restored for instructional uses when they are again needed. In applying this principle, bear in mind that the noneducational functions should be either temporary or easily moved to other locations on relatively short notice.

Adaptability

Adaptability refers primarily to the ease with which spaces designed for a given function can quickly be transformed to accommodate changes in methodology, student grouping, technology, teaching aids, and the like. For example, by installing uniformly spaced standards on the walls of a classroom, it is possible to convert a regular classroom with whiteboards and tack boards on two walls to a general physical science room with peripheral counters and wall storage simply by hanging counters, shelves, storage cabinets, sinks, and other needed accessories on these standards. Rubber hoses could be used to connect the science sinks to the various utilities.

Such a room is highly adaptable. Generally speaking, the concept of adaptability is confined to internal conversions. School planners refer to the adaptability of a school building as a whole. In this sense, the term is related to the ability to utilize a building designed for a specific purpose for yet another purpose. For example, can a current junior high school be readily converted to a middle school? If it can, then the building is said to be adaptable. In a broad sense, the concept is closely associated with multipurpose spaces, such as cafeterias, grass fields, general science rooms, athletic stadiums, and lobbies.

In planning for the unforeseeable, every effort should be made to include all features that facilitate internal changes in the instructional areas: the joint use of all walls, the ease of locating power and utilities in various parts of the room, the possibility that technology equipment may be hung from the ceiling, the control of internal lighting within a given instructional area, and the quick and simple rearrangement of furniture and equipment on the floor. How far to pursue this initial flexibility of design depends on the amount of funds the planning team feels it should invest in the unknown future.

Flexibility

Flexibility is closely related to adaptability but is somewhat broader in scope. Flexibility is conceived as a feature of a school building that facilitates extensive changes in the sizes and shapes of teaching areas without endangering the structural integrity of the building. Adaptability makes it possible to accommodate new functions in given spaces, while flexibility makes it possible to redesign old spaces to satisfy new educational needs.

The basic ingredient of flexibility is fluidity. Accordingly, many of the walls in a school building, with the exception of the outside envelope, should be conceived as temporary space dividers that are non-loadbearing. Ideally it should be possible, in a flexibly designed school, to relocate some of the internal walls without jeopardizing the structural system of the building. No conduits, pipes, ducts, or other service elements should be located in interior walls. Heating, cooling, and lighting systems should be concentrated in the floors, ceilings, and roofs.

It is not usually financially justifiable to provide all of these features throughout an entire school building. Furthermore, many walls may never be moved. Consequently, good school planning calls for the judicious application of the principle of flexibility. If movable walls are desired, it is imperative that supporting columns be strategically placed so as not to interfere with sight lines when the positions of the internal walls are changed to meet the demands of a changing curriculum.

The principle of flexibility should be applied to the equipment (fixed and technological), as well as to the building. The design of a school should facilitate the relocation of instructional equipment. For example, flat floors, rather than risers, are preferable in instructional areas because they permit flexibility of seating arrangements.

Practical Features of Modifiable School Plans

Some specific recommendations are presented in this section. These suggestions are focused upon those elements of school planning, discussed previously, that promote expansibility, contractibility, adaptability, and flexibility.

1   *Placement of a building on the site.* First and foremost, it is essential that school planners select a site of adequate size in accordance with the standards suggested earlier. Assuming that the area of the school site is large enough, the building should be placed so that additions can be made to it on all four sides. If not, additions should be possible on at least three sides of the school.
2   *The traffic pattern and location of corridors.* Corridors, stairways, and exits should be located so that the extended traffic pattern may flow naturally into any space added to the original structure. Also, the initial design of a school building should be aimed at keeping the costs of expansion at a minimum through the proper placement of corridors and stairways.
3   *The central utility core concept.* The establishment of a service core in the central part of a building is one method of providing for the unforeseeable. Wires, pipes, ducts, power, Internet, and cables can be easily extended to any part of the building from a centrally located service core.
4   *Anticipation of new instructional aids.* The imaginative school planning team endeavors to anticipate technological advances in instructional tools. There are currently a number of promising technological developments that should be taken into account in planning a school building. The use of technology in teaching is increasing at all grade levels of learning. The forms of social media will keep changing as new technologies emerge. Computerized teaching devices: iPads, laptops, Chromebooks, white boards, and many others are growing in popularity and usage. Some schools are now boasting of one to one ratios (students to electronic devices) and the amount of required bandwidth is literally doubling on a quarterly basis.

5 *Destructible partitions*. Partitions that are built durable are often used in lieu of the portable/movable partitions where the need for removing a partition is not immediate. The destructible partition is preferable to other types of walls from the standpoint of capital outlay when a movable or operable partition is not clearly required. A destructible partition is designed so that it can be removed and the structure of the building is not compromised. The problems of relocating pipes, ducts, wires, or cables that are often imbedded in ordinary partitions does not occur with these newer partitions.

The destructible partition has an important place in school design. Operable partitions that are only rarely used are costly and unnecessary. Conventionally designed permanent partitions that enclose ducts, wiring, and plumbing are very costly to eliminate and may even become a formidable barrier to change. The destructible partition, on the other hand, can provide an excellent acoustical barrier at a reasonable cost, one that can be easily removed at a later date without difficulty. Thus, the inclusion of a large number of destructible partitions in the design of a school building provides additional insurance that the building can help cope with the unforeseeable.

6 *The movable partitions*. The movable partition serves fundamentally the same purpose as the destructible partition, but the movable partition is salvageable, and it can be relocated without much difficulty. Several types are currently available. One type utilizes a nut-and-bolt assembly system that enables two men to move a 35-foot partition from one location to another in about four hours.

Another type of movable partition is quite ingenious in design. It utilizes a pneumatic rubber boot along the top. A section of the partition, with the boot deflated, can be moved easily by two men. When the new position is reached, the boot is simply inflated and the panel is automatically sealed at both top and bottom. From the standpoint of cost, the nut-and-bolt system still has an economic advantage over other types.

7 *Suspended ceilings*. Suspended ceilings provide great flexibility at a reasonable cost. In certain circumstances, suspended ceilings using tile may actually be less costly than some of the more common non-suspended types.

8 *Ideas that look toward the future*. Planning for the unforeseeable must focus on those design features that facilitate and encourage both minor and major changes inside of an educational facility. To conceive and create a design that readily lends itself to change, school planners must ask themselves, "What provisions in the design of the school should be made now so that certain changes can be made later at a reasonable cost?" "What special features should be incorporated in the plans at this time?" More specifically, they might ask themselves, What would we do:

a   If the heating capacity needed to be increased by 50 percent?
b   If air conditioning needed to be installed?
c   If utilities were needed in any part of the school where they are now lacking?
d   If electrical power of various voltages were required in any part of the school?
e   If WiFi access is needed in all of the classrooms?

f   If two-way interactive boards were to be installed in the science and engineering areas?

g   If fiber optics needed to be added between all of the schools in the district?

h   If computer carrels were to be provided for students in the ratio of one-to-one?

i   If individual offices were to be provided for all secondary school teachers?

j   If effective germicidal lamps were to be installed in instructional areas?

k   If 25 percent of the hardbound instructional materials were to be replaced with electronic software?

l   If 20 percent of the classified staff were composed of trained teacher aides who needed offices, equipment, and space for in-service training?

m If the school were to be expanded vertically?

n   If the library and classrooms were all connected with Internet for all parents and students?

o   If the school were to provide its own air pollution filtering plant?"

This list purposely contains suggestions that may seem revolutionary to the conservative and somewhat advanced for the liberal. But it is hoped these thoughts indicate the character of the ideas that should emanate from the educational planning team when it endeavors to cope with the problem of planning for the unforeseeable future.

DISCUSSION QUESTIONS

1   What are the enrollment numbers in your school district over the past five years?

2   Define the term "adaptability." How would this design help to accommodate a school change if needed?

3   Discuss four examples of the principles of modifiability. Were any of them included in your school design?

4   How is fad versus function a challenge for school architects? What are several examples of the fads that could cause a problem in the new school design?

NOTES

1. Wemer Rogers, "Education for the Future of America," *The Educational Facility Planner*, v. 30–1 (January–February 1992), p. 6.

2. Ibid., p. 7.

3. Merle R. Sumption and Jack W. Landes, *Planning Functional School Buildings* (New York: Harper and Brothers, 1957), p. 201.

Chapter 7

Adequacy, Efficiency, and Economy

Adequacy, efficiency, and economy are three related fundamental concepts in the planning of educational facilities. The adequacy of a school plant is measured by the degree to which it satisfies the quantitative and qualitative requirements of the educational program. Efficiency is related to the functional characteristics incorporated in the design of the facility. And economy is calculated by an estimate of the potential educational return per dollar expended for school facilities.

However, one cannot accurately measure the absolute educational return per dollar expended. At any rate, there is greater economy in school planning when the expenditure of funds is more likely to produce increased educational returns or greater utilization of space and materials over a longer period of time.

ADEQUACY AND SUITABILITY OF SCHOOL SPACES

The concept of adequacy is primarily concerned with the number, size, shape, and quality of educational spaces. Adequacy alone does not ensure a well-planned school facility. Suitability of instructional spaces with respect to function and operation of a school is a correlated consideration. In more specific terms, spaces for learning should be suitable from the standpoint of environmental controllability, shape, atmosphere, location, ease of maintenance, long-range economy, and the like.

Adequacy of Number

Educational specifications should state the number of the various types of spaces estimated to be both necessary and sufficient for the desired educational programs. Any reduction in the number of proposed spaces from the number appearing in the specifications results in a corresponding cutback in the educational program.

In addition to instructional spaces, a certain number of supporting spaces must be included, such as: storage areas, preparation rooms, faculty offices, research areas, washrooms, locker spaces, toilets, lounges, and the like. The number depends primarily upon the type and size of the school planned and upon the scope of the educational programs to be housed in it. These needs will be discussed in detail in later chapters. Suffice it to say at this point that a necessary and sufficient number of both instructional and supplementary spaces should be provided. The term "sufficient" suggests that spaces in excess of the number called for by the educational program may not be included.

Adequacy of Size

The size of an instructional space directly influences its proper functioning, particularly if the number of square feet falls below the minimum needed for the function. Suggested sizes for selected educational spaces are presented in chapters 10 and 11 for each type of school plan. These figures are based on accepted practices.

The functional analysis technique may also be utilized. The space required for each activity should be determined by actual net square footage measurements, under experimental conditions if necessary. It is surprising that the functional analysis technique, despite its relative simplicity, is not universally adopted.

For example, it may be necessary to determine the space required for ten student carrels. It is quite easy to compute the space needed for a table 3 feet wide and 2 feet deep. The dimensions required for a chair and circulation space can be estimated as 3 feet long and 3 feet wide. The total square footage per carrel and circulation space then becomes 15 square feet. For ten carrels, at least 150 square feet would be needed. If we add an estimated 50 square feet for circulation, the size of a room for ten student carrels would be approximately 200 square feet.

This procedure can be applied to any instructional space, provided the number of students involved and the estimated space requirement of each type of learning activity are known. In situations where new subjects are being introduced in the curriculum, experimental situations may be set up to determine the approximate amount of space needed. In some instances, the use of this method has revealed that spaces smaller than those suggested by rule of thumb were marginally adequate for the function under consideration.

Adequacy of Environmental Controls

Adequate environmental controllability is vital to effective learning and to healthfulness. Thermal, acoustical, and visual controls are directly related to the needs of the human body. Instructional spaces should be designed with ample thermal capacity, including individual room controls for both heating and cooling. In addition, they must have adequate illumination and optimum acoustical characteristics.

Details regarding the specific requirements associated with environmental control will be discussed in subsequent chapters. It is intended, at this point, simply to note the strong need for adequate heating, cooling, humidity, lighting, and acoustics.

Suitability of Shape

The shape of an instructional space should be suited to the function it is designed to serve. In general, rectangular, almost square, classrooms are quite suitable for classes of about thirty students engaged in non-laboratory-type instruction. Shape may be critical in some instructional spaces. For example, a combination lecture room-laboratory, where peripheral laboratory tables are desired, should be almost square. A music room should not be long and narrow. Elementary-grade classrooms can be supervised more effectively if the space is more "squarish."

On the other hand, a storage room should be long and narrow to make the most efficient use of floor space. In fact, a width of about 7 feet is preferable from the standpoint of economy. Characteristics of the various spaces are discussed in chapters 10 and 11 pertaining to the planning of elementary and secondary school buildings.

Suitability of Atmosphere

The environment created by an architect in the design of a school building should be psychologically stimulating to the students. Color, proportions, shape, lighting, fenestration, texture of interior surfaces, furniture, and furnishings all contribute to the atmosphere produced within an instructional space. Obviously, the total effect should both please and stimulate the student, who must sense that she or he is an integral part of the space and welcome in it. Instructional spaces should be warm, cozy, flexible, and attractive.

Color can be used most effectively in creating a proper psychological environment. Color coordination is a topic of major concern to school planners as they seek to create an environment suitable for learning.

Adequacy of Space Relationships

A school building should be designed so that it functions as a single organism. All of its parts should be located in proper relationship to each other in order that the activities in the building can be conducted efficiently, conveniently, economically, healthfully, and safely.

Clustering of Functionally Related Spaces

From the standpoint of economy, efficiency, and ease of communication between faculty and staff, it is highly desirable that spaces housing similar or closely related instructional activities be clustered together. For example, all science spaces, such as those for biology, chemistry, physics, and general science, could be located in a single cluster in a high school building. In general, it is recommended that an educational facility be conceived and designed as a series of clusters of related spaces. The relationship of one cluster to another will be treated in chapters 10 and 11 dealing with the planning of each type of school.

Separation of Incompatible and Unrelated Spaces

Incompatible spaces should be well separated from each other. For acoustical reasons, for example, it is necessary to separate spaces planned for noisy activities from those whose activities are quiet; for example, shop areas should not be near the library. For psychological reasons, it is highly desirable to separate the entrance to the guidance office from that of the principal's office, but for functional reasons, the interior areas of the guidance suite should be adjacent to those of the principal.

For aesthetic reasons, large masses may be separated somewhat. For reasons of economy, air-conditioned spaces would be separated from the power plant or mechanical rooms. From the standpoint of natural lighting, it might be necessary to separate adjoining wings by substantial distances, if natural lighting were to be the primary source of illumination. Sky lights should be utilized whenever possible to add light and save power.

The principle of separation should be applied judiciously in school planning, for example, by spacing the clusters or related spaces properly rather than isolating an individual space from the cluster to which it is closely related. The time necessary for students to travel from one space to another should be taken into account, too. If distances between classroom buildings become too great, it may be necessary to increase the time allowed between periods and possibly lengthening the school day.

Location in Relation to Safety and Health

In placing each function within the building or on the school site, planners should pay careful heed to the safety and health of the students and staff. For example, the location of storage space in lofts in shop areas can present a serious safety hazard. Spaces requiring service drives should be laid out with great care to ensure the safety of students and school personnel. Unloading zones should be properly situated in relationship to both sidewalks and main driveways. Students should not be required to cross driveways in traveling from the bus-unloading area to the building or in walking from the play areas to the gymnasium.

THE EFFICIENCY OF A SCHOOL BUILDING

At first glance, it would appear that efficiency and economy are virtually the same. Actually, they are similar only to the extent that both principles are designed to achieve the highest and best return for each dollar expended by the school district. For the purpose of this discussion, efficiency refers to architectural design that is likely to improve the instructional effectiveness or operational characteristics of the building.

Economy, on the other hand, has reference to actual savings in capital outlay that can be affected through architectural design. In a broad sense, therefore, efficiency is related to greater functional return per dollar expended, while economy is associated with the attainment of a given educational result at the lowest possible cost.

Greater educational return can be achieved in a host of ways through the creative design of a school building. School planners and faculty should keep efficiency of instruction in mind as they consider and discuss various proposals. The question that one should ask in relation to efficiency is, "Is this particular solution to the problem likely to yield the greatest educational return?"

To arrive at a proper answer, one should further ask such questions as, "Does the solution promote the learning of both teacher and students?" "Will most teachers find it simple to implement?" "Can the proposed solution be adapted to most of the situations that are likely to be encountered?" "Will the solution facilitate instructional or learning activities?" "Is the proposed solution too complex or elaborate in terms of the foreseeable need?"

Efficiency of Function

All school planners want to design a building that is tailor-made for the educational function of the school. Therefore, it is paramount that the functional aspects of the proposed school building be stated and described clearly in the educational specifications. Then the architect has no difficulty or uncertainty preparing concept drawings that are reasonably close to the desired design in terms of function.

As mentioned earlier, it is not possible to list functional features that apply to all educational facilities. A creative planning team and an imaginative faculty can supply the architect with hundreds of functional suggestions. In fact, it is not unusual to gather several hundred promising ideas from a faculty of fifty teachers, when the techniques of group dynamics are employed.

In planning for functional efficiency, school planners must also take into account the type of teaching materials, technology, and instructional equipment to be used. Functional efficiency demands that both the building and its equipment be conceived as a single, unified educational tool.

Many ideas related to functional efficiency will evolve as the faculty works with the planning teams. One idea suggests another. It might be helpful to describe two situations in which this approach was used. After a group of teachers had become thoroughly acquainted with the concept of functional flexibility, it was suggested that faculty offices and classrooms be supplied with uniformly spaced vertical standards, such as those used for bookshelves, so that whiteboards, shelves, cabinets, or coat hangers could all be hung on the walls (if desired). A faculty member could prepare charts and graphs on a small whiteboard hung in her office. She might then unhook it and carry it to the lecture room where she could hang it on the standards for instructional use.

In designing a gymnasium-natatorium, a faculty member posed the idea of locating the pool about 50 feet away from the gymnasium floor and parallel to it. The intervening space above the lockers and showers could contain folding bleachers that could face either the pool or the gymnasium. When the pool was being used for swimming meets, the bleachers could seat spectators in the natatorium. When the bleachers were reversed, spectators could face the gymnasium play area during basketball games. When the bleachers were folded, the space between the two facilities could be used for instruction in physical education. This example illustrates to some extent the variety of ideas that may be offered by the school planning team and the faculty associated with it.

EFFICIENCY IN MAINTENANCE AND OPERATION OF A BUILDING

School plants should be planned and designed to keep the cost of maintenance and operation at a minimum. Operational costs are directly related to the cost of services, fuels, expendable supplies, utilities, and the like. Maintenance costs refer primarily to the expenditure required to maintain the building and its equipment in its original state of utility.

Operational Efficiency

School planners should give a penetrating look to all matters related to the operation of a school. Services represent relatively large operational costs. Consequently, the building should be designed, the materials chosen, and the equipment selected on the basis of maximum human efficiency. For example, easily and quickly cleaned surfaces should be chosen over those that involve a lower initial cost but are more costly to maintain.

Features that save the time of employees who operate or occupy the structure are critical. For example, the placement of doors (using vestibules on all outside entry ways) and the location of service spaces with respect to entrances, driveways, unloading zones, and each other should be carefully studied to minimize unnecessary loss of time or motion. Fuels and utilities should be conserved as much as possible. Heat losses and gains must be taken into account, not only to provide sufficient heating or cooling capacity but also to achieve economies in the operation of the system.

Additional insulation or low-conductivity windowpanes mean greater initial costs, but the savings in operational costs over the life of the building will generally more than compensate for the additional initial cost. The design of the building should reduce waste of electrical power, gas, and water as much as possible. For example, the use of LED lights would permit the custodian to control all of the lights in a building from a single panel. By pressing a few buttons in the custodial area after a given hour, he or she could activate relays that extinguish some or all of the lights in a building, or the lights could be controlled automatically by the use of an app for a computer/tablet/smartphone.

Water conservation is also desirable, but not at the expense of function. Toilets and urinals with auto flushers save maintenance time and reduce odors in the restrooms. The use of spring faucets is a case in point. Having the water shut off automatically avoids using excess water, sinks that run over, and higher utility bills. Blow dryers to replace paper towels also saves money, reduces waste of paper, and cleanup of trash. The initial cost on these items may be somewhat higher, but the operation is both functional and economical.

Efficiency Related to Maintenance

Efficiency of maintenance is concerned with durability and cost of upkeep. Materials that are relatively maintenance-free should be given preference over less costly materials requiring greater care. The life expectancy of both materials and equipment is a basic consideration in the selection of such items. Those that have the lowest depreciation cost per year should be given first consideration, unless such choices adversely affect the educational function.

Efficiency in Storage and Handling of Materials

All materials should be stored as close as possible to the place where they are used. Storage rooms, therefore, should be strategically placed in a building with reference to *delivery, distribution,* and *utilization.* Sound business practice demands that storage spaces be controlled. Consequently, storage rooms should be designed and situated so that control is facilitated. It is also necessary to plan storage spaces to prevent spoilage or damage to materials stored in them. Unfortunately, architectural engineers often utilize storage rooms for ducts, transformers, distribution boxes, and the like. Besides reducing the effective size of storage spaces, the secondary use of these spaces may damage the supplies or materials placed in them.

Efficiency in the Design of Circulation Patterns within a School

The architectural design of student circulation space has a pronounced influence on the educational function of a school building. Circulation patterns must allow student traffic to flow rapidly from one part of the building to the other; however, extreme care must be exercised to ensure that the space provided for circulation is not only necessary but also sufficient. Excessive circulation space is wasteful from the standpoint of both initial investment and operation.

There seems to be a slight tendency among a few school planners to overdesign circulation spaces. In one instance, for example, there was a single-loaded corridor 10 feet wide surrounding three sides of a large cafeteria-dining area. In another school, two corridors were provided to serve three rows of classrooms. In both of these cases the excess corridor space added somewhat to student convenience, but in neither case did the circulation pattern indicate an efficient use of space.

Secondary corridors and lobbies should be carefully studied in any school facility plan. Hallway width can be adjusted to maximize the flow of student traffic. The main entry way may need a 20-foot hallway, whereas the back art hallway can easily function with a 10-foot corridor. Circulation space should be completely adequate, but, in planning the size of lobbies, corridors, and other circulation spaces in a school building, it should be remembered that efficiency in circulation space yields two bonuses—savings in initial capital outlay and reductions in operational costs.

ECONOMY

Every effort should be made by school planners to achieve maximum economy in both capital outlay and operation of a proposed school building. Economy, however, should be differentiated from cheapness. A building should be economical but not cheap. Economy, as used in this text, is not the acquisition of a school facility for a given enrollment at the lowest possible cost. Rather, it is defined as the achievement of maximum educational and utilitarian value per dollar expended. According to this concept, the lowest-cost building is not necessarily the most economical.

For example, one school district constructed a masonry school at a phenomenally low cost per square foot. When it was viewed after it was barely five years old, the mortar had crumbled so badly that a pencil could be pushed through an outside wall. The building had settled so badly that light could be seen through the walls in one of the rest rooms. Water damage had caused the window frames to rot, permitting cold air to enter the building. The superintendent of schools conceded that the school district had a serious problem on its hands, because the building was too new to abandon and yet too costly to continue in operation.

How Much Economy Can Be Achieved by Educational Boards?

Conscientious members of school boards spend months poring over plans and drawings in an effort to achieve real economies in school buildings. Their worthy efforts are concentrated on items of construction that represent only a small percent of the total cost of the project.

Human Effort and Potential Savings

Let us demonstrate the low potential savings that may be affected by educational boards in selecting less costly materials for walls, flooring, hardware, ceiling, lighting, acoustics, and the like. On the average, the total cost of a building is distributed as follows:

- Twenty percent for fees, furniture, furnishings and equipment, and site development.
- Eighty percent for construction, of which 30 percent is attributable to heating, ventilating, electrical, technology and mechanical equipment.

If we subtract 30 percent from the construction cost for heating, mechanicals, and the like, the remainder is 50 percent of the total cost. Assuming further that labor represents about one-half of the cost of construction, and also that a school board has practically no control over it, the cost of all remaining construction materials in a school is thus reduced to about 25 percent of the total cost. Let us assume further that about one-half of the materials cost is predetermined by the physical requirements, such as steel beams for framework, slabs of concrete, and the like.

Consequently, a board is left with about 12 percent of the cost of building materials over which it has some choice. If we also assume that it will cost at least one-half of the 12 percent to acquire basic materials over which the board has a choice, the maximum possible saving that could be effected by a school board appears to be 6 percent of the total cost of the school. Since most members of school boards are not professional engineers or architects, it is reasonable to assume that, at best, a saving of 2 or 3 percent in the total cost of a building might be effected at a personal cost to the board members in time and effort that is inordinately high in relation to such a savings.

The time invested in discussions, research, and study to effect economies is not always commensurate with the savings realized. All boards must review plans and specifications in terms of function, efficiency, and economy. It is suggested, however, that economy not be belabored. After initial corrections have been made, the return is disappointingly small when compared with the additional effort that must be expended. More substantial economies are possible through creative building design, long-range planning, use of new concepts, and the like, which are discussed subsequently.

True and False Economies

School planners must differentiate clearly between real and false economies. A true economy must meet the following two tests:

1 The reduced cost in capital outlay does not adversely affect the curriculum or educational efficiency of the school.
2 The reduced initial cost does not result in *increased* maintenance and operational costs.

The first test deals with intangible educational outcomes that are difficult to evaluate. Nevertheless, school planners should be fully convinced that an economy does not hinder or restrict the desired educational program. The second test, on the other hand, is quite objective and relatively simple to apply. For example, Pierce concludes that "the newer LED system (of school lighting) will probably cost slightly more initially, but the annual cleaning, relamping, and operating costs will more than offset this slight difference in less than a year's time."[1] This has been borne out in actual experience.

While this illustration is striking, many others are not so dramatic, nor so obvious. For example, the use of costly glazed tile on the lower part of corridor walls and in toilet rooms is a real economy. The installation of expensive ceramic tile on toilet room floors represents another real economy. The plastering of both sides of light-weight concrete blocks on walls between two classrooms is a real economy, because it significantly decreases noise interference between two adjoining instructional spaces.

The installation of suspended acoustical ceilings on a mechanical track system is another real economy from the standpoint of maintenance, replacement of tile, and adaptability of the space as a learning laboratory. The installation of wall-to-wall carpeting in certain areas of a school building also represents real economy from the standpoint of money saved, better acoustics, and improved educational function.

Economy Related to the Design of a School Building

The design of a building strongly influences its cost. In discussing cost reduction by educational boards, it was assumed that the design of the building was approved and fixed before board members sought to effect economies by selecting less costly equipment, furniture, and interior surfaces. Not only does the design of the building have a profound influence on the initial cost of a school, it also affects its cost of operation.

The Compact Design

The School Design and Planning Laboratory has found a close relationship between "compactness of a school building and both subsequent maintenance and operation expense," in elementary and secondary schools.[2] There was also a strong negative correlation between initial cost of a building and compactness. In these studies, the index of compactness was obtained by dividing the perimeter footage by the square footage within the walls.

The compactness effect was more pronounced in the larger buildings than in the smaller structures, as might be expected. In designing economical buildings, therefore, it is desirable to keep the linear feet of perimeter per square foot of enclosure as small as possible. The architectural profession has applied this principle of economy to school design for many years. Many architects have turned to the cube, the circle, and more recently to the sphere, as exemplified by the introduction of the geodesic dome by R. Buckminster Fuller, in their efforts to achieve maximum compactness.

In designing educational facilities, however, school planners should bear in mind that the primary purpose of a school building is to educate students. No predetermined design should be adopted unless it satisfies the requirements of the desired educational program. If the compact plan satisfies the educational need just as well as the rambling type of school building, then the principle of economy would dictate that the compact design be selected.

On the other hand, there may be circumstances, particularly in the design of elementary schools, where the rambling single-story, finger plan is particularly suitable. It is believed that school planners should give a strong preference to the compact plan but should not insist upon it in all situations. It is also felt that a rambling school cannot be justified in terms of economy unless its design meets a specific educational need.

The compact design does not mean that the entire school must be designed as a single large cube or hemisphere. Indeed, architects have utilized this principle in many ingenious ways. They have used a series of cubes varying in size. They have planned circular school buildings. They have employed combinations of spheres, cubes, and cylinders. Of course, the influence of compactness on economy of school construction is less pronounced in school buildings having areas under 15,000 square feet.

For secondary schools containing less than 50,000 square feet, the correlation between cost of construction and compactness was −0.78, while schools with areas in excess of 100,000 square feet yielded a coefficient of correlation of −0.90.[3] A similar research project was conducted at the School Design and Planning Laboratory using data related to elementary schools, which are generally substantially smaller in area than secondary schools. Even in these cases, the economy due to compactness was quite pronounced. The coefficient of correlation between compactness and the cost of elementary schools was −0.41.[4]

The principle of compactness suggests that greater economy of initial capital outlay and operational cost with respect to heating and cooling is obtained when the perimeter of a building is kept as short as possible. For this reason, jogs should be avoided. Long, narrow wings are less desirable than structures in which wings are combined to form a more compact building. For example, arranging classrooms so that the narrow end faces the corridor tends to promote compactness and economy. The geodesic plan is another illustration of compact design in school planning.

Planned Economy for Capital Outlay Programs

Economy can be the result of educational planning that takes place long before a building is conceived or proposed. In fact, economy is an important aspect of long-range planning. The strategic location of new buildings, the judicious rehabilitation of facilities with educational potential, and the abandonment of obsolete school buildings contribute to educational economy.

A few highlights of economy related to long-range educational planning are reviewed. A more detailed account appears in chapter 5, where many elements of long-range planning are discussed. Economy in long-range planning is promoted by acquiring school sites in advance of need. An educational board should obtain an option on property that may be required for expansion or a new school as many as five years prior to the anticipated need, if possible.

New schools should be located properly in relation to the area of future population growth of the school district and to existing buildings that are likely to be abandoned in the foreseeable future. Economy may be improved through the development of a long-range financial plan designed to keep the credit rating of the school district as high as possible. Such a plan can provide for advantageous timing of financial transactions.

Economy can be achieved by selecting the proper type of grade organization for the educational program offered and in relation to existing school buildings with educational potential for future use. And finally, the economy is substantially improved when new facilities are designed for real, as contrasted with pseudo expansion.

In fact, a few dotted lines showed exactly where expansion could occur, but there was little or no consideration, in most cases, as to exactly what educational functions would be housed within the space enclosed by the dotted lines, or how they would be related to existing functions. All that the architect did, in such cases, was to point out that there was sufficient land to expand at the end of a corridor. Educators must help architects envision specific educational uses for the space contained within such dotted lines. Such planning fosters economy.

Another aspect of economy that precedes the planning of a building is the employment of an architect who can prepare a proper set of final working drawings and specifications. Economy is substantially improved if the architect prepares plans and specifications that are complete, detailed, and easy to understand. A school board never really knows how many additional dollars contractors add to bids simply because they want to be on the safe side in translating ambiguous specifications into the cost of labor and materials. Also, drawings and specifications that lack sufficient detail may lead to change of orders and misunderstanding during construction, both of which are costly.

Suggestions for Improving Economy in School Planning

It would be a monumental, if not an impossible, task to list every conceivable method of enhancing an economy in the planning of school buildings. A few suggestions are presented here with the expectation that many other money-saving ideas will evolve during the planning process:

1   *Economy is improved when instructional spaces can be designed to serve several functions.* In such cases, the room utilization factor is likely to be increased and, under certain conditions, fewer spaces may be needed.
2   *Classroom ceilings can be lowered to 9 feet or 9 feet 6 inches without any harm to the educational program.* Such a change would result in savings of both initial capital outlay *and in heating and cooling costs.*
3   *A reduction in the amount of sliding glass windows in a school building decreases the cost of both maintenance and operation.* The use of fixed glass is more economical than the installation of movable window sash.
4   *The quantity of ventilation should be kept as low as possible but consistent with minimum needs, about 10 cubic feet of fresh air per student per minute or less in some states.*
5   *Construction materials should be selected on the basis of ease of maintenance and durability.* As mentioned earlier, substituting materials that reduce the cost of initial capital outlay does not necessarily achieve economy.
6   *Stock floor plans should be avoided since they do not save educational institutions money in the long run.* According to Pierce, "The cost of a project can be reduced by using stock plans only when the school is willing to settle for inadequate and incomplete planning; and, therefore, willing to settle for less than the most appropriate functional provisions in the building."[5]

Where stock plans have been used, the results have been less than encouraging. The amount that can be saved is insignificant. For example, if the architect's fee is 6 percent, one-quarter of the fee, or 1.5 percent, is reserved for construction oversight. Consequently, a school district can effect savings on only the remaining 4.5 percent of construction cost.

Since sites and soil conditions vary greatly, some revision will be required in the structural aspects of stock plans. If we assume that it would cost a school district about 1 percent for the adaptation of stock plans to a given site and orientation, then the school district would have a potential savings of 3.5 percent, providing its educational specification is exactly the same as the one for which the original stock plans were designed.

Changes in stock plans will probably be needed, because the educational needs in any given district are likely to differ. Perhaps another 2 percent of construction cost would be needed to employ an architect to modify the stock plans to satisfy the educational needs of the school district. At this point, it would appear at first that a school district can save about 1.5 percent of the construction cost of the proposed school after all changes are made. However, stock plans must be designed and continuously kept up-to-date at the standard cost of architectural services. This cost must be shared and borne by the school districts using such stock plans.

Consequently, potential savings of about 2 percent are virtually wiped out by charges made to the state or school districts for the original stock plans. When it is realized further that the modifications required to meet local needs represent at best a series of compromises between the changes that *need* to be made and those that *can* be made, because of the necessity of adhering to the basic concepts of design in the original stock plans, the appeal of stock plans almost disappears.

It is often not realized that even conventionally planned buildings use some prefabricated to a large extent. The major difference between the so-called prefabricated buildings and those of modular design lies in the extent to which the parts of a building are preassembled at the factory. Under prefabrication procedures, relatively large sections of walls and ceiling structures are preassembled. In both conventional and prefabricated buildings, practically all of the component parts are prefabricated. For example, bricks, steel framing, doors, window sash, and tiles of various types are prefabricated in any type of construction.

In all fairness, it should be stated that the process of prefabrication possesses at least three important advantages over other types of construction. First, large parts of a structure can be assembled in a shop under ideal conditions. Second, a minimum amount of labor is needed on the site. Third, the time required to erect a prefabricated structure on the site is dramatically reduced (by over 50 percent) using mass-production techniques.

The technology underlying prefabricated buildings has advanced by leaps and bounds over the past few years. Predesigned plans can now be changed at once and at will to meet the special needs of any school district. CAD (computer-assisted design) software assists architects in preparing architectural and engineering drawings. For this reason, they are now able to design and redesign plans of prefabricated structures more quickly and inexpensively. Since computers are also used to control robots that fabricate the components of prefabricated structures, these two technological advances combine their computer power to produce prefabricated units that can be readily designed to meet the specific requirements of any educational program.

Operational Economy

The rapidly increasing costs of labor, materials, and energy over the past two decades have placed a high premium on certain aspects of school planning. Formerly, these matters were inconsequential. Labor was cheaper so that a school building could tolerate a number of items that were low in initial cost but relatively costly to maintain. School planners were able to overlook possible savings in heat, light, and power, because the cost of energy was insignificant in relation to the operational costs of a school building.

Today, the situation is quite different. The high cost of labor and the dwindling availability of energy place an extremely high value on the cost of maintenance and on the selection of energy-saving equipment. There is also a greater emphasis on the ways and means of conserving energy. See chapter 8 for energy-saving measures.

Planning for Minimal Expenditures for Maintenance

The design of school buildings that are not costly to maintain entails much more than selecting materials that are easy to clean. To be sure, the choice of such materials is an important consideration, but that is just the beginning. There are many other important aspects of planning that can produce dramatic savings in the cost of maintaining a school facility.

Let us look, for a moment, at the placement of equipment, lighting, plumbing, shrubbery, or lawns. With high labor costs, time represents money. School planners would be richly rewarded in the form of substantial savings in maintenance costs if the architect were required to design a building in which each item requiring routine maintenance is installed so that the time required to maintain it is at a minimum.

There are hundreds of such items in a school building, including light fixtures located in the high ceilings of an auditorium, trees and shrubs that hinder lawn mowing. These undesirable design elements consume hours of valuable time. Every effort should be made to eliminate all design features that increase the time required for maintaining the facility or the equipment associated with it.

It is not practical in this publication to describe the many ways by which savings in maintenance cost can be achieved. If the principle stated above is kept in mind in designing a school building, the appropriate solutions will evolve naturally in the course of the planning. The application suggested by the above principle—design features that promote efficiency—undoubtedly reduces the time required for maintenance and bolsters the operational economy of the educational facility.

The Principle of Least Probable Maintenance

It often pays high dividends to determine the potential cost of maintenance over a long period of time. Indeed, the practice of selecting materials that are durable in quality and economical in maintenance is an application of this principle. But the potential savings or losses over the life of the building are not always known. For example, many materials that are enduring and easily preserved are also more costly in initial capital outlay. The added initial cost, however, should be balanced against the estimated savings in cost of maintenance over a period of at least twenty to thirty years. Once these two figures are determined, the answer becomes self-evident.

Until recently, very little thought was given to the potential cost of maintaining building equipment. The functional specifications of specialized equipment were prepared by the architect, and the contractor was obligated to conform to the desired products. Accordingly, the contractor could simply select the specified equipment that was the lowest cost. Potential maintenance cost was of little or no concern to the contractor. In the interest of greater long-range economy, it is suggested that all persons involved in planning educational facilities consider the overall maintenance cost of equipment.

It might be quite advantageous for a school district to include some statements concerning the "frequency-of-repair" characteristics of potential maintenance costs, in addition to the usual functional specifications of all equipment to be installed in a school building. This practice may encourage some manufacturers to include long-term maintenance guarantees on their equipment. Thus, in selecting the equipment for a school facility, the contractor would be responsible for selecting products that are both low in maintenance and functional in design.

In general, the cost of maintaining equipment is directly related to the level of sophistication of the equipment. The more complicated the equipment both mechanically and electronically, the more important it is to determine the potential cost of maintaining such equipment in accordance with the principle of least probable maintenance.

DISCUSSION QUESTIONS

1   How do school planners prepare for the task of requiring operational efficiency for the unforeseeable future?
2   Define "true economy." How would you determine if it meets the associated tests?
3   Discuss five ways that could help to achieve an "improved economy" in school planning.
4   How is operational economy a challenge for school contractors? What steps are needed to be in place to avoid problems with the purchase of inefficient equipment?

NOTES

1. David A. Pierce, *Saving Dollars in Building Schools* (New York: Reinhold, 1959), p. 88.
2. School Planning Laboratory Research, Reports 3 and 4 (Stanford, CA: Educational Facilities Laboratories, Inc., Stanford University, 1961).
3. Ibid.
4. Ibid.
5. Pierce, *Saving Dollars*, p. 32.

Chapter 8

Planning for Energy Conservation and Management

Prior to the Middle East embargo on oil shipments to the United States in 1973, architects, educational facility planners, and school officials were not fully aware of the eventual depletion of world sources of energy derived from fossil fuels. At that time, energy was of no particular concern to the public or school officials. There was an overabundance of fuel and the cost was relatively low. Accordingly, there was no reason for anyone to become apprehensive about energy consumption.

Under these conditions, architects and school planners were concerned only with the form of energy that would be supplied to a proposed school building; oil, natural gas, or electricity. School boards often asked architects and utility companies to make studies in depth to determine the cost-effectiveness of each form of energy for a particular school facility in a given location. In this context, it is interesting to note that the electric companies were very aggressive and often successful in promoting "all electric" school facilities. They spared no effort and were ingenious in their attempts to convince local school officials that electricity was the clean, cost-effective heating energy of the future.

Recently, the future outlook on energy has changed completely. The recognition by the public and leaders of the world that the supply of fossil fuels is finite has been shocking. The dwindling supply of energy from fossil fuels such as oil or gas has become a major concern of the industrialized nations.

Scientists predicted that there would be a serious energy shortage before the year 2000 and that the world supplies of fossil fuels would be completely exhausted about the middle of the twenty-first century, assuming that the demand for energy continued to grow in the future at the same rate it did in the past. And still, no one believed them! And why should they? After all, more and more reserves were being discovered. The supply of oil far outstripped the demand, and fuel prices were quite low. Automobile makers were producing high-powered vehicles with very low efficiency.

The predictions of when the present known reserves of oil and gas would be completely depleted varied from the beginning of the twenty-first century to about the year 2100. These predictions were based on the increased demand for energy caused by the growth in world population and by the foreseeable industrialization of underdeveloped countries. Under these circumstances, the energy outlook for the future was rather bleak. It has been interesting to see how the more recent discoveries of the Bakken oil reserves and other previously unavailable fossil fuel sources have affected the use of alternative energy solutions.

Solar energy, biomass energy, wind energy, geothermal energy, and energy from the sea are all now viable alternatives. While there have recently been some break-throughs in these alternative energy sources, cost is still an issue in any of these potential approaches. For school districts, however, energy conservation is much more than planning for the future. For them, energy conservation is imperative, if they are to cope successfully with the relatively high price of fuels.

In concluding this introductory narrative on energy consumption and conservation, it might be enlightening to take a brief look at the unbelievable rate at which energy is consumed, compared to the time required to produce it. A real situation will be cited to illustrate this point. A family in New England is using an efficient, airtight Fisher wood stove to heat a Cape Cod–style house with an area of about 1,000 square feet on the first floor and 600 square feet of space developed in the attic. The total floor area of the house is about 1,600 square feet.

During the coldest part of the winter, this wood stove maintains the temperature of the house at about 70° Fahrenheit and consumes one cord of hardwood in four weeks. Foresters have found that it takes an average of five trees between 35 and 40 feet high to produce one cord of fire wood.

The time required for an oak seedling to become a tree of this size is between fifteen and twenty years depending upon soil conditions. For the purpose of this discussion, let us assume that the growing time for such a tree is about seventeen years, or 200 months. Thus, it takes 200 months to produce five trees that will heat one average-size house in New England for one month! In this case, energy is consumed 200 times as fast as nature can produce it through the process of photosynthesis.

For school officials and school boards, conservation of energy has both external and internal implications. Conserving energy contributes to the well-being of the industrial nations throughout the world. But, internally, conservation of energy becomes an absolute necessity in terms of fiscal considerations. The dramatic increases in energy prices make energy conservation an unconditional imperative of modern educational management

THE ESSENCE OF ENERGY

A few years ago, the word "energy" was primarily restricted to the routine vocabulary of the scientist and the engineer. Today, "energy" has become a household word for something that is of vital concern to everyone in the industrialized nations of the world. Energy is something whose cost has at times doubled and redoubled over a very short period of time. Energy is also that elusive something that appears and disappears at the whim of circumstances beyond our control. And it is becoming more and more evident that energy, whatever meanings and forms it may take, is something that is being taken seriously by everyone living in the industrialized nations.

Scientifically energy is that which is capable of doing work. But, to superintendents, school boards, school officials, and school planners, energy is oil, gas, electricity, solar power, and other alternative sources. It is also lighting, heating, cooling, and power for communications devices and mechanical equipment. Few people realize that our own sun is and has been the only primary source of energy for our earth ever since the world was formed millions of years ago.

The sun is a nuclear furnace that continually radiates a substantial amount of energy in the form of light and heat onto the surface of the earth. It must be remembered that the supplies of fossil fuels found in the crust of the earth in the form of oil or gas are the products of solar energy that took thousands and thousands of years to accumulate. It is frightening to face the stark reality that, at the anticipated rate of consumption, all of these accumulated reserves could be completely exhausted in the foreseeable future.

A number of geological scientists have already predicted that this will occur during the twenty-first century. The exact time at which our fossil fuels will be totally consumed is still open to question. But, despite the glut of fuel that appears on the market from time to time, there is absolutely no question whatsoever that the time will come, perhaps sooner rather than later, when there will be no more gas, and no more oil that can be economically extracted from the crust of the earth.

While the energy outlook of the world is not particularly bright at this time, there is every reason for looking toward the future with optimism and renewed hope. We still have the nuclear furnace on the sun that is producing energy at an enormous rate. The world is indeed blessed by the abundance of energy that the sun continually showers upon its surface every day. In fact, the sun is daily supplying the earth with an amount of energy that is many more times the amount of energy that the world is likely to need in the foreseeable future.

This energy arrives in the form of light and heat, and some of it reappears in the form of vegetation, wind, weather, ocean waves, ocean currents, and temperature differentials both in the oceans and in the atmosphere. With these forms of energy in mind, the future is really exciting and challenging. There is indeed an abundant source of energy—the sun. In due time, human creativity and ingenuity will discover the ways and means of converting this vast source of energy into new forms of energy that can best serve the inhabitants of the earth.

Energy Management

The management of energy has emerged as a crucial and multifarious operation in the administration of educational facilities. Before the energy revolution in the mid-1970s, the conservation of energy was of no particular interest to school officials or educational facility planners. There was really no reason to be concerned. The cost of energy was low and the supply was plentiful.

At that time, architects rarely considered the use of insulation materials, for example, in the walls and roofs of school buildings. In many instances, they summarily rejected them by stating categorically that the addition of insulation materials was not cost-effective. While that may have been true, no research findings were produced by such architects substantiating their contention that the pay-back period for the added cost of insulation would have exceeded the usable life of the educational facility.

The energy crisis, however, produced fundamental changes in the planning and modification of educational facilities. It also had a salubrious and stimulating effect on educational facility planners concerning matters related to energy. They were no longer apathetic and indifferent about design features that had the potential of reducing energy consumption. They became deeply involved in the selection of building materials, equipment, and control devices that contributed to the conservation of energy.

They were receptive and responsive to any feasible concept or innovation that promoted energy conservation. They vigorously searched for promising solutions to the energy problem. Their concerted and sustained efforts were quite successful. In a relatively short time, they were able to bring the total cost of energy down to tolerable levels in many school districts across the United States.

Architects and engineers evaluated a wide variety of feasible and achievable solutions to the energy problem confronting school officials and school boards. During this process, they identified two major categories of energy-conserving measures. The *first* group included items related to changes in building design or materials and to the replacement or alteration of selected parts of the heating, cooling, ventilation, and electrical equipment.

The *second* category, on the other hand, was focused primarily on energy management techniques that were designed to reduce energy consumption by *controlling* the use of available energy. This control was accomplished through carefully selected changes in some of the operational policies of the institution and through the use of a variety of promising energy control systems.

It might be helpful, at this point, to clarify certain terms that are currently associated with matters related to energy. Whenever fundamental changes occur in any field, new terms and expressions are likely to emerge. The energy conservation movement is no exception. Retrofitting refers to any change in an *existing* building or equipment that saves energy. The term *energy management* has been widely adopted by educators. It refers to *any* measure or procedure that effectively reduces the energy budget of the school district.

Strictly speaking, of course, any measure that saves energy is generically a form of energy conservation, regardless of whether it is accomplished by major changes in the building and its equipment, by implementing policies designed to save energy, or by the installation of energy control devices. For the purpose of this text, however, the terms "energy management" and "conservation of energy" are used synonymously. The end result is the same—lower energy costs for the school district.

There are many sound and reliable procedures, techniques, and practices that are frequently employed in counteracting the higher cost of energy. These are discussed in considerable detail in the latter sections of this chapter. School officials would be well advised, however, not to implement any of the suggested solutions before completing an energy audit, such as the one described later in this text.

Special attention is directed to *step one* of the energy audit. As will be discussed later, the information derived from this preliminary study can be helpful to the local staff in many ways. Among them is the disclosure, perhaps for the first time, as to how much, where, in what form, and for what purpose energy is being used in an existing educational facility.

The information included in the next section under "Energy Needs in School Facilities" is intended to assist local personnel in conducting the step one of the energy audit. While this material may seem redundant to persons familiar with educational facility planning, it is hoped that it will be practical, useful, and informative to local personnel assigned to the task of completing step one of the energy audit and for graduate students in the planning and maintenance of educational facilities.

Energy management appears in many forms. In addition to the suggestions made under "Retrofitting" and "Planning Energy Efficient School Buildings" later in this chapter, studies have shown the application of computers in controlling the use of energy in school buildings is quite cost-effective.[1] Later studies confirm these results.[2] The use of wireless electronic timers that control the consumption of energy in various parts of the educational facility is another type of energy management.

Finally, the modification of existing school policies may sometimes play an important part in the management of energy. For example, a substantial number of school districts have adopted changes in their academic calendars whereby schools open the fall semester during the last week of August instead of the traditional date in September. Through this change in policy, these institutions operate their facilities in August when there is little or no requirement for heating and close them in December when the cost of heating educational facilities in cold climates is quite high. The net result is a substantial saving in the cost of energy for heating purposes.

ENERGY NEEDS IN SCHOOL FACILITIES

In order to conserve energy intelligently in any educational facility, it is helpful to identify and locate all fixtures, appliances, and equipment that consume energy, including all types of teaching aids that need power. In general, the items that use energy fall into two major categories. Most of the energy supplied to a school building is associated with the health and comfort of the occupants. This group includes energy for heating, cooling, ventilation, and lighting.

The second category consists of a multitude of items that are used in conjunction with the teaching process. Since the amount of energy consumed by each teaching aid is often relatively small, the total amount of energy required by such items is frequently underestimated. But when it is realized that instructional equipment includes power tools, shop machinery, kitchen ranges, clothes dryers, computers, and other electronic systems, the amount of energy consumed by such equipment is no longer negligible. It must be taken into account in any plan designed to control energy.

Uses of Energy for Health and Comfort

As indicated previously, the major portion of the energy required for an educational facility is devoted to the health and comfort of the occupants. The energy is used for heating, cooling, ventilation, lighting, and various types of automated control mechanisms (see chapter 9).

Energy for Heating

Throughout the United States, a considerable portion of the energy budget is allocated to heating, which includes mechanical heating, water heating, and heat for food preparation. Ordinarily, this energy is derived from gas, oil, or electricity or from various combinations of these. In addition to the energy required to produce heat, power is required to distribute the heat to various parts of the building.

This ancillary equipment consists of fans, various types of pumps, and automatic valves. Power for these items is almost always electricity, which activates motors of one sort or another. Finally, controls such as thermostats, automatic valves, internal and external photoelectric devices, and various types of gas-detecting systems consume electricity even when on a standby mode.

Energy for Ventilating

Ventilating systems generally consume energy in two ways. Heat must be provided to all incoming fresh air so that cold drafts are avoided. Some designers are using a number of ways of recovering heat from air that is being exhausted from the building. This *first* approach will be discussed in more detail in this chapter under the section entitled "Planning Energy Efficient School Buildings." The *second* major use of energy in a ventilation system is to maintain a supply of fresh air in all the classrooms and other parts of the building, such as the gymnasium and auditorium.

A substantial amount of energy is consumed by scores of electric fans that move air from one point to another at predetermined rates of flow. All air movement is not by fan, however. In some of the older school buildings, gravity systems still provide ventilation in classrooms. Regardless of the functional merits of this system, it cannot be denied that it is energy efficient. However, it should be resurrected and included in the design of future schools.

Energy for Artificial Lighting

An enormous amount of electrical energy must be supplied to hundreds of lighting fixtures in school buildings. A proper visual environment is extremely important from the standpoint of health and educational function, and adequate levels of illumination should be maintained despite the energy cost involved. There is an upward trend in the use of skylights to reduce the energy required for artificial lighting.

Artificial lighting is found almost everywhere in a school building. It appears in closets, in storage rooms, in crawl spaces, and pipe trenches. It is seen in attics, in the corridors, above the stairways, inside of walk-in safes, and hidden behind panels for the indirect lighting of walls. Artificial lighting is also widely used for local illumination on various articles of furniture or equipment, such as sewing machines, shop tools, kitchen ranges, table and floor lamps, microscopes, art and drafting tables.

There are also many special applications of artificial lighting. Athletic fields are highly illuminated for night games. The auditorium is supplied with thousands of watts of artificial lighting. Many of the spaces occupied by students and teachers during the learning process are well illuminated by artificial lighting. This partial list of the more common applications of artificial lighting clearly indicates that its use is widespread throughout an educational facility and represents a substantial saving potential of the total energy supplied to the building.

Energy for Cooling

In certain parts of the United States the amount of energy used for cooling school buildings during the warm months accounts for a relatively larger part of the energy budget. To be sure, the designers of air-conditioned school buildings are cognizant of the high energy consumption of cooling equipment. In an effort to reduce the cost, they have installed insulating and mirror glass. Unfortunately, in past years architects have rarely insisted that all exterior walls and roofs be heavily lined with thermal insulation.

In fairness to the architects, however, it should be pointed out that they were deeply concerned about the high energy consumption of cooling equipment long before it became an expensive and precious commodity. Consequently, architects and engineers devised several ingenious methods of reducing the cost. Among them was the use of heat for cooling.

This paradox was accomplished through the application of the diffusion principle using high-pressure steam. On a more conventional note, engineers developed heat pumps to transport heat out of the building in the summer months. During cold weather, the same pumps can be used to heat the building by simply reversing this cycle.

Energy for Instructional Uses

Some of the instructional uses of energy have already been mentioned in connection with artificial lighting. But illumination is only part of the energy requirement of the many pieces of teaching equipment. To be sure, many types of electronic teaching devices consume relatively small amounts of power. But the aggregate of all these low users of power becomes quite important, particularly in a fairly large secondary school enrolling over 1,500 students.

For example, one flat screen computer monitor may use as little as 200 watts of power, but 100 such units in various classrooms of a school would consume 20,000 watts or 20 kilowatts of electricity per hour. One electric iron in the home economics lab uses about one kilowatt of electricity, but thirty of them would consume 30 kilowatts of power per hour. The same reasoning applies to electronic equipment in the science laboratories, kilns in the arts and crafts room, and specialized equipment in the physical therapy rooms. Computers, laptops, tablets, and other technological devices for large-group instruction consume an appreciable amount of energy.

One area of a secondary school where large amounts of power are used for instructional uses is that devoted to vocational education and industrial arts. Relatively large machines and numerous power tools are found in this area. Finally, the amount of energy required by the home economics areas for instructional purposes is probably second to that expended by industrial shop areas. Ranges and other kitchen equipment consume thousands of watts of electricity per hour. However, the cost of energy required to operate these items over the course of a year can easily be one of the larger utilities budget items.

From the standpoint of energy conservation, the primary purpose of calling attention to the wide variety of instructional equipment, teaching aids, and learning devices that consume energy in a modern school facility is to alert school officials to the hundreds of outlets that must be monitored and controlled in effecting energy-saving measures. The object of energy conservation is not to reduce the number of teaching aids but rather to make certain that power is not expended uselessly.

Other Uses of Energy in School Buildings

In addition to the major uses of energy in a school facility mentioned earlier, there are a few less obvious energy needs that are worthy of note. In most states, elevators are required for the physically handicapped. The custodial workshop is often equipped with various types of power tools. The physical education area may have equipment for washing and drying towels, and the training room may have several whirlpools and other specialized equipment. Signaling devices such as bells, chimes, fire, smoke, and CO_2 alarms are all users of energy, albeit the amount of power consumed is quite small.

Although the transportation of students is not considered part of a school facility, the amount of energy consumed by this school service is enormous indeed. Many school districts in the country own and operate their own school buses, though many larger districts are outsourcing student transportation. It is not within the scope of this book to discuss this educational service. Suffice it to say, however, that school officials and school boards can save a substantial amount of energy by streamlining bus routes, reducing the number of bus stops, improving bus maintenance, and operating each vehicle at optimum speed and capacity.

A STEP-BY-STEP APPROACH TO ENERGY CONSERVATION

Energy conservation will not just happen. It must be planned as a series of sequentially related steps. The techniques for conserving energy range from measures that are simple and inexpensive to those that are more extensive, more costly, and more technical. Unfortunately, the specific measures or changes that lead to energy conservation are not always obvious.

Consequently, some kind of systematic examination of a given school facility is required in order to determine the exact nature of the changes that promise to help conserve energy. Such a study would also include a cost analysis of such changes and what effect they are likely to have on the educational function. Several questions must be raised before any energy conservation action is taken: "Does the proposed action interfere with the educational process in any way?" "Does the proposed action create an atmosphere that is not conducive to learning?" "Is the proposed action really energy-effective?" "Is the proposed action cost-effective?"

A "no" answer to one or more of the preceding questions denotes that the proposed energy-saving action may not be in the best interest of the school district from the standpoint of economic efficiency educational impact, or the well-being of students and teachers. Energy conservation should not outweigh educational function or the healthfulness of a school building. A three-step process for energy conservation is discussed in detail in the following sections.

Step One: The Preliminary Energy Survey

A team of local school staff is organized to conduct a preliminary survey of a specified school building. This team is usually made up of a representative from the administrative office, such as the director of building maintenance and operation, or equivalent, and the maintenance and custodial staff of the building being surveyed. Similar groups are established to survey each school building in the district.

The organization and structure of the energy survey teams for each school are designed to facilitate the implementation of desirable energy conservation measures. These teams accumulate a wide variety of practical information about energy conservation. They become highly knowledgeable groups who can provide the basic data for some of the more technical energy audits that may be conducted at a later date for every school building in the school district.

The primary responsibility of each school team, however, is to recommend and implement energy-saving measures that are relatively simple to execute. These measures often require little or no capital outlay funds. For example, one larger district performed such an energy audit in each of their buildings. Mini-refrigerators were found in most of the classrooms. The removal of these mini-refrigerators saved the district thousands of dollars in energy costs each month. Finally, since each school team has been involved in the energy conservation program from the time of the program's initiation, they are informed about the various techniques associated with energy conservation. Furthermore, they will be in a better position to implement energy-saving measures that are more complex and comprehensive in nature than those introduced in the above step one, if and when a more sophisticated energy audit is made by experts at a later date. In completing step one, it is suggested that the team use a comprehensive checklist for conducting a preliminary energy survey.

Let us review what has been accomplished in step one. In this step, a team of local staff members, knowledgeable in the maintenance and operation of school buildings, has attended workshops sponsored by the appropriate state and local agencies on energy conservation. Each team has acquired as much knowledge as possible on immediate steps that could be taken in order to conserve energy. Each team surveyed a school facility and made recommendations back to school officials of the local school district on how energy could be conserved. Some, if not all, of these recommendations have been implemented for each school surveyed.

Step Two: The Mini-Audit

Local school officials can select a few school buildings where substantial savings in energy could be made. These officials must also make a study of whether or not these selected school buildings are part of the long-range school facility needs of the district. As a result of a comprehensive study by school officials and the school board, a decision can then be made to take additional steps to conserve energy in certain school building(s).

The local maintenance and operational staff must take and perform every conservation measure within its level of expertise and budgetary limitations. There can be computer-generated information to indicate that sizable potential savings in energy and tax dollars could be realized in certain school buildings in the district. Thus, the school board can authorize the school officials to study the matter further and return it with recommendations. They can approve a "mini-audit" of selected school facilities in the school district.

The "mini-audit" is a sound and well-conceived step in meeting the urgent and pressing needs of saving energy, as well as public funds. The mini-audit is conducted by a small number of highly trained professionals over a short period of time. This team of professionals usually consists of a structural engineer, a heating and ventilating engineer, an architect, and a representative from the utility company.

This group, together with one or two school administrators, walk through a given school building over a period of two or three hours, concentrating primarily on two aspects of energy conservation. They focus on measures that can be accomplished quickly and on those that are not costly, such as operational practices, eliminating unnecessary energy-consuming equipment, and reduction of inefficient light fixtures in certain areas. This team also searches for ways and means of reducing energy consumption that can be accomplished easily and with relatively small amounts of capital outlay.

There are several reasons underlying the use of a mini-audit. First, the overall cost is reasonable and has the potential of being highly cost-effective. Secondly, the team consists of experts who normally are not readily available in most school districts. Thirdly, this audit is an extension of the survey conducted in step one by local school personnel.

In the mini-audit, the survey includes high-level technical expertise not available in step one. In both instances, however, energy-saving measures that are feasible and not too costly are recommended. It seems natural, systematic, and logical that the process related to energy conservation should be a continuum that ranges from the simple to the more complex and from the least expensive measures to those of greater magnitude and cost.

Step Three: The Maxi-Audit

The maxi-audit is the sine qua non of retrofitting an existing school building in cases where substantial amounts of capital outlay funds are required. Relatively inexpensive retrofitting measures such as adding insulation, caulking doors and window frames, and installing clock-controlled thermostats may be taken at any time. Extensive retro-fitting may be either partial or comprehensive.

In either instance such action should be the direct result of a maxi-audit. This audit is generally conducted by a competent and experienced team of experts in the fields of: architecture, structural engineering, mechanical engineering, and solar engineering. It is important that each person on this team whose expertise is required for the audit be thoroughly scrutinized. Not every architectural or engineering firm is capable of conducting a maxi-audit for the school district.

Besides the building, the maxi-audit includes a close examination of the educational uses of energy such as technology equipment, shop machinery, home economics appliances, business machines, and kilns. The pattern of power usage in the facility is examined very closely from the standpoint of energy conservation. Also, the possibility of using a piece of equipment more efficiently and at a maximum capacity is explored in every instance. An example would be running a dishwasher with a partial load versus waiting until it is full of dirty dishes.

The maxi-audit differs enormously from any of the approaches to energy conservation mentioned thus far. It is actually a quantified scientific investigation of the energy savings as an invaluable piece of information for school officials and the school board in assessing energy conservation measures. This detailed information enables them to make intelligent decisions regarding the expenditure of capital funds for retrofitting of their school buildings.

One of the most important end products of the maxi-audit is a cost analysis of the pay-back period required to retrieve the cost of capital outlay and interest through the savings in energy brought about by recommended capital outlay expenditure.

The energy consultant provides a wide variety of data. It includes a description of the existing pattern of energy consumption and current unit costs for each major energy use within the building. The consultant prepares and submits a considerable number of energy-conserving recommendations. Each recommendation has a price tag attached to it, together with a realistic financial analysis of each aspect of the recommendation.

The information submitted with each energy-saving recommendation includes the anticipated annual reduction in energy consumption, cost savings per year, cost of capital outlay required to implement the recommendation, length of the pay-back period, and the priority of a given recommendation among the other items recommended.

The cost of a maxi-audit is not modest. It represents a substantial initial investment that has the potential of returning savings that are many times the initial cost over the remaining life of a school building(s). Despite the cost, there is really no other way of obtaining the information required for retrofitting an existing building(s). The cost of a maxi-audit is fully justified, however. *First* of all, the audit must be conducted by highly trained, competent, and experienced architects and engineers. *Secondly,* the work required by these experts is often greater than that which would be required if this same team were asked to design a new building of the same size and shape as the existing facility.

In designing a new building, the team makes all of the required computations for achieving maximum energy efficiency. These computations involve all forms of energy to be consumed in the building, such as: lighting, heating, cooling, mechanical equipment, appliances, and electronic devices of various and sundry types. In conducting a maxi-audit, these same computations and studies must be performed for an existing building.

This aspect of the maxi-audit addresses itself to the question, "How much energy, of the various types, would be required to operate the existing structure under optimum conditions?" Obtaining the answer to this question is time-consuming and relatively complicated. But, in a maxi-audit, the answer is only the beginning.

Phase two of the maxi-audit represents another segment of the study, which involves a high level of creativity and expertise and requires a great deal of time on the part of these team experts. The question to be answered in phase two of the maxi-study is, "In what ways can the existing building, equipment, and pattern of energy use be modified in order to conserve and save energy?" This phase demands a concentrated study of the use and operation of the building and calls for an extended period of observation by the team of experts.

As can well be imagined, phase two also takes considerable time. It is time that would not be spent on the planning of a new building. The maxi-audit includes a phase three that develops the data obtained in phase two and compares the information with the corresponding information prepared under phase one. The questions to be answered in phase three is, "What energy-saving measures are feasible, how much will it cost to implement them, and what is the pay-back period for each one of them?" The response to this question is highly technical, fiscally oriented, and broadly based.

More specifically, the consultants must look at all alternatives for each recommended measure and select the one(s) that seems most appropriate. They must make detailed cost studies of capital outlay funds and interest needed to effect the recommended changes. Finally, they must compute the anticipated amount of energy saved by each recommendation, convert these energy savings into dollar savings, and estimate the number of years needed to compensate the school district for the funds expended to implement the proposed energy-saving measure.

All of this work takes time and costs money for the services of this respective team of experts. In view of the extensive nature of the maxi-audit, it can be an expensive venture for a school district. But it can also be one of the most rewarding investments a school district makes. If the savings in the cost of energy to the school district are quite substantial, the pay-back period for the cost of the maxi-audit can be very short, indeed. But the school district will never know this for sure unless a maxi-audit is completed!

PLANNING ENERGY-EFFICIENT SCHOOL BUILDINGS

As mentioned earlier, conservation is needed not only to extend our present supply of energy but also to soften the economic impact that the increasing cost of energy is having on school budgets throughout the United States. In attempting to conserve energy, however, care must be exercised to make certain that all conservation measures really save energy. Some of them may appear to be very attractive and appealing at first glance.

But, upon further study and consideration, they may actually waste more energy than they purportedly save. On the other hand, there are many energy-saving measures that are sound and stand the test of scientific analysis. Both false and real energy conservation measures are discussed in this section.

Questionable Energy Conservation Practices

1   *Reducing the weekly use of a school building.* Various plans have been advanced by school boards and school officials to reduce energy consumption by rescheduling the use of educational facilities. Under one year-round plan, schools would be closed entirely for a four or five-week period during the coldest part of the winter and the school year would be extended through the summer.

Another proposal would operate the schools four days per week and extend the time for each of the four days to compensate for the lost day. In this plan, school buildings would be closed from the end of the school day on Thursday until the following Monday morning. To be sure, the cost of energy consumed in a school building can be substantially reduced by these measures, but does it really conserve energy within the boundaries of the school district?

There is reason to believe that closing school buildings may actually waste energy in some situations. If the net gain or loss in energy consumption is measured *within the boundaries of the school district* rather than within the boundaries of the school site, the conclusion may be quite surprising.[3]

A hypothetical case illustrates the questionable nature of the four-day school week from the standpoint of energy conservation. Let us assume a school district has an enrollment of 2,000 students and the school board has introduced a four-day school week and increased the length of each of the four days to compensate for the time lost on Friday. Under this plan, all of the school buildings could be set on "lowest heat" from Thursday evening to Monday morning. Beyond any doubt, the amount of energy saved *on the school site* would be substantial and measurable.

This represents an impressive plus for the school budget. Let us now look at the negative side of this alleged energy-saving measure. What happens to the 2,000 students who are not in school on Friday? It can be assumed that most of them will be home on these colder days. Many students will be at home watching television, cooking snacks, and consuming energy. Some of them will be in their room with the thermostat raised high, the lights turned on, and consuming energy. And some of the high school students will be driving their automobiles and consuming fuel.

When the additional consumption of energy by these 2,000 students on their Friday holiday is compared to the amount of energy saved in the school buildings, studies reported by Denning and LeBlanc suggest that, on the whole, it is highly probable that the total increase in energy consumption within the "boundaries of the school district" due to these Friday closures will far exceed the amount of energy saved on the school site.[4]

This would represent an *energy loss* within the boundaries of the school district as a result of the Friday closure. The burden of the cost of energy for the Friday holiday is simply shifted from the school district to the parents of the 2,000 students enrolled in that school. No useful purpose would be accomplished by this kind of "energy-saving" measure.

On the other hand, real savings could be affected if a school facility were planned initially for maximum energy conservation. Educational services could be maintained at optimum levels and the cost of supplying energy to a school building could be held at a minimum. This approach is realistic in function, promising in concept, and effective in economic efficiency.

2 *Reduction in educational services.* **Some** school districts have seriously considered closing the school building promptly at the end of the school day during the cold winter months. In these instances, students would be deprived of extra help from teachers and the use of library and other school facilities. Some students might not be able to participate in extracurricular and athletic activities.

Under close scrutiny, it is questionable whether or not this practice would result in any noticeable savings in the energy budget at the end of the year. And even if some savings were effected, would the amount of money saved compensate for the loss of educational opportunities suffered by the students? This energy-saving measure and others like it should be carefully examined relative to educational values lost and the number of dollars gained, if any.

Sound Energy Conservation Practices

There are several effective and well-founded techniques for keeping the amount of energy consumed in a school facility to a minimum. Each one is presented from the standpoint of energy conservation. It is realized, of course, that it may not be possible to implement all of them in all cases. It is hoped, however, that this list of techniques will serve to stimulate the creative thinking of educational facility planners in designing school buildings that are both educationally effective and energy efficient.

1 *Shape of the building.* Heat loss or gain is directly proportional to the total square footage area of the walls, floors, and ceilings of a structure. Theoretically, the external surface area should be kept at a minimum. A sphere meets this requirement. It contains maximum volume within minimum exterior surface. For obvious reasons, a spherical school building, though possible, is not too practical. The most practical shape that provides maximum volume with a minimum of exterior surface is the cube.

In view of the foregoing considerations, the ideal shape of a school building from the standpoint of energy conservation is one consisting of a large cube or a combination of varying sizes joined together to form a single, contiguous structure. Consequently, the long and narrow, single-storied buildings of yesteryear should be avoided. The high-rise tower building is also not consistent with the principle described above. Neither is it desirable to design a building with jogs or indentations. Not only is this practice wasteful in energy but it is uneconomical to construct. A building constructed in the shape of a hemisphere could be considered if there were some ingenious way of utilizing the odd-shaped spaces along the curved walls.

2   *Orientation of the building.* For maximum absorption of passive heating from the sun, one side of the building should face east and the other side should face west. The south wall should also be exposed to the sun. Care should be taken to control heat gain in the summer and permit maximum energy gain from the sun in the winter.

Whenever possible, passive solar heating features should be designed into the building. These characteristics are discussed later in this chapter, but the orientation of the building should be such that passive solar heating can become an important part of the heating and cooling system of the school building.

3   *Insulation in the building.* It is a well-known principle of physics that the conductivity of heat varies from substance to substance. From the standpoint of energy conservation, the transmission of heat from one side of a wall or window to the other should be held to a minimum. The transfer of heat from within the building to its exterior through roofs, basements, and walls should be kept as low as possible.

Our present perceptions of brick and concrete should be reexamined. Indeed, from the standpoint of maintenance and durability these materials are economical, functional, and desirable. But in terms of thermal efficiency, looks are deceiving. Visually, it would appear that brick, mortar, and concrete are good insulators of heat. Quite the opposite is true. In fact, heat travels through concrete nine times as fast as it does through an equal thickness and area of wood. And stone conducts heat about 20 times as fast as wood.

In other words, a wooden board 1-inch thick is thermally equivalent to concrete 9 inches thick and to a stone wall 20 inches thick. It is not suggested that stone and concrete be abolished in the construction of school buildings, but simply to point out that these materials are not good heat insulators despite their massive appearance. When these materials are used, they should be lined or filled with highly insulating substances, such as fiberglass and insulating panels.

Wood, on the other hand, is a good insulator and may have a wider application in school construction, particularly in areas where wood is plentiful. The penalty for using wood, however, is its relatively high cost of maintenance. The architect is in an excellent position to advise school officials as to how to create the best balance between the use of wood and concrete.

Materials of construction should be chosen so that heat losses from the building to the atmosphere in the winter and heat gains from the atmosphere into the building in the summer are kept at a minimum. Exterior walls and ceilings exposed to cold attics should be heavily insulated. The amount of glass on the north side of the building should be reduced as much as possible but not below that required for good seeing conditions through the use of natural light. Basements should be designed so that the heat transfer between the building and the earth is as low as possible.

4   *Selecting and installing windows and doors properly.* The loss or gain of energy within a school building is greatly affected by the design, construction, and method of installation of windows, doors, and ventilation units. Unless special precautions are taken in the selection and proper installation of doors, windows, and ventilation units, the transfer of heat through these openings by conduction and by the infiltration of air could result in substantial losses of costly energy.

Conduction of Heat Energy through Windows and Doors

Windows and doors should be designed to severely impede the flow of heat from one side to the other. Since windows must be constructed of transparent substances such as glass or special plastics, the choice of materials is quite limited. However, great strides have been made by the glass industry in restricting the flow of heat through windows by providing alternate layers of glass and air in a sandwich-like panel of glass or plastic sheets.

Ideally, a vacuum between two sheets of glass separated by 1 centimeter (just less than one-half inch) would effectively impede the flow of heat through the window by conduction. Technologically, it is impractical to construct such a window panel due to the tremendous force of the atmospheric pressure on both sides of the panel tending to shatter the glass into the evacuated space between each sheet.

Thus, the glass industry has created an acceptable substitute that is relatively easy to produce but which is not as thermally efficient as the ideal situation described earlier. Insulating glass, as it is called, consists of two sheets of glass separated by about 1 centimeter of moisture-free air or nitrogen and is sealed along the edges. Such glass panels are also produced with two layers of gas separated by three sheets of glass. In this case, the window panel would consist of an outer sheet of glass followed by a layer of dried air or dried nitrogen, then another sheet of glass, followed by a second layer of gas and covered on the other side by another sheet of glass.

This combination of alternate layers of glass and gas effectively impedes the flow of heat through the panel and conserves energy. Sometimes these windows fog up from the inner seals breaking down allowing moisture to enter between the layers. If this occurs the window(s) will need to be replaced, costing the school district if it happens after the warranty period has expired.

The construction of insulated doors is much simpler than that described earlier for windows from the standpoint of heat transmission. First of all, doors need not necessarily be transparent. Thus, the choice of materials of construction is less restrictive. Weight and thickness of doors is somewhat less stringent than that for windows. Consequently, the door industry has produced a wide variety of insulating doors from light, hollow doors filled with insulating materials, to the more massive solid doors that are fabricated from highly insulating substances.

If a door requires that a person should be able to see through it for safety reasons, small panels of insulating glass can be installed at the proper height to meet this specification. Thus, from the standpoint of energy conservation, all exterior doors in a school building should have the capacity of severely impeding the flow of heat from one side to the other.

Infiltration of Air around Windows, Doors, and Ventilation Units

In any building, substantial amounts of heat are transmitted through the infiltration of air around the perimeter of windows, doors, and ventilation units. In general, there are two major sources of infiltration. One is around the window sash, the door, or the cover of ventilation units, that is, the element that opens and closes. This source can be effectively corrected by specially designed edges of windows, doors, and covers and by the use of weather-stripping.

The other source of infiltration is also around the perimeter of windows, doors, and ventilation units, but it occurs at the interfacing of the frame within which the window, door, or cover is mounted, and the building itself. This source of infiltration of air can often be remedied by properly installing the frames specially designed to keep the infiltration of air at a minimum, and by caulking the edges where the frames interface with the building. The caulking material should be vermin-proof, long-lasting, weather-resistant, and capable of withstanding a fairly wide range of temperature changes without cracking or crumbling.

5   *Selecting efficient heating, cooling, and ventilating equipment.* The heating and cooling of school buildings is accomplished by converting one form of energy to another through the use of an appropriate contrivance. Fuel is one form of energy that can be burned on the site to produce heating and cooling for the building. Or energy produced offsite in the form of electricity can be transported to the school building and then be transformed into heating and cooling.

The contrivance commonly used to convert fuel directly into heat is the gas furnace. Electricity, on the other hand, can be transformed into heat by the resistance method (heating coils) or by a heat pump. Cooling is usually produced either by a diffusion process utilizing high-pressure steam or by a heat pump that is powered by electricity.

Some type of specially designed contrivance is necessary to convert fuel or energy from one form to another. While the heating and cooling industry is experimenting with a number of more sophisticated contrivances designed to conserve energy, the heat pump is still the major practical contrivance for generating heat or cooling. Thus, in designing a heating and cooling system for energy conservation, special care should be exercised to specify the contrivance with the highest energy output for a given input of energy.

The more efficient the contrivance, the less fuel or electricity consumed to produce a given result and the more energy conserved in the process. The continued improvement of heat pumps holds much promise with respect to increased energy conservation. The contrivance itself is simply a machine that moves heat from one location to another.

The electricity consumed by this machine is not directly converted into heating or cooling. It simply powers the pump that moves heat from the ground or atmosphere into the building during cold weather or transports heat from within the building to the ground or atmosphere during warm weather. Consequently, the efficiency of the heat pump can be far greater than that resulting from other means of converting energy into heating or cooling.

Ventilation is another important aspect of energy conservation. The amount of fresh air required per student per hour in the past can be substantially reduced in most instances. In some states the amount of fresh air required per student is modest, realistic, and economically justifiable. Some states specify 10 cubic feet per minute per occupant when the outside temperature is above 35° Fahrenheit, and no fresh air is required for temperatures below 35°. In these instances, the lower volume of air required per student reduces the amount of energy needed for ventilation.

The efficiency of heating, cooling, and ventilating equipment is a major consideration in energy conservation. Ideally, the maximum amount of usable energy should be extracted from the amount of available energy supplied to a given school facility. Hence, when the source of energy is intended to heat the building, all of it should be utilized for that purpose.

Electrical heating most closely approaches this ideal. When resistance electrical heating is used, all of the energy purchased provides heat for the building, except when the transformers and meters are placed outside of the building. When various fuels are used for heating, the efficiency of the boiler and heat distribution systems can greatly affect the amount of heat that actually reaches the spaces where such heat is required.

This reduction stems from two causes. A certain amount of heat is lost through the stack in the combustion process, and cold air from the outside is needed to support the combustion. During this necessary and essential chemical action, the outside air tends to cool the heating equipment. And finally, when heat is transmitted from the furnace room to the classrooms, for example, some of it is lost en route where it is not needed or wanted. Cooling, heating, and ventilating equipment does not always use energy efficiently. For this reason, care should be exercised in selecting high-tech equipment that possesses a high energy efficiency rating.

6   *Utilizing electric power efficiently.* The major part of the electrical energy consumed within a school building for purposes other than heating or cooling is attributable to artificial lighting and to the operation of mechanical equipment associated with the heating and cooling of the school building.

The proper design of an artificial lighting system provides fertile ground for conserving energy in a school building. First of all, the number of foot-candles of light intensity striking the task of students engaged in learning activities in school has been raised continually since the end of World War II. When energy was inexpensive, the increase of intensity of light in classrooms from 30 foot-candles to 70 or 80 foot-candles was not a major cause for concern.

The research conducted by various groups of lighting engineers was well done, in most cases, but the nature of the tasks for which the various light intensities were applied tended to be focused on specialized activities that occupied only a small portion of the students' curriculum. And, since energy at that time was still quite inexpensive, increases in the overall intensity of light in a classroom presented no real problem.

Today, the situation is quite different. The question posed to educators and school boards due to circumstances beyond their control is, "What is the minimum intensity of classroom illumination that is healthful and provides a good visual environment for the tasks normally performed in the teaching-learning process?" With this objective in mind, it can be seen that the intensity of high-quality LED lights at the task level of the student could be reduced to 30 foot-candles in regular classrooms.

It is well known that the acuity of elementary- and secondary-age-level students in general is very high. Hence, high light intensities are not needed for such students. However, in view of the cost of energy, it might be well to plan certain spaces for use by both young people and staff. In spaces for both young and staff, additional lighting could be switched on when mainly adults are occupying the space. Otherwise, the 30-foot-candle intensity could be maintained when the regular school is in session.

7   *Controlling energy distribution effectively.* Both electrical and heat energy should be readily available in sufficient quantity at any location in a school building where it is needed at a given time. Conversely, energy should not be supplied and consumed in any part of the building where it is not required. These two considerations suggest that a sophisticated system of control in the distribution of electricity and heat (also cooling) be made an integral part in the design of the building. Such controls can be provided at a relatively small additional cost through the use of remote relays and controls activated by a low-voltage wiring network or a wireless device. Also, electronic clocks can control energy availability at various points in the school. There is one drawback in the use of clock controls, however. Power outages can also stop clock movements that are not battery-operated. This, in turn, changes the real time at which such clocks turn the energy on and off. Consequently, these systems run by a clock need constant monitoring by school personnel who may find it necessary to reset them from time to time.

Control over the temperature of hot water is another way of saving energy. Rather than allowing the individual mixing of hot water with cold water at every point of usage, it might be advantageous to supply hot water to each faucet at a temperature that requires little or no mixing with cold water. In widespread, strung-out buildings, this arrangement may be somewhat more difficult to achieve, but special consideration should be given to devise ways of conserving energy by controlling waste of hot water.

Such waste often occurs when the temperature of the water at the mixing faucet is higher than needed or when the hot water faucet is left partially open. Even in large buildings, it might be possible to bring relatively long hot water lines close to a point of usage and mix hot and cold water centrally at that point, so that water flowing from the hot water spigots, in toilet rooms, for example, is at the proper temperature for handwashing.

8   *Recovering normally wasted energy.* School planners should always be on the alert for ways and means of recapturing heat that may be lost to the atmosphere or ground. For example, a certain amount of fresh air is required to ventilate classrooms. Normally, warm air inside of the building would be exhausted in order to provide space for the fresh air. Some architects exhaust the warm air through spaces above the ceiling in order to minimize the loss of heat from the classroom through the ceiling.

If the plenum chamber is used to distribute air throughout the building, the heat from the exhausted air could be exchanged with the fresh cold air being drawn into the building. In this way, the heat from the exhausted air could be recovered and transferred back to the classroom while the so-called stale air could be exhausted—minus heat.

There are often spaces within a school building that are unavoidably warm, such as furnace and mechanical rooms, kitchens, vocational welding labs, and food laboratories. This excess heat is ultimately dissipated through the walls and by natural infiltration. It might be worthwhile to design a school facility so this excess heat could be redistributed to other parts of the building. This feature would make it possible to reduce the temperature to comfortable levels in areas where excess heat is generated or accumulated and transfer this excess energy to other parts of the building where it is needed. Thus, energy that is normally wasted could be recovered.

9   *Exploiting humidity control to save energy*. Humidity control has been widely used to promote comfort within homes, schools, and other types of shelters. Humidification has not been used very extensively for the purpose of energy conservation. It is well known that human comfort within an enclosure is a function of both temperature and humidity. Discomfort occurs when both temperature and humidity are high. It is also recognized that the human body controls its comfort level and temperature through the process of perspiration. Discomfort sets in when the body cannot cool itself by the evaporation of perspiration due to high humidity.

The school planners of the future should utilize the effect of humidity on human comfort in an effort to save costly energy. During the heating season, the room temperature can be dropped and the level of humidity can be increased to the level of comfort for the occupants of the building. It is realized, of course, that the level of the humidity should be kept within limits so that furniture, doors, and equipment are not affected in any way. But even a temperature drop of 3° or 4° Fahrenheit could produce substantial savings in the cost of energy in a school building over the heating season.

The same principle could be applied to cooling. It might be possible to use dehumidifiers instead of air conditioners in certain areas and save the cost of energy to operate high-capacity condensers that are found in air-conditioning equipment.

PLANNING SCHOOL BUILDINGS FOR SOLAR ENERGY

The energy from the sun is free, but collecting it and putting it into practical use still costs a considerable amount of money. The outlook for solar energy is promising and very optimistic. The solar energy industry is making rapid strides in the development of more efficient and less costly solar energy systems. For this reason, all new school facilities should be designed and oriented so that solar energy systems could be incorporated into them at a later date.

A Brief Look at Solar Energy

It is indeed difficult to imagine the enormous amount of solar energy that reaches the surface of the earth every day. To be sure, the intensity of the solar energy is not uniform the world over. It varies from place to place, from day to day, and from hour to hour. But the accumulated amount of solar energy falling on 1 square foot of horizontal surface per day, even in February in the northern hemisphere, is surprisingly high in many parts of the world.

Looks are sometimes deceiving as we feel the pleasant and soothing warmth from the sun in a sheltered area even in the middle of the cold season. Under these circumstances, the sunshine looks gentle, pervasive, and innocuous. Actually, the light and heat produced by the nuclear furnace on the sun is very intense. In fact, it is so intense that the retina of the human eye can be burned and permanently damaged if one stares directly at the sun for any length of time.

Without getting deeply involved in the technical aspects of solar energy, it might be helpful to readers to describe the active collecting of solar energy in more meaningful terms. Let us place 1 gallon of water in an insulated wooden box whose interior is painted black and is covered by a sheet of glass having an area of 1 square foot. Let us further assume that the box is level, has been exposed to the sun for a full day in February, has not lost any of its heat to the atmosphere, and is located out-of-doors in the northern part of the United States.

If the initial temperature of 1 gallon of water from a faucet was 40° Fahrenheit, the temperature of the water would have risen to 150° Fahrenheit at the end of a clear day! This idealized but realistic situation clearly shows that the amount of energy available from the sun annually is enormous. In extracting energy from the sun, however, allowances should be made for a variety of heat losses.

In practice, the temperature of the gallon of water in our example would have lost a considerable amount of heat directly from the box to the atmosphere. An additional amount of heat would have been lost in transit while pumping the water from the box to the inside of the building, where it could be put to practical use. In this hypothetical situation, the temperature of the water reaching the inside of the building at the end of the day could conceivably have dropped to 78° Fahrenheit, which is still sufficiently high to heat a building.

Solar Energy Collectors

Realistically, the efficiency of a commercially produced solar energy system is surprisingly high, but it varies with the ambient temperature of the atmosphere. Consequently, panel-type solar energy collectors are more efficient during periods of warm weather than they are in the winter months. But it must be remembered that, no matter how well solar energy systems are designed and engineered for efficiency, they cannot develop more energy than was available at our hypothetical box described above. But solar energy engineers have been very ingenious in capturing the energy from the sun.

A few of the more advanced manufacturers of solar energy collectors have virtually created "solar energy traps." Once the energy enters the collector, very little energy escapes. The transfer of energy from the collector to some storage device within a building is accomplished with as little energy loss as possible. Sophisticated temperature devices control the rate of flow of water or air through the collector unit so that the temperature of the water or air returning to the building is as high as possible. The total area of the collectors is determined by the geographical location of the system.

The area of the solar collectors may range from several hundred square feet for heating water to several thousand square feet for space heating. Although the technology underlying solar heating and cooling is well developed and scientifically sound, cost is still a barrier to the widespread use of active solar energy systems. These systems are discussed in detail in the following section.

Photovoltaic Energy

Within the past few years, the efficiency of photovoltaic cells has risen from 7 percent to 20+ percent for crystalline silicon, the most widely used cell material. The still experimental gallium cells have an efficiency of 37 percent, but further research is needed to reduce their production cost.

The future of solar energy from photovoltaic cells is promising. The efficiency of photovoltaic cells has been increasing steadily and new cell materials are being developed at several research centers. Photovoltaic energy has a great potential for reducing our dependence on energy from fossil fuels.

Windmill Farms

Wind energy is being harnessed in many localities where strong winds are continually present. Windmill farms, which consist of hundreds of windmills operating in a given area, are both practical and commercially profitable.

The Core Features of an Active Solar Energy System

Any active solar energy system must perform three basic functions. (1) It must be capable of collecting the energy of the sun efficiently and transforming that energy into a form that can be easily transported from one place to another. (2) The system must be able to move the energy from the collector to the interior of a building. (3) Finally the system must provide some means of storing the energy, once it has been conveyed from the collector to the interior of the building. Each function is discussed briefly in the following sections.

Solar Energy Collectors

There are basically two types of solar energy collectors on the market. One of them concentrates the solar energy at a point or along a straight line through the use of lenses or reflectors. The other type is simply a flat, boxlike structure that entraps the energy that enters the box. The concentration-type collector is complex and must always be aimed directly at the sun, while the flat solar panel is relatively simple to construct and functions well in a fixed position. For this reason, solar panels are more practical for heating purposes in school buildings.

There is a wide variety of solar panels on the market today. Some are very sophisticated and highly efficient. Some trap the solar energy inside evacuated glass cylinders that resemble fluorescent tubes. Others consist of copper tubing soldered onto a sheet of copper that is placed inside a box whose sides are about 6 inches high. The bottom and sides of the box are covered with insulation. The copper sheet, with the pipes facing the top of the box, is laid on the insulation. The pipes and copper sheet are sprayed with a special type of heat-absorbing black paint. The top of the box is sealed and covered entirely with glass or sheets of plastic. In simpler terms, the box resembles a miniature greenhouse.

The working medium in a collector is either liquid or air. The heat is removed from the box by passing cold or cool liquid through the copper tubing that is soldered to the copper base. There are many variations of the arrangement described above on the market, but the principle is always the same. Black, heat-absorbing pipes or plates are sealed in a well-insulated, glass-covered box. The collected heat is removed from the enclosure by passing air or a liquid through the box. The heated air or liquid is then brought into the building.

For those interested in obtaining more detailed information about the many types of solar panels on the market, it is suggested that brochures be obtained from the various manufacturers of solar energy equipment. The Department of Energy distributes lists of solar energy suppliers. Incidentally, these brochures are a rich source of information on solar energy. Not only is the reading exciting for the solar energy enthusiast but it clearly demonstrates the creativity and ingenuity of the manufacturers of solar energy equipment in a free enterprise system.

Transference of Solar Energy

After solar energy is collected, it must be moved from the collector to the inside of the building where it can be stored or used as desired. The medium for conveying solar energy is usually air or a liquid. When air is selected, fans are used to circulate the air from the building to the collector and back to the building through a closed system of ducts. These ducts are well insulated to minimize loss of heat during the process.

Water, however, is more commonly used as the medium for transporting solar energy from the collector to the building. Water is pumped through the sun-heated collector and is returned to the inside of the building after absorbing heat from the solar panel. The pipes connecting the building storage unit to the collector are heavily insulated in order to keep heat losses from the water in transit at a minimum. Antifreeze is usually mixed with the water during cold weather.

In both liquid and air systems, temperature control devices prevent the transfer of heat from the building to the collector. When the temperature of the medium in the collector is close to that in the building, the fans and pumps become inoperative. In some water systems, there are controls that drain the water from the pipes when the temperature of the water in the collector approaches the freezing point. In some systems, there is also a computer-controlled flow valve that keeps the amount of water or air flowing through the collector at an optimum volume at all times.

Storage of Solar Energy

Since solar energy is available only during daylight hours, it is necessary to store some of the collected energy for use at times when solar energy is not available or insufficient in quantity. This situation may arise when the sun is not shining brightly, during the night, or when the outside temperature is so low that the amount of energy collected is not sufficient to maintain the proper temperature within the building.

Solar energy is commonly stored in water or in stones. There are also physical-chemical methods of storing energy, but the problems associated with these methods plague those who experiment with them. Consequently, large tanks of water (ranging from 10,000 to 15,000 gallons) are used for storing solar energy for space heating if water is chosen as the transporting medium. When air is the transporting medium, several tons of loosely piled stones in or adjoining the basement of the building are used to store the solar energy. Warm air from the collectors is filtered through the stones, which absorb the heat.

The retrieval of the stored heat is a relatively simple process. The hot water is pumped to other parts of the building where the heat is required. Or air from the building is circulated over the warm stones and returned to other parts of the building where additional heat is needed.

Practical Considerations Related to Active Solar Energy Systems in School Buildings

Theoretically, solar energy is ideal. It is free and nonpolluting. It is constant and renewable. It is abundant. It can be used for both heating and cooling. It reduces our dependence on fossil fuels. Ultimately, solar energy will greatly improve the quality of the air we breathe, when its use becomes widespread.

There are, however, practical limits to the extent that solar energy can be utilized in school buildings at this time. The major drawback is cost. The cost of solar panels, pumps, controls, and storage systems is still very high. To be sure, the federal government and some states are paying part of the cost, but the full purchase price for a total solar energy heating and cooling system may still be beyond the budgetary reach of many school districts. But future prospects look promising. With the advent of more efficient equipment and improved design, the cost of solar energy systems should drop considerably and become more affordable for more and more school districts in the nation.

On the other hand, the possibility of utilizing solar energy at this time must not be overlooked. It should, however, be limited primarily to hot water heating. This application of solar energy is economically justifiable and very practical for a number of reasons. First of all, *no* special storage system is needed. The existing hot water tank also serves as the heat storage tank, assuming, of course, that the water tank is not less than 500 gallons. Secondly, the cost of purchasing the limited number of solar panels that are needed to supply energy for hot water purposes is cost-effective. And thirdly, the heat transfer system can be very simple, uncomplicated, and relatively inexpensive.

Solar energy for space heating need not be ruled out entirely, however. If space heating is planned, it should be done judiciously. It is suggested that a conventional backup heating system supplement the solar energy system. By so doing, the size of the solar energy system can be scaled down to one that is economically efficient. In this instance, a considerable amount of money can be saved by eliminating almost all of the solar energy storage. Under these circumstances the solar energy panels can supply solar heat to the building during daylight hours in varying quantities.

Any deficiency in heat is automatically compensated for by the standby system. Under this arrangement, whatever energy is collected from the sun represents a saving in the cost of energy for the building. On the other hand, purchasing the number of solar panels and ancillary equipment required to heat the building on a 24-hour basis, employing extensive storage and distribution facilities, may not be economically efficient until manufacturers of solar energy equipment can find ways of reducing the cost per Btu of heat delivered to the point of need within a school building.

Planning School Buildings for Passive Solar Energy Heating

Thus far, the major focus has been on active solar energy systems. In these instances, as mentioned earlier, solar energy is collected at some location outside of the building. It is then transported into the building and stored in water or stone for distribution within the building wherever it is needed at a later time. Passive solar energy heating, on the other hand, is primarily a function of building design and requires no special equipment.

Under the concept of passive solar heating, no effort is made to pump solar energy in from the outside. However, through ingenious building design, solar energy is allowed to enter the building naturally and is trapped within it by various methods. A number of typical methods for capturing solar energy at little or no extra cost are listed here. Passive solar energy is achieved primarily by building orientation and design.

1   *The south window wall.* The admission of heat through the south wall warms objects and surfaces within the building when the sun is shining. The heat is trapped within the enclosure by the so-called greenhouse effect. In classrooms, special care should be exercised to keep the glare away from student desks through the use of Venetian blinds or their equivalent. Also, reflecting shades should be closed at night to keep the heat within the building.

    The architect should design the proper overhang along the south-facing windows so that sunlight will not enter the building during the summer months when the sun is high in the sky. The dimensions of the overhang will depend upon the location of the building on the earth with respect to the solar plane. Solar angle tables should be consulted in determining the proper angle of the shadow line for winter and summer.

2   *Using a roof reservoir for sun heating.* Flat roofs can be made into shallow water reservoirs by forming a watertight glass- or plastic-covered box 2 or 3 inches deep over part of the roof area. The box would be filled with water. Since the roof could

already be coated with black asphalt, which absorbs heat, the temperature of the water would rise and store solar energy.

The specific application of this concept depends upon the climate where a given building is located. An insulated and reflective cover could slide over the box at night, during which period the accumulated heat in the water would be radiated into the building. This application assumes that outside temperatures do not fall below freezing. In colder climates, however, it may be necessary to add antifreeze to the water. If covering the reservoir with reflective material at night is not feasible, the sun-heated water would still reduce the amount of heat that would be lost through the roof during daylight hours when outside temperatures are low.

3   *Air heat collectors.* An air heat collector, consisting of a simple box about 4 feet wide, 8 feet long, and 12 inches deep, insulated on the inside, could be located on the roof of the building. Its interior surfaces would be painted black and the top would be sealed with a glass or plastic transparent covering. This box would be tilted to the proper angle depending upon the latitude of its location. Two ducts would be attached to the box. The inlet duct would receive cool air from within the building while the exhaust duct would force air warmed by the sun into the building. No fan would be needed since the air would be moved by natural convection.

4   *Skylight solar heating.* Solar energy could be admitted and stored at various points within the building through the expedient use of skylights. Ideally, the solar energy should fall on massive stone or masonry walls or on floors that are painted in dark energy-absorbing colors. During the daylight hours, heat from sunlight entering through the skylight would be absorbed by the floors, walls, and other materials. At night the stored solar energy would be released into the building.

5   *Collecting solar energy in containers of water.* Several 55-gallon drums of water could be stacked inside the building along a window wall facing south. These barrels would be painted black on all sides. At night, insulating doors covering all of the windows could be closed. The warm water would then radiate heat within the building and keep it warm. Aesthetics would be a matter of concern. However, any imaginative architect utilizing this approach to passive solar energy would find no difficulty creating a pleasant, aesthetic atmosphere.

6   *Going partially underground.* It is well known that the temperature of the soil a few feet below the surface rarely falls below freezing in most of the United States. It is also a recognized principle of physics that the flow of heat through a wall, floor, or ceiling is directly proportional to the temperature difference between the two sides of the surface. For example, if the temperature is 70° Fahrenheit inside a building, and 0° Fahrenheit outside, the amount of heat lost to the atmosphere per square foot of surface is approximately twice as much as that lost to the ground 5 or 6 feet below the surface. Consequently, the more of the building that is underground, the less will be the loss of heat from the building during cold weather.

It is not recommended, however, that school buildings be entirely underground. Two important considerations should be borne in mind when school planners think about partially underground school facilities. As more and more of the building is constructed below the surface, more and more energy will be required for artificial lighting. On the other hand, as more and more of the building is constructed below the surface of the ground, less and less heat is lost from the building in cold climates. Moisture may penetrate inside the building envelope if any cracks occur in the foundation walls.

It may be of interest that there have recently been a number of proponents for school facilities built completely underground. Their reasons have considerable merit. Underground schools are ideal as civil defense shelters, not only for the students but also for the residents of the community. Underground schools conserve land use, particularly for parking. Underground schools are free from noise pollution. And underground schools are purportedly less expensive to build and maintain.

In warm climates, the supporters of partial underground schools contend that the added cost of energy for artificial lighting is more than compensated for by savings in the cost of energy for air conditioning aboveground buildings. At some point, there may be a balance between heat energy saved and electrical energy consumed for lighting.

The concept of building at least part of the structure underground has merit from several points of view. Some heat energy will be saved for reasons mentioned earlier. Passive solar energy features can be incorporated into the facility, because part of it is still above the topographical grade. In fact, light wells extending below the surface of the ground can be designed so that they may become effective solar energy traps.

DISCUSSION QUESTIONS

1   What is being done in your school district (where you reside) on their implementation of energy practices?
2   Define the term "energy." How could a step-by-step approach be designed to benefit your school district?
3   Discuss three sound energy conservation practices. Which of these would you push to implement in the design of a new school?
4   What are six examples of sound conservation practices? Prioritize each of these from the most to the least desired ones.

NOTES

1. "Report of Energy Management Information Center, Honeywell, Inc.," *CEFP Journal* (November–December 1980), p. 14.
2. Edward Churchill, "School's Energy Costs Cut Two-Thirds with No Capital Investment," *CEFP Journal* (March–April 1985), p. 21.
3. Charles K. Denning and Edmond A. LeBlanc, "Community Education and the Energy Problems," *CEFP Journal* (January 1980), p. 10.
4. Ibid.

Chapter 9

Safety, Health, and Comfort

The safety of those occupying a school building is of prime concern to the architect, educators, and school boards. Safety hazards in schools may be due to building design, site planning, selection of floor materials, or location of obstacles such as fire extinguishers, water fountains, electrical floor stubs, and protruding pipes. No school planner or architect can justify such hazards on the basis of design or aesthetic unity. Although safety cannot always be completely assured, every effort must be made to achieve as high a safety level as possible. For example, a service driveway must be located near a school building, even though it introduces a safety hazard and it is difficult, if not impossible, to plan the crossings of walks and drives at grade level so that students are absolutely safe.

HAZARDS ASSOCIATED WITH THE MOVEMENT OF PEOPLE

The safety of people moving from one part of the school to another is discussed in the following paragraphs.

Ramps

Ramps, like stairways, are an integral part of the circulation system within and outside a school building. Their use is receiving increased attention from both architects and educational planners, especially as a means of meeting the needs of physically handicapped students where students must travel from building to building. Ramps should be designed for wheelchair use and should be covered with nonslip materials.

According to federal standards, the slope of a ramp should not exceed 8.3 percent, which is equivalent to a rise of not more than 1 foot for a horizontal run of 12 feet in length. Elevators are preferred for people with physical handicaps. However, where the change in elevation within a building is less than three risers, a ramp is preferable to stairs for the safety of *all* students traveling from one level to another.

Architects and school planners should give additional thought to the problem of wheelchairs outside the building. While elevators are adequate within the building, ramps should be provided for wheelchairs to reach the elevators from out-of-doors. Sidewalks and outside areas should be planned with the handicapped student in mind. It should be possible for such a student to travel by wheelchair from the bus-unloading zone on the campus to any other point within and outside of their school buildings.

Stairways

Stairways can be dangerous, so certain precautions should be taken in their design. Stair runs should not exceed sixteen risers, nor should they be less than three. The riser height on all main stairways should not exceed 6½ inches, and treads should not be less than 10½ inches deep, exclusive of nosing or overhang. Experiments conducted in a major department store in Boston revealed conclusively that accidents on stairways were reduced when the riser heights in a stair run did not vary by more than 1/8 inch.

The engineer conducting the experiment was convinced that uniformity in riser height was fully as important as the riser height itself. Stairways should ensure a rapid and safe egress from a building when emergencies arise. Speedy evacuation from a school is imperative in the event of fire, the escape of noxious fumes, or other dangers. Stairways, therefore, should be specifically designed for such emergencies.

Multistory buildings should have at least two main stairways located well apart from each other. At least two independent and smoke-free paths to safety should be provided from any point in a school building where students are located. For example, some state codes require that a door be located in every partition between classrooms adjacent to the wall opposite the corridor. In the event that hot gases filled the corridor, students could travel from room to room until they reached a smoke-free stairway in multistory buildings.

Two stairways terminating on the same landing should be considered as a single stairway. Stairways should run at right angles to main corridors and should be enclosed in fire-resistant stairwells. Handrails may be composed of combustible materials. It is also important that main stairways be open to egress and that they lead to an exit on the ground floor.

Stairways should be at least two lanes in width, with 44 inches between handrails. Handrails should be installed between 26 and 30 inches above the nosing on the stair tread. When pupils of many ages attend a school, two handrails, one at the normal height and one at a lower position, should be provided for the safety of both younger and older children.

Corridors

The mass movement of students from one point to another on the same floor level usually takes place through a corridor. Corridors should be wide enough to accommodate the traffic and free of obstructions and bottlenecks. It is generally accepted among school planners that main corridors should be at least 8½ feet wide. In schools with enrollments exceeding 200 pupils, they should be wider. The width of secondary corridors, on the other hand, is governed by the number of classrooms served by each corridor, and by its length. In any case, secondary corridors should not be less than 7 feet wide.

There should be no projection into the corridor greater than 8 inches beyond the face of the corridor wall. Doors should be installed so that they do not project into the corridor by more than 8 inches. In addition to being a safety hazard, doors opening farther into a corridor create a bottleneck and thus appreciably reduce the effective width of the corridor. Also, radiators, fountains, fire extinguishers, and the like should be completely recessed in corridor walls.

Dead-end corridors are very dangerous and should always be avoided in planning. Corridors should always terminate at an exit or at a stairway leading to an egress. Doors that open onto a stairway or tend to block passageways create safety hazards and should, therefore, be avoided. Double-loaded corridors that have rooms on both sides should be wider than single-loaded ones. Twice the number of students could utilize them requiring the width to be around 10 feet for good circulation flow in the respective hallway.

HEALTH HAZARDS DUE TO GASES, CHEMICAL AGENTS, RADIOACTIVITY, AND DUST-LIKE PARTICLES

The danger from commercially produced heating gas in school buildings is well recognized, but the hazards resulting from inhalation of fumes produced by some cleaning agents, insect sprays, and paint thinners are not quite so obvious. Every effort must be made to minimize the hazard from any noxious fumes. Admittedly, it is often difficult to cope with the problem of poisonous vapors because it is not always possible to determine the type, origin, or location of the source of such fumes.

Heating Gases

The presence of detectable amounts of heating gas in the atmosphere creates a potentially explosive situation, particularly in the case of propane gas. Since bottled gases are heavier than air, they spill over onto the floor and are, therefore, difficult to smell until the accumulation has reached dangerous proportions. Regardless of the type of heating gas used, the selection of the equipment, the installation of the distribution system, and the attachment of equipment/appliances to the outlets supplying such fuel should be performed with the utmost care by a competent person.

Noxious Fumes

The problem of noxious fumes in schools is elusive. Architects have worked diligently to minimize the health and fire hazards from noxious or combustible vapors, particularly in areas where the need for special precautions is obvious, such as bus garages and paint-spraying shops. There are, however, a number of other spaces in an educational facility where the problem of harmful vapors is present.

While hoods are provided in chemistry laboratories, special provision for the escape of noxious gases is not always made in the preparation rooms. Special attention should also be given to the exhaust of fumes from cleaning agents and chemicals used in the physics and biology laboratories. The custodian is often required to refinish furniture, but rarely does one find a well-ventilated custodial workshop. Maintenance personnel often clean parts of light fixtures and rugs using agents that emit noxious fumes, but one does not often find a properly designed space for this function.

All of the places where noxious gases should be exhausted in a school building cannot be listed. It is hoped, however, that school planners will make a mental note of the areas that might require additional ventilation. Electronic sensors should also be provided in each of these areas of concern.

Radioactive Gas—Radon

Radon is a colorless, odorless, radioactive gas that occurs naturally in low concentrations almost everywhere on earth.[1] It is the first product generated by the normal radioactive disintegration of radium. In nontechnical terms, radon might be envisioned as the grandchild of uranium. In more precise language, however, it is the result of a chain reaction that starts with uranium.

When uranium decays radioactively, one of its products is radium. Radium, in turn, decays radioactively and produces radon. Unfortunately, the process does not stop at this point. The radon gas continues to decay radioactively and produces a new generation of radioactive materials. Thus, if a person inhales radon gas, this new generation of radioactive particles releases small amounts of radiation that can damage or kill normal living cells. Although research on the effects of long-term exposure to low-dosage radiation is not conclusive, "People exposed to significant amounts of radon for a long time run an increased risk of lung cancer."[2]

Radon can be found in major regions of the United States and Canada. Radon gas is discharged from rocks containing even infinitesimal quantities of radium. High concentrations of radon have been traced to granite or sillimanite rock. To further complicate matters, radon gas has a great affinity for water. It is readily dissolved in it. For this reason, it is often found in well water that has permeated through rock formations containing radioactive materials.

The corrective measures are effective, reliable, and technologically sound, and the outlook is positive and reassuring. More specifically, the remedies are uncomplicated, straightforward, and doable.[3] Furthermore, the presence of radon can be easily detected and accurately measured without difficulty. Finally, even high concentrations of radon gas can be rendered harmless through a combination of increased ventilation and effective control of the points where the gas enters the building.

When educational facilities are being planned in radon-prone regions, it is imperative that the architect determine at the outset whether or not radon is present on the site. In the event that radon gas is present, corrective design features can be incorporated in the plans. In pursuing this preliminary investigation, educational facility planners will find health agencies to be of invaluable service. Local and state health officials have the staff and apparatus to detect and measure the quantity of radon present in well water or in the air at a given site.

Fortunately, the presence of radon gas is not nearly as troublesome in school buildings as it is in tight, energy-efficient homes. School buildings are almost always mechanically ventilated, while homes generally rely on the incidental infiltration of outside air. More specifically, the amount of ventilation currently required for instructional spaces in educational facilities is sufficient to overcome the deleterious effects of nominal concentrations of radon gas.

However, there may be areas within the building that are usually not as well ventilated, such as custodial workshops, storage areas, and equipment rooms. These spaces may require special attention by educational facility planners. As a rule of thumb, normal ventilation requirements for instructional spaces are generally sufficient to offset the radon problem when the concentration of radon gas is not very high, between 1 and 2 parts per liter.

On the other hand, in areas where higher concentrations of radon are present, additional measures may be required. These remedies are aimed primarily at sealing the pathways of gas entry into the building. It is not within the scope of this text to deal with the engineering aspects of this type of remedial action. Suffice it to mention, however, that the usual points of entry of radon gas include porous cinder blocks, loose-fitting pipes, unsealed slab joints, cracks in walls and floors, exposed soil or granite, and from radon-contaminated ground or well water entering the building.

HARMFUL DUST-LIKE PARTICLES

Dust is a pulverized form of solid that is suspended in the air. Some types of dust are distressing but harmless. Some kinds of dust are temporarily irritating and potentially harmful. Some forms of dust can be deadly. These types of air pollutants are discussed briefly in the following paragraphs.

Non-Cancer-Producing Particles

Wood dust is perhaps one of the most prevalent forms of solid air pollutant that is encountered in educational facilities. Other forms of noncarcinogenic dust are sometimes found in spaces where students are working on arts and crafts projects and, to a lesser degree, in some of the home economics rooms where lint and various powders may be present in the air.

Although the symptoms created by non-cancer-producing dust are usually temporary, their effects may be potentially harmful to persons who are repeatedly subjected to such irritants.

Dust particles affect people in different ways, depending upon the concentration, type, and chemical content of the particles. They may irritate the skin, the eyes, and the respiratory system. Generally, the pain and discomfort associated with dust inhalation disappears when the person is no longer exposed to such irritants.

Educational facility planners have always been concerned with air pollution in school buildings. Their efforts to combat it have often been rewarding. For example, they were able to overcome the health hazards caused by wood dust by applying modern air purification methods. First, most of the dust particles were removed at the point of origin by a vacuum system. Then, air filters were installed in dust-producing areas to further improve the quality of the air.

Architects and engineers successfully coped with this problem because they were aware of it during the planning process. For this reason planners should systematically examine each function housed in an educational facility and identify locations where harmful dust particles are likely to be produced. Once this review is completed, corrective measures can be taken.

Radon-Laden Particles

The effects of radon in its gaseous form have already been discussed in considerable detail. There is, however, another phenomenon related to radon that should be mentioned. Radon molecules frequently attach themselves onto dust particles present in the air. Thus, concentrated radon gas could increase to significant levels through the accumulation of radon-laden dust in any nook or crook of the building.

Obviously, if radon gas is prevented from entering the building, radon-laden dust is nonexistent. But it is important for planners to be aware that radon gas may be carried by dust particles and to be on the alert, therefore, to situations that allow radioactive dust to enter the building; for example, fresh air ducts in the ventilation system or other openings.

Asbestos Dust Particles

Asbestos dust is highly carcinogenic. As long as it remains solidified on pipes, walls, ceilings, and other surfaces it is relatively harmless. But when it crumbles and appears in the form of dust moving freely in the air, it becomes a deadly health hazard.

The removal of asbestos from a building creates treacherous conditions somewhat difficult to control. It presents a health hazard not only for those directly involved in removing it but also for others elsewhere in the building. Thus, special care is required. Furthermore, asbestos dust is so menacing to public health in general that a prescribed procedure must be followed in its removal, transportation, and final disposition. Licensed asbestos removal firms must be contracted to handle these projects.

The difficulty in dealing with asbestos stems from the nature of the material itself. After asbestos has been in place for a number of years, it becomes extremely friable. Consequently, as soon as it is disturbed, it pulverizes and forms a high concentration of dust that quickly permeates the air and ultimately spreads throughout the building. For this reason, it would be ideal to remove the asbestos when classes are not in session. If this is not possible, *extreme* care must be exercised, to prevent the asbestos dust from reaching locations occupied by students and staff.

Lead Paint and Lead Dust

In school buildings constructed prior to World War II, the paint used for aesthetics and wood preservation usually contained lead. It has been found that even small amounts of lead ingested by children can have a deleterious effect on their mental and physical development. Research is currently being conducted to determine the extent to which lead is harmful to students and adults. Lead paint can be either removed or sealed.

In either case, special precautions prescribed by national codes must be taken in eliminating the source of lead poisoning. When lead paint is disturbed, even slightly, there is the possibility that dust particles containing lead may be formed. Lead paint was being removed from a high bridge passing through a city in the Boston area. Special precautions were taken by state authorities to catch dust-laden particles in canvas sheets suspended below the bridge structure.

Meanwhile, city officials continually monitored the air near homes located in the vicinity of the bridge and discovered that the amount of lead-laden particles escaping from the bridge area was becoming a health hazard. State officials were forced to take additional precautions to minimize the dispersion of lead-laden dust particles.

It is suggested, therefore, that any removal or sealing of paint containing lead be done when school is not in session. Furthermore, it is prudent that precautions similar to those employed by asbestos-removing contractors be specified in any contract awarded for the removal or sealing of lead paint. Custodians should not be expected to remove lead paint unless they are properly trained to do so and they must wear protective clothing, air filters, and goggles to shield them from the effects of lead-laden dust.

HAZARDS ASSOCIATED WITH NORMAL SCHOOL ACTIVITIES

Hazards are associated with many activities normally conducted in a school building. While such potential sources of danger cannot always be completely removed, they can and should be minimized or controlled as much as possible. School planners may wish to prepare a comprehensive checklist of specific dangers to be avoided in the design of school buildings in relation to students, faculty, clerical staff, and custodians.

Students

In reviewing plans of school buildings, each detail should be checked with the safety of the student in mind. A few questions suggest major areas of concern. If hot gases in the corridors block student egress from an instructional area, is there another means of escape? Are doors designed so that they cannot be accidentally slammed into the faces of students? Are floors slippery in the corridors, wet shower areas, main entrances, and in the classrooms? Are there dangerous projections or protrusions in the corridors, classrooms, and other areas where students congregate? Are electrical circuit boxes and other controls properly shielded and located away from student access?

Has every safety precaution been taken in normally hazardous areas such as shops, gymnasiums, laboratories, playgrounds, and stairways? Has adequate provision for first aid been made in the chemical laboratories? Is lighting in the various shops and laboratories adequate for the learning tasks to be performed? Is supplementary local lighting provided on power machines in the shops? Are electrical floor stubs avoided in teaching areas? Are catwalks, balconies, and other elevated areas fully protected and locked off for student entry? Can large expanses of glass be easily shattered by direct bodily contact by students? Are walks and drives planned for maximum safety, with a minimum of crossing of foot and vehicular traffic? Do driveways separate the building from play areas, thus causing a safety hazard?

Faculty and Staff

Many of the hazards listed earlier also apply to the faculty and staff. For the most part, schools are still designed without the work of the custodian in mind. Oftentimes, lights/bulbs in auditoriums and gymnasiums are difficult to change and require the use of extra-long ladders. Heat pipes are seldom color-coded. Without such coding, custodians may be seriously burned by hot water lines. Pipe trenches may be unlighted and studded with dangerous projections.

Electrical equipment is not always completely free from shock hazards. Mechanical controls and equipment are not always located for maximum safety. In multistory buildings, elevators are not always provided for the conveyance of heavy equipment from one floor level to another. These are a few of the hazards confronting custodial personnel. The health dangers produced by the use of cleaning agents in certain parts of the school are also of major concern to school planners.

PLANNING FOR COMFORT AND CONVENIENCE

Functional school planning has long been considered a fundamental concept of school design. However, in planning educational facilities, it is also important to include the dimensions of comfort and convenience. It is generally agreed among educators that human comfort is conducive to effectual learning. Consequently, a school should feature comfortable lighting, humidity and temperatures, comfortable seating, light colors, ventilation, and acoustical environment. A well-planned school should also provide for the convenience of its occupants.

Convenience is important in location of the rest rooms, design of traffic patterns, layout of equipment, location of storage and shelving, and grouping areas of related activity. Convenience deserves careful consideration, especially when thoughts related to the functional aspects of the school are being crystallized. For example, while the functional aspects of the heating system are being discussed, it would be wise also to consider the safety and convenience of the custodian and engineer who will eventually operate the equipment.

It is hoped, of course, that school planners will evolve a plan that is aesthetic, efficient, and convenient. Architect Louis Sullivan believed that 'form follows function'. The wisdom of this axiom cannot be overstated. Aesthetic integrity deserves careful consideration in the design of any educational facility, but if there is an unresolvable conflict between aesthetics and function, aesthetics must inevitably yield to function.

Sanitary Facilities

School planners are concerned with both the physical and the mental hygiene of those for whom schools are planned. Consequently, architects and engineers work as a team to create conditions that provide for the physical well-being of the occupants of a school building. By and large, the healthfulness of a building is determined by the design and function of the heating, cooling, and ventilating systems, and by its visual and acoustical environment. Healthfulness is also promoted by the selection of easily cleaned interior surface materials whose design reduces the accumulation of dust and air polluters. A building designed with the health of its users in mind also provides for emergency situations involving sudden illness or injuries.

Plumbing Requirements

Plumbing requirements are often reduced to a simple formula with respect to the size and number of facilities, lengths of pipe runs, proper pipe pitch, and dollars and cents. Admittedly, all of these considerations are important, but the so-called slide rule approach to school planning often falls short of ensuring thoroughly healthful conditions in the schools.

Local and national codes specify the plumbing requirements in various types of buildings. These requirements are realistic and are designed to meet the needs of modern society. The codes are reviewed by the plumbing industry periodically in order that the latest techniques and newly developed materials are incorporated in such codes. Consequently, there may be a wide discrepancy between the codes of today and those of a quarter of a century ago.

Many school buildings currently in use are over thirty years old, and some of them may even be older than fifty years. Unless a building has been remodeled recently, the number of plumbing fixtures may not be sufficient to meet current needs. For those school administrators who wish to ascertain whether the existing number of plumbing fixtures in the older buildings is sufficient, tables 9.1 and 9.2 are offered as guides.

If the discrepancies between the number of existing fixtures and those specified in these tables are large, it is suggested that local building departments be contacted to request a copy of the latest plumbing code requirements. With this information in hand, school administrators are in a position to review them with their architects so that an appropriate action to remedy any serious deficiencies can be taken.

Nationally recognized standards call for the following allocation of plumbing fixtures as specified in table 9.1. The minimum quantity of plumbing fixtures in school buildings serving adults, such as office buildings, and vocational labs, varies with the number of students attending class in the respective building(s). The minimum plumbing fixture requirements for public or state buildings in which large numbers of persons are engaged in gainful pursuits are given in table 9.2.

Toilet Facilities

A toilet room should be easy to clean, attractive, well ventilated, properly equipped, and uncongested. Every effort should be made to select fixtures, wall materials, and flooring that can be kept spotlessly clean with ease. The choice of colors in a toilet room is also quite important. The more attractive the space, the less likely it is to be defaced.

Congestion may be a problem in poorly designed toilet rooms. For example, the location of mirrors over lavatories contributes to congestion. It might be better to

Table 9.1. Plumbing Facilities

Type of Occupancy	Water Closets (Fixtures per Person)		Urinals (Fixtures per Person)	Lavatories (Fixtures per Person)		Drinking Fountain Facilities (Fixtures per Person)	Service Sink
A-4*	**Male** 1 per 75 for the first 1,500 and 1 per 120 for the remainder exceeding 1,500	**Female** 1:1–25 2:26–50 3:51–100 4:101–160 Over 160 add 1 fixture for each additional 40 females up to 1,520 and 1 per 60 for the remainder exceeding 1,520	E Over 900: 1 additional urinal for each additional 300 males; all required can be in place of required water closets	**Male** 1 per 200	**Female** 1:1–100 2:101–200 3:201–300 4:301–500 5:301–500 6:651–750 7:751–1050 Over 1,050, add 1 fixture for each additional 150 females	**Female** 1:1–250 2:251–500 3:501–750 Over 750, add 1 fixture for each additional 500 persons	1
E**	**Male** 1 per 50 UPC	**Female** 1 per 30	**Male** 1 per 100 IBC	**Male** 1 per 40	**Female** 1 per 40	1 per 100	1
Color legend	UPC		IBC	Combination of IBC and UPC			

* A-4 Assembly area within a school (auditoriums, gymnasiums, etc.)
** E Education facility (school)

Sources: 2016 Idaho Plumbing Guide (IPC), 2012 International Building Code (IBC), 2012 Uniform Building Code (UBC)

Table 9.2. Ratio of Students per Plumbing Fixture

IBC	Male WC	Male Urinal	UPC	IBC	Female WC	UPC	IBC	Female Lav	UPC
1–75	1		1–100	1–40	1	1–25	1–150	1	1–100
76–150	2		101–200	41–80	2	26–50	151–300	2	101–200
151–225	3		201–400	81–120	3	51–100	301–450	3	
226–300	4		401–900	121–160	4	101–200	451–600	4	201–300
301–375	5		901–1300	161–200	5	301–500	601–750	5	300–500
376–450	6		1301–1600	201–240	6	501–750	751–900	6	501–750
451–525	7			241–280	7	751–1250	901–1250	7	751–1250
256–600	8								

Sources: 2012 International Building Code (IBC), 2012 Uniform Building Code (UBC)

locate mirrors elsewhere in the toilet room. A shelf could be installed under mirrors for purses and other articles. In addition to distributing students within a toilet room, relocating the mirrors reduces maintenance of lavatory drains because less hair will be dropped in the lavatory. Then too, there is a significant increase in the potential utilization of the lavatory when the stations are separated. One student can be engaged in washing, while another is combing his or her hair at a location removed from the lavatory fixture.

Cleanliness and ease of maintenance must be kept in mind in planning toilet rooms. Good lighting and attractiveness are desirable even there. School maintenance personnel affirm that attractive and well-illuminated toilet rooms are usually cleaner than those that are drab and dark. The use of interior surfaces that are easy to clean tends to improve the healthfulness of toilet rooms. Floor drains and hose outlets also promote cleanliness, because they permit custodial personnel to wash the floors with ease. Floor surfaces should be impervious to moisture and acid-resistant, particularly in areas surrounding urinals.

The type of toilet fixtures selected may have an important bearing upon the healthfulness of toilet rooms. Although floor-type urinals possess many advantages, they present one serious drawback. Because of the difference between the coefficient of linear expansion of the china and the flooring material into which the unit is imbedded, a small crack eventually develops at the juncture between the floor material and the urinal.

In time, body wastes collect in the crack and sometimes seep under the floor surface, producing an unpleasant odor, which can be removed only by tearing out the floor covering or tile. Wall-hung urinals avoid this problem and are less costly to purchase and install. Also, they are easier to clean the areas near the urinals. Wall-hung toilets are also more desirable, because they permit the custodian to keep the toilet area clean more easily than the ordinary pedestal-type toilet fixtures. Wall-hung toilet fixtures are somewhat more costly than other types, so economy may dictate the pedestal-type fixture.

Ventilation is vital in toilet rooms. A mechanical ventilating system capable of producing about 20 to 25 complete air changes per hour in the room is essential. Natural ventilation through open windows would appear to be acceptable, but the lower portions must be kept closed for security and privacy, especially in single-story buildings. The upper sections, which are controlled manually, are not always open enough to provide the necessary ventilation. Mechanical ventilation, on the other hand, is effective and automatic.

Toilet seats and flush mechanisms should provide for maximum sanitation. Toilet seats of the open-front variety are highly desirable. Automatic flushing devices have now been in operation in some institutions for years without presenting any unusual maintenance problem and are preferred over the lever type on both urinals and toilets.

The location of the restrooms deserves careful thought from the standpoint of their relationship to the educational function, public or school utilization of such areas, nature of the users and convenience. The accepted location of all gang toilets in most schools constructed before World War I was in the basement of the building—the boys' area on one side and the girls' on the other.

After World War I, gang toilets were removed from the basement areas and distributed, in stack formation, on each floor. Generally, there was one set of gang toilets for each sex on every floor level. In most cases, such toilet facilities were placed adjacent to each other for reasons of economy. After World War II, however, toilets became more widely distributed throughout school buildings, and the use of single water closet toilet rooms became common.

Moving toilets from the basement to more convenient locations throughout the building was an improvement, but did not go quite far enough. The convenience of faculty was all but ignored in planning schools, although many teachers' rooms or lounges have been provided with toilets. But, in many situations, the toilets in the teachers' room are the only ones designated for faculty members.

In large high schools, the teachers' lounge may be located far from many of the classrooms where teachers spend most of the school day. It would be highly desirable, therefore, to locate a lockable, unisex faculty member restroom on each wing of the school. Such an arrangement would satisfy both the distribution and convenience requirements of such a facility.

Special attention should be given to the location and type of toilet facilities provided for students in kindergarten through third grade. Toilet facilities for these grades should be located adjacent to the classrooms to which they are assigned or within each of the kindergarten rooms themselves if possible. The size of the toilet fixture and the height of the lavatory should be scaled down to accommodate the level of physical development of the children. In some instances, one common toilet room serves two adjoining classrooms.

While this arrangement is economical, it increases the burden of supervision. The two teachers are never sure that the toilet is unoccupied when a student requests to use it. If the toilet is occupied, the student must return to his or her seat, disturbing the class twice. This may seem trivial, but if repeated several times day in and day out in the two classrooms, the disturbance is significant.

There is, however, a possible solution to the problem. If an unobtrusive light or electronic vacant or occupied sign were installed in each classroom indicating the toilet is occupied, unnecessary class interruptions could be reduced to tolerable levels. This suggestion seems straightforward but is really not that simple. The question arises, "How would the lights be triggered?" In airplanes, for example, the triggering occurs when the occupant of the toilet locks the door. In primary grades, toilet doors must be left unlocked for safety reasons.

Perhaps the lights could be controlled by opening and closing the doors. Each door could turn the light on when it is opened the first time and off when it is opened a second time. But what if someone enters the toilet area through the door in classroom A and leaves through the door to classroom B? Do the lights remain on in both classrooms when no one is in the toilet room? It is up to the electronic engineer to find a functional solution or to suggest an entirely different approach. Incidentally, there is always the better alternative of providing one toilet and lavatory facility for each classroom in the primary grades.

Lavatories

Most lavatory fixtures found in educational institutions are not designed for both healthfulness and economy. While a few installations do satisfy the need for sanitation, they do not provide for economy of water consumption. A few installations reduce the waste of water, but ignore requirements of sanitation. The standard two-spigot faucets, one for cold water and the other for hot water, produce the most unsanitary conditions under normal school use. In this case, the student must plug the drain and fill the lavatory with a mixture of hot and cold water at the desired temperature.

A lavatory used in this fashion soon accumulates dirt, since students do not ordinarily clean the lavatory after use. The spring-type or delayed-closing faucets, on the other hand, save water but do not permit students to wash their hands under sanitary conditions. When two spigots of this type are employed, the student can leave the drain open but cannot control the temperature of the water flowing from either spigot. Therefore, unless the hot water supply is tempered, he or she must wash with cold water. The other alternative, of course, is to close the drain and fill the lavatory bowl as described earlier. This procedure creates the same unsanitary conditions mentioned earlier.

What is desired in a handwashing lavatory is an installation that saves water and promotes healthfulness. In public toilets, no student should have to wash his or her hands in water collected in a basin that is not thoroughly clean. Consequently, the use of a drain plug in a wash basin is ruled out. If economy of water consumption is not a major concern, an ordinary mixing faucet with a single spring-loaded spigot solves the handwashing problem. Students do not habitually leave faucets running after use but the spring-loaded ones prevent any overflowed sinks.

Certain other parts of handwashing needs merit attention. Soap may be provided in one form or another at locations convenient to lavatories. Liquid soap systems facilitate the distribution of soap, but added maintenance is required to keep the system from becoming clogged. The location of these units should be over the sinks so that spills do not go onto the floor requiring daily cleanup.

Some provision should also be made for hand drying in toilet rooms. Ordinarily, students use cloth rollers, paper towels, or electric hand dryers. Towels generally create a maintenance problem. The cloth roller must be laundered. Paper towels will be scattered over the floor or stuffed into lavatories and toilets. In either situation, however, the maintenance problem is not intolerable. Electric hand dryers are functional and satisfactory, provided they are furnished in sufficient numbers. Electric dryers are noisy and require more time for hand drying than other methods. Therefore they usually create some congestion, but maintenance is low and littering is avoided. The initial cost of such units is offset because there is no expense for paper towels, laundering of cloth rollers, or paper waste cleanup.

Drinking Fountains

Water fountains should be readily accessible in areas where strenuous physical activity is carried on, such as playgrounds, gymnasium foyer, and playrooms. Avoid water fountains inside the gymnasium above the wooden floor to prevent any overflow possibilities. They should also be distributed throughout a school in convenient locations where water is already available.

The choice and installation of drinking fountains are of utmost importance in maintaining healthfulness in school buildings. They should be constructed of impervious materials and be designed to minimize the chance of contamination. Orifices should be located appropriately so that students' mouths do not come in contact with them and so that waste water does not fall upon the nozzle. The installation of water bubblers on the periphery of work sinks is not recommended, because students washing hands or equipment are apt to contaminate the bubblers during the washing process. Spring-loaded bubblers help prevent overflow of water as well.

Nozzle heights are very critical, particularly in elementary schools, where there is a wide range in the age and development of the children. Acceptable heights for water fountains are as follows:

a   24 inches (above the floor) for kindergarten and primary grades.
b   28 inches (above the floor) for upper elementary grades.
c   32 inches (above the floor) for junior high schools.
d   36 inches (above the floor) for senior high schools.

Water Supply

Unless the water supply system is part of a municipal system, it should be planned by a competent mechanical engineer. Where wells are used, a minimum supply of 25 gallons of water per day is required for each student for normal needs. Additional capacity of adequate storage is needed for firefighting equipment and special educational uses, such as laboratories, home economics areas, and vocational shops.

For obvious health reasons, drinking water should be free from nitrogenous or undesirable mineral content and harmful bacteria. It is of extreme importance that the plumbing system be designed to prevent back-siphoning from toilet fixtures, swimming pools, and the like.

Sewage Disposal

Unless it is part of a municipal sewer system, the sewage disposal system at any school should be designed by a competent sanitary engineer. Sewage disposal fields on school property can become a serious health hazard unless the system is properly designed. Soil percolation and terrain are critical factors in the design of a sewage disposal system. Only a well-qualified sanitary engineer can interpret the results of soil tests and drainage characteristics of the site in designing a healthful sanitary system.

THE THERMAL ENVIRONMENT

The effectiveness of the teaching-learning situation and the efficiency of school personnel are greatly influenced by the climate produced within the school building. The thermal environment should be designed to provide for the health and comfort of the individual. Comfort is determined primarily by the rate of exchange of heat between the individual and the environment. Thermal control of the environment simply regulates the net body heat loss or gain for given conditions.

Contrary to popular belief, comfort is not necessarily a function of the air temperature alone. The temperature of the walls and of other interior surfaces is more directly related to comfort than is the temperature of the air itself. For example, on very cold days, the exterior walls are relatively cool. Hence, the body radiates more heat to them than it receives and therefore experiences an uncomfortable cooling effect, even though the temperature in the room is about 72° Fahrenheit. Clothing insulates the body and reduces the loss of heat by radiation, thus producing comfort on cold days.

Discomfort, on the other hand, may be produced when the heat gained exceeds the heat lost. There is a considerable variation among individuals with respect to thermal comfort in any given set of conditions. This variation is due primarily to differences in basal metabolism that are dependent upon sex, age, activity, and individual characteristics.

Comfort and health are related, as noted above, to the equilibrium of heat exchange between the individual and the environment. The exchange is affected mostly by convection and radiation and to some extent by conduction when the individual is sitting or lying down. Consequently, the temperature of the air and that of large surfaces become the major contributors to comfort. When walls are cool, air temperatures must be kept at a level considerably higher than normal if comfort is to be maintained.

When wall and ceiling temperatures can be held close to that of the atmosphere within the room, an air temperature of 65°–68° Fahrenheit at shoulder height for kindergarten and primary grade students, and of 68°–70° for older students, is both healthful and comfortable. Convection causes air temperatures to vary with height in any given space. The difference in temperature between the floor and the 5-foot level should not vary by more than 3° Fahrenheit.

The relative humidity in a space for learning strongly influences the comfort of the individual. The comfort index varies with respect to both temperature and humidity.

At temperatures of about 72° Fahrenheit, a relative humidity of 60 percent is quite acceptable. As air temperatures rise, however, the relative humidity should decrease if comfort is to be maintained.

The human body utilizes the principle of evaporation in order to achieve a comfortable equilibrium. Since evaporation is much more accelerated when the humidity is low, spaces in school buildings requiring higher temperatures, such as drying rooms and special science laboratories, should be dehumidified, if necessary, to keep the humidity in the vicinity of 40 percent. Automatic thermostats with day/night setbacks for non-occupancy hours will help save money and increase efficiency of the mechanical units.

Ventilation Requirements

Until recently, schools in many areas have been over-ventilated. The old rule of thumb specifying that every classroom provide 30 cubic feet of fresh air per minute for each student is now being replaced by fresh-air requirements that are more reasonable. Where state codes govern the ventilation capacities of mechanical systems in public schools, the ventilation requirement has been substantially reduced, because it is generally accepted among school planners that the 30-cubic-foot-per-student requirement is excessive and unnecessary in the ordinary school classroom.

The purpose of ventilation in schools is twofold. It is well recognized of course that a major function of ventilation systems is to remove body odors from classrooms and obnoxious odors from toilets, laboratories, and kitchens. It is not as generally recognized, however, that cooling is really one of the most important functions of a ventilating system. When it is realized that human beings generate about 250 Btu (British thermal units) per hour, the need to remove heat from classrooms assumes new proportions.

For example, the amount of heat generated by 300 persons occupying a multipurpose room can be as high as 75,000 Btu per hour, which equals the heating capacity of many home furnaces. Once a given instructional space in a school is heated to the desired temperature, ventilation for cooling must be provided unless the heat loss of the room exceeds the amount of heat generated by its occupants. In some spaces in a school building, such as shower rooms, drying rooms, and basement storage areas, it is necessary to provide ventilation to remove excessive moisture, as well as heat.

It is fairly well agreed among school planners and designers that a ventilation system providing between 10 and 15 cubic feet of fresh air per student per minute is adequate for the dilution and removal of obnoxious substances from the air in classrooms.

HEATING, COOLING, AND VENTILATION SYSTEMS

It is not within the scope of this book to discuss the engineering aspects of the various mechanical systems commonly installed in school buildings, but a certain amount of descriptive information regarding these systems may be helpful to educational planners. As a rule, heating, cooling, and ventilating are conceived as a single system rather than three isolated and independent systems.

Each could operate quite satisfactorily as an independent unit from the standpoint of engineering design, but it would not be economical, since many parts of an integrated system can be designed for dual or triple use. Basically, the mechanical system consists of a source of heat, a device for cooling, a method for ventilating (window, fans, closed systems), and a means of conveying heat from one point to another.

The design of mechanical equipment has reached a high level in terms of efficiency and automation. The choice of equipment is no longer as simple as it was a quarter of a century ago. While wood and coal were the only common fuels some time ago, today's heat energy can be derived from oil, gas, electricity, radioactive material, the earth's surface, the atmosphere, and the sun.

The debate regarding the best source of heat continues. Electricity is no longer a serious challenge to oil and gas as a heat source. The choice of fuel is primarily a matter of economics, involving both the cost of the fuel and the operation of the equipment that converts the energy into heat. For example, while the cost of electricity per Btu of heat developed is generally higher than it is for other fuels, this system does not require the employment of a stationary engineer in a school as would a boiler system. It is the total cost over a period of time that should have a strong bearing on the selection of a fuel or form of energy. Again, the mechanical engineer can make an important contribution in this selection (see chapter 8).

Heating

There are at least five basic types of heating systems, ranging from the heat pump to forced hot air. Each system has features that are best suited to a particular situation. For high schools having a capacity of 1,000 or more students a hot water system can be used advantageously. In smaller educational facilities, it is possible to install forced hot air, hot water, or low-pressure systems.

The two less commonly used heating systems are heat pumps and resistance-type electrical heating units. The heat pump basically operates on the same principle as does a refrigerator. Heat is taken from one temperature zone and moved to another through the use of a compressor and a special fluid. During the winter, for example, heat is taken from coils placed in the ground or exposed to the air and conveyed to the interior of a building. During the summer, the cycle is reversed. Heat is taken from the interior and conveyed to the coils.

Thus, a heat pump serves as an air-conditioning unit in the summer and as a heater in the winter. Another promising type of heating system consists of individual resistance-type, electrically heated baseboard convectors. In some instances, electrically heated coils are used to heat water contained in a radiator-type heat exchanger. This method provides so-called wet-type heat electrically.

Radiant-heat systems merit serious consideration for use in educational facilities. The system consists of a network of piping that is usually embedded in the floor or ceiling of the space being heated. When hot water is pumped through the pipes, the entire floor or ceiling is heated. Radiant-heated floors are ideal in kindergarten rooms where children often sit on the floor. The major advantage in radiant heating is comfort. Heat radiated from a large surface does not depend upon the intervening air medium for its effectiveness. Thus, it is conceivable that persons occupying spaces heated by radiant panels may be quite comfortable when the air temperature is several degrees below the usual 68° Fahrenheit.

Cooling

General air conditioning is receiving much attention in the planning of educational facilities. The prospect that some school buildings are now being used year-round strongly accentuates the need for cooling, as well as heating. For this reason, general air conditioning is commonplace in modern school buildings. The central air-conditioning system using ducts, which is found in home air conditioning, is not very economical when entire sections of large buildings are involved.

The most common method of cooling such buildings involves the use of chilled water. A three-pipe system with air handlers and traps to collect the condensate from the moisture in the air seems to be one of the most effective and economical methods of providing cooling in the various spaces in a school building. The additional cost of the third pipe and provision for trapping the condensate is nominal. If funds are not available to purchase cooling equipment during construction, it might be prudent to plan for future air conditioning by installing the third pipe and specially designed air blowers at the time of construction. The cooling unit may then be installed later.

The cooling unit is usually located on the roof. Two basic types are currently available. The compressor type, which is mechanically driven, is quite common in both home and industrial units. A second type is a diffusion method that uses heat to produce cooling. In this instance, the same mechanical units are used to produce space heating in the winter and space cooling in the summer.

Ventilation Methods

Many ingenious methods of ventilating buildings have been devised. In one instance, warm room air is drawn through the space between the top of the suspended ceiling and the bottom of the roof. Thus, the exhausted air provides a warm buffer between the ceiling and the roof. Another method simply exhausts the air through the corridors and ultimately out of the building.

Whenever air is exhausted, there is a corresponding intake of fresh air. In general, fresh air is preheated before it enters the classroom. The fresh air is often mixed with a certain proportion of recirculated air before it is introduced into the spaces to be ventilated. One frequently used method of providing a mixture of tempered fresh air and recirculated air is the unit ventilator.

These units are generally installed along the outside wall of a building with a direct intake of fresh air from the outside. The unit can be adjusted to mix predetermined proportions of fresh and recirculated air. When unit ventilators are employed for air cooling, they can be set for the recirculation of air only. It should be pointed out, however, that a certain amount of fresh air is desirable even when the system is in the cooling cycle.

Special attention should be given to the ventilation of certain areas in school facilities. The gymnasium and natatorium are two facilities that merit special design considerations. The obvious problem in the natatorium, reduction of moisture, can be handled through an exhaust system which simply forces moisture outside of the building, or through a dehumidifier whose condensate can be fed back into the pool.

Locker and shower areas also deserve special consideration. Air is sometimes exhausted through the locker so that odors from soiled clothing are exhausted to the outside. Excessive moisture is also a problem in these spaces. Kitchen areas require ventilation primarily for cooling but also to prevent food odors from permeating the school building. And finally, special ventilation is required in spaces where noxious fumes are likely to be present, such as a paint room, chemistry laboratory, biology laboratory, and the like.

Control of Humidity

Although architects are currently not paying special attention to general humidity control in school buildings, both comfort and teaming can be appreciably improved if complete air conditioning, including humidity control, is provided in the new and renovated schools.

DISCUSSION QUESTIONS

1   How do school planners and architects prepare a school for the highest degree of safety for of all its occupants?
2   Define a "double-loaded corridor." How is the mass movement of students dependent on the corridor width?
3   Discuss four features that must be considered when designing a toilet room (also called a student restroom).
4   What is the ratio of students per plumbing fixtures? Include toilets, urinals, lavatories, and drinking fountains for both boys and girls.

NOTES

1. William Turner and Terry Brennan, "Radon's Threat Can Be Subdued," *Solar Age* (May 1985), p. 19ff.

2. Marguerite SmoUen, "Radon Remedies," *New Shelter* (June 1984), p. 28ff.

3. Steve Bliss, "Breathing Free, Part I," *Solar Age* (November 1984), p. 42.

Part IV

PLANNING AN EDUCATION FACILITY

Chapter 10

Planning Elementary and Middle Schools

It is becoming increasingly difficult to classify schools, particularly at the elementary level. At one time, there were basically two types of common schools: the grammar school with grades 1 through 8, and the high school with grades 9 through 12. Then, after World War I, the junior high school, serving grades 7 through 9, emerged as an answer to the educational needs of the 1920s. As a result, three types of schools came into being: the school serving kindergarten or grade 1 to grade 6 became known as the elementary school; the school attended by students in grades 7 through 9, the junior high school; and the school housing grades 10 through 12, the senior high school.

These grade-level organizations are by no means universal. In many parts of the United States the so-called 8–4 (eight-grade grammar school and four-year high school) organization persists. In several states, there are even separate elementary (1–8) and high school (four-year) districts within the same geographical area. In recent years, another type of school has emerged, the middle school, which usually houses grades 5 or 6 through 8.

The grade structure associated with the adoption of the middle school concept is usually a K-5, 6–8, 9–12 organization. Under this grade grouping, the former elementary schools become neighborhood units that serve kindergarten through grade 4, and the high school houses grades 9 through 12. The case has yet to be made as to which grade organization is best. It does not matter what one calls a school. What really counts is the quality of education the students receive within the school building.

The authors have seen both superior and mediocre instruction in all types of schools. An excellent educational program can be provided under any of them. The organization for a given school district should be one in which the existing usable school facilities best serve the physical requirements of the educational program. Educators may honestly favor one type of organization on the basis of experience, personal preference, or conviction.

There is to date, however, no documented evidence that strongly favors one type of grade organization over another. Often the reason for changing grade organization is to make the most effective use of available educational facilities within the school district. In some situations, such a change may significantly reduce the cost of maintenance and operation of the school plant without affecting the quality of the educational programs. In a few instances, it may even improve the variety of learning experiences to which some students are exposed.

Fundamentally, it is believed that instructional effectiveness depends far more on the interaction between students and teachers than it does upon the number of grade levels housed in a given building. Until educational psychologists uncover evidence demonstrating that a higher quality of learning occurs under a given grade organization, school planners should feel free to recommend the organization that best suits the respective needs of the educational program from the school district's standpoint of cost, economy, student convenience, and safety.

For the purposes of this discussion, elementary schools refer to school buildings that are designed to house students under the age of thirteen, regardless of the grade organization. Under this definition, the elementary school building must provide for students at various stages of physical and mental development. School planners should be aware of these variations when they plan elementary school buildings. Table 10.1 indicates the magnitude of the differences among students who are likely to attend elementary schools. From table 10.1 is clear that the elementary school must be quite versatile if it is to satisfy the diverse needs of its occupants.

In height, children will range from about 46 inches to almost 6 feet. In weight, they will range from a scant 27 pounds in kindergarten to a hefty 150 pounds in grade 6. Most seat heights in kindergarten will be 10, 11, or 12 inches above the floor; seat heights in grade 6 will be in the 13-, 14-, 15-, and 16-inch range. These differences in physical characteristics are accompanied by different levels of intellectual and social development. The range of differences does not seem to present any problems where the self-contained classroom is used, that is, where a group of students of a given age or intellectual level are taught in a single room by one teacher.

Until recently, the self-contained classroom was considered quite adequate for instruction at the elementary level, but educators are beginning to doubt the effectiveness of this concept. The elementary school program is undergoing an orderly and systematic transformation. For this reason, school planners should give greater emphasis to the likely shape of the elementary school of tomorrow than to the pseudo stable instructional practices of today.

Table 10.1.   Range of Physical Differences between Students in Selected Grades

Characteristics	Kindergarten	Grade 3	Grade 6
Weight in pounds	46.1	68	156
Height w/shoes (inches)	45	53	70
Eye height standing—above floor (inches)	35	49	65
Shoulder height standing—above floor (inches)	30.6	42.5	58
Seat height above floor (inches)	9.8	14	18.8
Eye height seated—above floor (inches)	26.6	31.3	49.6
Elbow height seated—above floor (inches)	13.5	18.6	29.6

Source: Children's Body Measurement (U.S. Department of Education)

THE CONTEMPORARY ELEMENTARY SCHOOL

A number of emerging concepts, which are discussed in the next section, are altering the conventional pattern of elementary schools. In some situations, the administrative organization seems to have changed, but the traditional practices still prevail. For example, a school district recently constructed a middle school. Actually, it was a middle school in name only. Grades 5 and 6 were still being taught in the same manner as they were in the former sixth-grade elementary school, and grades 7 and 8 in the new middle school were being treated as they were in the junior high school with almost complete departmentalization.

The lower grades, under this arrangement, did not reap many of the benefits claimed for the middle school, and the upper grades experienced none of the significant educational changes predicted by the proponents of the middle school during the referendum that authorized construction of the school.

Practices and Concepts

The Multipurpose Self-Contained Classroom

Under the traditional concept of elementary school education, between twenty and thirty children in one grade (lower in kindergarten and higher in upper grades) are assigned to a single room and a single teacher for all of the experiences they will undergo at that grade level. In some of the more advanced schools, supervisors of science, mathematics, and social sciences regularly meet with the teachers to assist them with their work. More often, the regular teacher in the self-contained classroom receives assistance and advice in the areas of music and art. Generally, students assigned to single classrooms in a conventional school use a common multipurpose room for physical education and indoor recreation.

Groupings within the Regular Classroom

Even in the traditional self-contained classroom, there is a provision for grouping. First of all, if there are two or more classrooms per grade, some school districts assign students of high learning ability to one room, average students to another, and possibly slow learners to a third, if three sections per grade are needed.

Once the children are grouped in classrooms, the teacher in each classroom subdivides them into two or three other smaller groups. Two methods are generally employed. (1) The teacher may organize three permanent groups according to ability, in which case each group stays together regardless of the subject being taught. Or (2) the teacher may organize three levels of instruction for each major area of teaching and assign students according to their ability in that area. For example, one could be a member of the top group in reading, the middle level in science, and the lowest group in arithmetic. This provides more effectively for individual differences than the first method. Both groupings, however, are aimed at meeting the individual needs of the students.

Functional Aspects of the Self-Contained Classroom

Under the aforementioned grouping, the teacher works very closely with about ten plus students at a time. When a group of about ten is being instructed by the teacher, the other fifteen to twenty or so are studying, reading, drawing, or doing independent work.

Many activities take place within the conventional elementary classroom. Individual or group projects are conducted in science, social studies, or language in one part of the room. Report preparation and small-group work may be taking place in another. Construction of simple instructional projects is one part of the learning experience of the student. These projects may involve making plaster of Paris topographical maps, use of simple machines and levers, cutting mathematical shapes out of cardboard to demonstrate the concepts of area and volume, using water to show the relationship of the volume of cubes and spheres, and work with musical strings.

To summarize, the self-contained classroom must be highly versatile and easily adaptable to a multitude of purposes. It must accommodate several activities simultaneously without excessive interference between them.

Application of Promising Concepts

Elementary school education is approaching the threshold of a golden era. New concepts are challenging time-honored traditional practices. Multipurpose teaching aids are making a significant impact upon the quality of modern education through the enrichment of student experiences in the classroom. Newly developed techniques aimed at large-group instruction, effective use of electronic teaching aids, and cooperative instructional practices among groups of teachers are being tested.

A more sympathetic attitude toward democratic administration on the part of principals and supervisors is also changing the character of the elementary schools. Several promising concepts and practices were discussed in chapter 2. A few of them are particularly suitable for elementary schools. When the administration and staff are receptive to new ideas, discussion of innovative practices can prove quite stimulating and often produce dramatic improvements in the curriculum. Where this adventurous spirit exists among staff, administrators, and generally in the community, the introduction of new concepts, studied carefully and implemented wisely, often generates a deep sense of pride within the community.

It is suggested that the concepts and practices described in chapter 2 be reviewed and seriously considered in planning an elementary school. Special attention should be given to computer-oriented instruction, team teaching, the nongraded school, variable class sizes, and the epideictic (inquiry-demonstration) concept. The planners of elementary schools that are futuristic in concept should also review and consider other potentially sound and promising practices and concepts that may be in the developmental or emergent stage when an elementary school facility is being planned.

PLANNING CONTEMPORARY ELEMENTARY SCHOOLS

At some point architects and school planners must become concerned with the physical requirements, such as how many spaces are needed, how large they should be, and where they should be located in relation to each other. This type of information is contained in this section. Also, review chapter 8 for energy conservation measures.

The school discussed in this section is based upon the self-contained classroom concept currently popular throughout the United States. The conventional elementary school is a proven concept that should not be viewed as obsolete or inferior in any way. It has had a long history of success and, it might be added, some leaders today are still the product of either the self-contained classroom or the one-room school, which is a single classroom housing eight grades under the guidance of one teacher.

It should be pointed out that the promise of the concepts discussed in the preceding section has yet to be validated through research findings. These newer concepts have much in their favor and may become universally accepted in the not-too-distant future. For this reason, whenever a traditional school is being planned, it should be designed with the newer concepts clearly in mind so that changes in the building floor plans can be made at a reasonable cost.

The Site

The minimum size of an elementary school site should be at least five acres plus one acre per 100 students of *ultimate* (includes future additions to the school) enrollment. In growing urban and suburban areas, school boards should pinpoint the location of future school sites and make purchases of them, so that sufficient acreage will be available when and where it is needed. In locations where land is available at a reasonable cost, the above rule of thumb could be modified to read: "10 acres plus 1 acre per 100 students of ultimate enrollment."

While these rules of thumb are helpful, they are not based on rigorous scientific study. More and more state agencies involved in educational facility planning are moving toward different methods in determining the size of school sites. They are relying less and less on empirical rules of thumb. The functional approach in determining the optimum size of a school site is discussed in chapter 5. At the risk of being repetitious, it seems that it would be more cost-effective to spend capital outlay funds for educational improvements in the design of a school building than to purchase a school site that is larger than can be justified on a functional basis.

Building Height

A single-story building is preferred at the elementary school level. Some elementary schools, for example, have direct access from the classroom to an outside "classroom" during good weather. The outside classroom, separated from other outside classrooms by shrubbery, serves as a laboratory in the study of plants, solar heat, and weather. From the standpoint of building cost, there is a small significant difference in the cost per square foot of usable area between the single- and multiple-story schools.

In cases where land is at a premium, a two-story building is preferable. The cost for elevators, stairs, and higher roof lines (of a two-story building) can balance out the cost for less roof, less spread of the school, and less acreage that is needed over a single-story school.

Maximum Size of School

There is, to date, no substantive research that specifies a maximum or optimum size for an elementary school. It is generally accepted, however, that an elementary school of optimum size is one with about fifteen teachers. The maximum size is considered to be about three rooms per grade, including kindergarten, or approximately twenty or twenty-one teachers. In cities, where the density of students is extremely high, the maximum size of an elementary school will necessarily be considerably higher than twenty-one teachers. In these situations however, it is strongly suggested that two schools within the same school be planned.

For example, if a school of fifty classrooms is needed in a given area, two separate and distinct administrative units could be provided. When such a school is being designed, space could be provided for two principals or a principal and vice principal, two secretaries, two teachers' rooms, and so on.

Required Spaces

Table 10.2 includes specific information about spaces commonly found in elementary schools.

Space Relationships

In the elementary school, with its self-contained classrooms and common spaces for indoor recreation, assembly, and hot lunch, the problem of space relationships is not over-complicated. Figure 10.1 suggests a desirable arrangement of spaces in

Table 10.2. Types, Number, and Sizes of Spaces in an Elementary School

Type of Space	Number Needed	Normal Class Size	Suggested Net Area in Sq.Ft.
Kindergarten	1 per 20 pupils	20	1,000–1,200
K-storage, wardrobe, toilets	1 per room	25	300–350
Classrooms	1 per 25 students	6–10	850–900
Library	1 per 15 or fewer teachers	12–15	900–1,000
Remedial room	1 per 5 teachers		350–450
Special Ed (including gifted)	As needed		900–1,000
Storage for SpEd classroom	1 per SpEd classroom		150–200
Auditorium	a) 1 separate unit for schools		8 sq.ft. per person
Stage	with more than 21 teachers. Capacity: 50% enrollment		600–800
	b) Combined with cafeteria in schools having 15–21 teachers		
	c) Multipurpose rooms in schools with less than 15 teachers		
Physical education	1 full-time use unit per		2,400–2,800
PE storage	15 teachers		400–450
	1 per PE unit		

(Continued)

Table 10.2. (Continued)

Type of Space	Number Needed	Normal Class Size	Suggested Net Area in Sq.Ft.
Cafeteria	a) One unit having capacity		10–12 per diner
(1) Dining	of 1/3 of enrollment		1½ per meal
(2) Kitchen	b) Combined with		½ per meal
(3) Food storage	auditorium in schools		0.8 per diner
(4) Serving area	with 15–21 teachers		
	c) For smaller schools,		
	combined also with PE		
	and assembly hall		
	1 per dining unit		
	1 per dining unit		
	2 per dining unit		
Administrator office	1 per 21 or fewer teachers		200–250
Outer-office clerk	1 per school		250–300
Additional clerk	1 for schools w/ 15–21		100–150
Health suite	teachers		500–550
Teachers' workroom/lounge	1 per school		500–600
Custodial office/workshop	1 per school w/ 15 or fewer		500–550
Storage of outdoor	teachers		300–350
maintenance equipment	1 per school		0.8–1 per pupil
and instructional	1 per school		80–100
equipment	1 or 2 per school		150–200
Central storage of	1 per wing and or floor		
instructional materials	1 per school		
Book storage near classrooms			
Receiving rooms—			
incinerator			

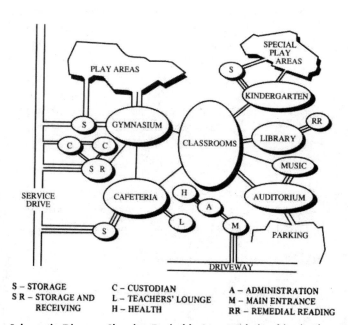

S – STORAGE   C – CUSTODIAN   A – ADMINISTRATION
S R – STORAGE AND   L – TEACHERS' LOUNGE   M – MAIN ENTRANCE
    RECEIVING   H – HEALTH   RR – REMEDIAL READING

Figure 10.1. Schematic Diagram Showing Desirable Space Relationships in Elementary Schools

an elementary school. The degree of relationship is indicated by the number of lines between any two spaces. No lines signify that there is no close relationship.

The architect, in this case, may locate the space or cluster of spaces where they best fit into the plan. One line between two spaces denotes a weak relationship. The two spaces, for example, could be located on the same floor or wing. Two lines between any two spaces or groups of spaces mean that there is a close relationship and that such spaces could be located across the corridor from each other. Three lines between two spaces denote a very close relationship, in which case they should be contiguous.

Special Design Features

A school planning committee routinely explores many special ideas in the planning of an elementary school. A few of these special features are suggested in this section.

1   *Video/Internet connectivity.* Today every classroom, and the multipurpose room as well, should be equipped with video/internet connectivity. Video/Internet connections should be wired into each classroom and other spaces when the school is constructed.
2   *Acoustical environment.* It should be said at this point that a suspended acoustical ceiling should be considered in the planning of elementary schools. The space above the tiles can be used for many purposes, such as exhausting warm air from the room, so that a blanket of warm air covers the classroom ceiling in winter. Above a suspended ceiling there is also adequate space for installing pipes, cables, and wires at a later date. Furthermore, such a ceiling is not very costly. It provides a well-controlled acoustical environment for classrooms where students may learn with fewer acoustical distractions and where teachers may teach with less fatigue.
3   *Visual surroundings.* The proper use of light color is essential in any elementary school. Color can stimulate learning in the classroom, and its psychological effect upon learners should be explored in planning interior decoration. Age of the students, orientation of the classroom, and its purpose are all important in this regard.
4   *Health room.* The health room is frequently located near the administrative offices without much regard to its function. In smaller elementary schools where a nurse is not on duty even part time, the health room should be adjacent to the office of the principal so that either the principal or the secretary can quickly help or supervise a sick child. A lockable medicine cabinent is recommended.

    The first-aid function should not be ignored. A general-use lavatory is not adequate for this purpose. It is suggested that a deep sink with a gooseneck be installed in the health room area. Ordinary lavatories may be included in the toilet rooms, which should be adjacent to the health room. A small room separate but adjoining the examination room in the health suite should be provided for children who become ill during the school day.
5   *School library.* A library that is not staffed is really nothing more than a book storage room. As such, it does not serve the purpose of a library. Libraries should be provided in elementary school buildings and should be staffed by competent

persons on at least a half-time basis. In surveying school districts, one is often dismayed when the superintendent of schools has to unlock the library room before it could be entered while school is in session. A library is essential in an elementary school, and groups of students should be allowed to use it under the guidance of the librarian. A rotating collection of library materials can be furnished to classrooms through properly designed library displays on casters. Such carts are loaded in the library and rolled into the classrooms where they may remain for a few days before being replaced by the librarian with another set of materials.

6   *Storage*. Two methods are in general use for storing students' outer clothing during the school day in elementary schools. The most common method, particularly in the lower elementary grades, is to provide a coatroom accessible from the classroom. This arrangement is quite adequate from the standpoint of supervision of students and their belongings, but it entails the loss of a wall for the use as a whiteboard. Even when an interlinked system of horizontally swinging doors is used, it is difficult to keep exhibits attached to the doors. On the other hand, if a long counterbalanced panel that slides up and down is used, the wall space of doors enclosing the cloak closets becomes usable.

The second method involves small corridor lockers for storing wraps. The corridor location for lockers is not as widespread at the elementary level as are wardrobe closets or cubbies installed within the classrooms. There are three drawbacks to the use of corridor lockers in elementary schools. (1) It is more difficult for teachers to supervise children in the corridor. (2) The children, particularly in the lower grade levels, often forget combinations or lose their locker keys. Lastly, (3) unless rubber bumpers are provided on the doors, lockers are rather noisy. On the other hand, corridor lockers can utilize space already available in corridors and increase the amount of usable wall space in the classrooms.

7   *Multipurpose room versus a lunchroom and a PE space*. The multipurpose room is sometimes called the "triple-threat" room, because it seems to be a threat to the three activities normally conducted in it. For example, the flat floor provides poor sight lines to the stage when this space is used for an assembly. The chairs and tables must be removed before this space can be converted from a cafeteria to a play area and vice versa when the room is transformed from a play area to a cafeteria. The use of in-wall tables facilitates this conversion, but they are expensive, can be unsafe as they get older and they are not particularly suited to a good social situation during meals.

A serious objection to the multipurpose room is that it gives the appearance and assurance that all of the extra-classroom needs of an elementary school can be met by that single room. It is easy to assume that the single "triple-threat" room can meet certain extra-classroom needs. In reality, of course, such is not the case. In general, however, one multipurpose room can meet the needs for assembly, indoor recreation for the students for two periods per week, and dining for a school of about twelve classrooms.

Beyond this point, a second large gym space is needed for a school of twenty to twenty-one classrooms. In this instance, two of the three functions are combined in one space. In the interest of operational efficiency, the assembly function and physical education are combined. There are several advantages to this arrangement of two different spaces. The tables and chairs can remain in the lunchroom, but if another assembly capacity is needed, the tables may be replaced by chairs. Finally, during inclement weather, the physical educational space could be used by other students before school and would not interfere with those who arrive at school for breakfast before school starts.

8   *Classrooms.* It should be borne in mind that all student experiences, with the exception of physical education, eating meals (breakfast and lunch) and music, take place within the self-contained classroom. Consequently, the room must be designed for instruction in art, science, language, social sciences, and mathematics, if these activities are not conducted elsewhere. The rooms should be furnished with a work sink and work counters on both sides of it, primarily for experiments in science and art. There should also be a smaller alcove where students construct paper, cardboard, and wooden models of various types for science, art, arithmetic, and social sciences.

The classroom should be spacious and functional. It should, if possible, approach the shape of a square to simplify supervision. It should be designed to include two or three well-defined locations, such as a science and art area, a project area, a reading area, and an adjoining small tutoring room (with glass walls into the classroom and hall) is where helping volunteers may assist the teacher in working with small groups.

Fenestration has received much attention in recent years. Emphasis has ranged from one extreme to the other—from the complete window wall to the windowless classroom. Architects argue that it is easier and more economical to control the environment in a windowless or inoperable windowed classroom. This may be valid, but educators are mixed on this point. Some argue that it is not desirable to remove children from the world in which they live for the sake of easy temperature control.

A few maintain that students are subjected to fewer distractions in a windowless school than in a conventional building; others counter this argument by pointing out that an inspiring teacher can hold the class's interest anywhere, even in a classroom where students may look out the window. The thinking on this matter is quite confused. Perhaps a compromise solution is in order. If artificial light is the primary source of illumination, it might be desirable to provide a simple vision strip across the outside wall of a classroom. In this case, the window sill should be about 6 inches below the eye level of the seated students, and the top of the vision strip should be approximately 6 inches above the eye level of a teacher standing in the classroom.

Again, it should be emphasized that a proper brightness balance must be maintained within a classroom. Brightness balance should apply to the mobile and movable furniture and equipment, as well as to the room itself. Color, acoustics, and brightness balance are all matters of major concern in planning classrooms that are conducive to effective learning.

9   *Site development.* In some instances, site development is left to chance or to "if funds are available," but site development is an integral part of a well-planned school. It seems ridiculous to acquire a site of, let us say, 14 acres without

developing a major portion of it for recreation, parking, parent pick-up/drop-off, bus loading/unloading and other educational purposes. In fact, the school site could also be planned for use by the public for Little League baseball, outings, and other recreation when it is not being used for school purposes. Summer recreational programs could also be accommodated on a well-developed school site.

The natural assets of a school site, such as trees or brooks, should be preserved whenever possible. Brooks lend beauty and interest to a school site, but too many school planners regard them as a liability that must be eliminated. A few imaginative architects and school planners have converted a liability to a beautiful asset by preserving, widening, or providing of a brook.

THE MIDDLE SCHOOL

The middle school, well established in the United States, is an educational entity. It is neither an elementary school nor a junior high school. It is a school that is focused primarily on the educational and psychological needs of students in the ten- to fourteen-year age group. As a rule, middle schools are designed to house students in grades 6 through 8. In some instances, middle schools are planned for students in grades 5 through 8 or 7 through 9. These grade groupings may suggest that the middle school is a substitute for the upper elementary or the lower high school level. It is not. The middle school, properly planned, is not a substitute for anything. It is uniquely a middle school.

Planning a Middle School

A long step may be taken in the direction of the middle school concept without seriously alarming teachers, students, or parents in a stable, conservative community. After public acceptance of the middle school concept has been achieved, the school board and superintendent of schools should develop policies governing the reorganization or redefining of the attendance areas for each of the respective schools.

The Special Characteristics of an Effective Middle School

The transition from the conventional elementary-junior high school concept to the middle school should be careful and evolutionary. The changes in instructional pattern may occur gradually at a pace that is comfortable for teachers and students. The middle school seems somewhat different but in reality is closely related to traditional patterns in many ways.

Grade Grouping. A gradual transition from the existing 6–3–3 or 6–2–4 to the 5–3–4 organization can be planned. It would not be surprising, therefore, to find that a middle school planned initially for grades 6 through 9 would later house grades 6 through 8.

Student Separation. Most modern middle schools are planned so that the lower grade is assigned to one side of the building and the upper two grades to the other. While this practice has some merit, it should not be carried to such an extreme that specialized rooms, such as shops, homemaking suites, and science laboratories, are decentralized for the sole purpose of preventing a sixth-grader from crossing the path of a seventh-/eighth-grader. In passing, however, it may be noted that parents who often protest against intermingling students of various age groups in school, where they are highly supervised, rarely seem to question the practice of transporting children of all ages in the school buses, where practically no supervision is provided.

Team Teaching. Some provision is included in the modern middle school for the beginning of a team-teaching program. Seminar rooms are usually provided for the group activity of the team teachers, and a workroom of about 400 square feet is often located in the vicinity of the teachers' lounge. It is furnished with work tables and chairs and equipped with copiers, computer stations, a drawing table, art supplies, and photographic devices. The teaching team would thus be able to produce some of its own instructional materials. In the beginning, at least, most of the team teaching would be focused upon the upper two grades, but in time all of the students in the school could be exposed to some form of team teaching.

Variable Group Size. The effective middle school can include provision for a limited amount of instruction in larger groups of about sixty to eighty students. In general this is accomplished simply by including a few movable partitions between pairs of regular classrooms. A space about 78 feet long and 23 feet wide could be provided for teaching a group larger than the conventional twenty-five or thirty students simply by opening a partition. Provision for teaching in larger groups could also be made in the cafeteria, library, gymnasium, and auditorium spaces. The expansible spaces may not seem very exciting or extraordinary at first glance, but in the hands of creative teachers and administrators their potential for educational improvement is greatly enhanced provided their widths approximate 30 feet.

Number of Instructional Spaces for the Effective Middle School

In planning a middle school, some regular, self-contained classrooms are usually retained while others are specialized. The distribution of regular and specialized classrooms of course depends upon the desired middle school grade program. In the middle school it can be assumed that:

(1) students in grade 6 will spend 25 percent of their time in specialized rooms and the remainder under a single teacher;
(2) students in grade 8 will spend half their time in regular classrooms and the remainder in specialized spaces; and
(3) students in grade 8 will spend two periods (about 25 percent) of their time under one teacher and the remainder with several others. Under these conditions, the approximate distribution of instructional space is as follows:

Sixth grade: *Three units* of regular classrooms to *one unit* of specialized space.
Seventh grade: *One unit* of regular classroom to *one unit* of specialized space.
Eighth grade: According to programs—using the following formula.

   a) *Number of teaching periods needed.* The following formula may be used to determine the number of faculty periods per week required for each course:

$$Pwk = \frac{En}{C}$$

where:

Pwk = Number of periods per week required to staff a given course

E = Number of students enrolled in the course

C = Desired class size

n = Number of class meetings per week for the respective course.

b) *Teaching stations needed.* To convert Pwk into the number of teaching stations required, simply divide the sum of the Pwk for each subject by the number of instructional periods each classroom is available per week multiplied by 1.20. The computed number of teaching stations incorporates a surplus of 20 percent in order to provide sufficient leeway for scheduling difficulties and unavoidable variations from the desired class size.

To illustrate the application of the aforementioned formula, let us assume that the desired educational program for students in grade 6 is as given in table 10.3 that follows:

Table 10.3. Data Table for Formula Usage

Number of students to be served	120
Total number of periods in the school week	45
Desirable class size for all courses	30
Number of periods per week each student attends physical education classes	2
Periods per week per student for assembly, conferences, etc.	3
Number of academic instructional periods per week	40
Periods per week per student under a single teacher	30 (in a regular classroom)
Periods per week per student in specialized science room	5
Periods per week per student in specialized art room	2.5
Periods per week per student in specialized music room	2.5

The number of spaces required to house the program and enrollment in the example set forth above is computed as indicated in table 10.4:

Table 10.4. Formula Calculations—Periods

Regular classrooms—periods	$\frac{120}{30} \times 30$	$=$	120 periods per week
Science periods	$\frac{120}{30} \times 5$	$=$	20 periods per week
Art periods	$\frac{120}{30} \times 2.5$	$=$	10 periods per week
Music periods	$\frac{120}{30} \times 5$	$=$	10 periods per week

To convert these period requirements to classrooms, divide each result by 40 and multiply by 1.2. Thus, the spaces needed for 120 students in grade 5 are as given in table 10.5:

Table 10.5.   Formula Calculations—Teaching Stations

Regular classrooms	$\dfrac{120}{40} \times 1.2$	=	3.6 teaching stations
Science classrooms	$\dfrac{20}{40} \times 1.2$	=	0.6 teaching stations
Art classrooms	$\dfrac{10}{40} \times 1.2$	=	0.3 teaching stations
Music classrooms	$\dfrac{10}{40} \times 1.2$	=	0.3 teaching stations

Diagrammatic Features of a Middle School

The computerized sketches presented in this section display selected components of a middle school planned for a capacity of 1,200 students. They also show how provision can be made for unforeseeable future needs. While the square footage figures shown for each type of space are within the normal range of the area needed for such spaces, they can be construed as being fixed or standard sizes.

The actual size of each space should be determined by local educational planners strictly on the basis of the area requirement perceived for each type of space. It is advised, however, that local school planners take a second look at their figures if they deviate by more than 50 percent in either direction, from those shown on these diagrams. Such large deviations are not necessarily out of line. They only need to be confirmed and fully justified on the basis of unique local educational requirements.

Figure 10.2 presents the layout of several major components of an idealized middle school. It shows the degree of relationship between various parts of the educational facility. Three lines connecting two elements of the plan indicate a very close relationship. Two lines between two parts of the facility signify that a close relationship exists between them, while a single line means that the relationship is weak. The diagram also shows where future expansion should be located in order to preserve the educational integrity of the building.

It should be pointed out that the individual components of the school specified in figure 10.2 do not necessarily represent separate and distinct buildings. They simply denote function. Actually, all of the architectural components of the plan could be enclosed in a single building. The architect and local educators should determine how each component can best be integrated into a functional educational unit while preserving space relationships. It is realized, of course, that the topography of the site and cost considerations will have a direct bearing on the final design of the facility.

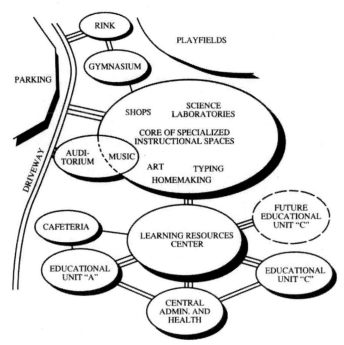

Figure 10.2. Idealized Middle School Layout

If any part of a school does not contribute to the educational function of the building, prudence dictates that it should not be built. A school should contain only those elements that are necessary and sufficient to house the desired curriculum.

Figure 10.3 focuses primarily on certain operational aspects of the educational facility. Only four major components are shown. These clusters were selected because they are especially sensitive to any weaknesses in their internal space relationships. Special attention is directed to the planning of cafeteria and custodial facilities. Sometimes, for example, there are situations where cafeteria food supplies must be wheeled through corridors because there is no direct access from the service drive to the food storage room. Similarly, custodial spaces are often planned without fully considering the functional requirements of such facilities.

Figure 10.3 also calls attention to two other crucial components of a middle school: the administrative cluster, which represents a complex of closely integrated functions; and the learning resources center, which is surrounded by a cluster of ancillary spaces for remedial education and for the maintenance and storage of audiovisual materials. The most common deficiency within this complex is the lack of adequate space for storing specialized technology instructional equipment and materials associated with remedial education.

Figure 10.4 displays several clusters of highly specialized instructional spaces. Shop clusters deserve special consideration. They must be easily accessible from the service drive. It is frequently not realized that woods and metals shops receive and store a

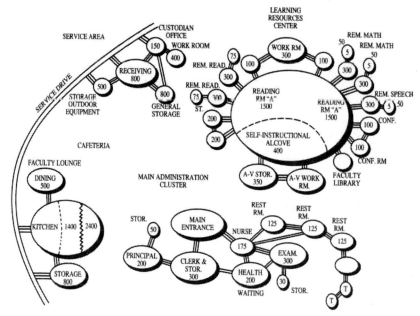

Figure 10.3. Administrative Cluster

Note: The numbers in the bubbles represent square footage of those rooms. The bubbles with "5" in them have the square footage noted on the outside of the bubble.

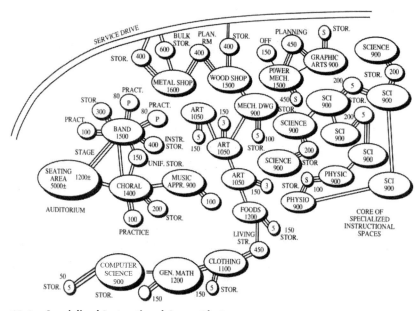

Figure 10.4. Specialized Instructional-Space Clusters

Note: The numbers in the bubbles represent square footage of those rooms. The bubbles with "5" in them have the square footage noted on the outside of the bubble.

substantial amount of materials in bulk form. For this reason, direct access from the service drive to these two shops is mandatory. If the mechanics shop deals only with small motors and electrical appliances, access from the service drive is desirable, but not essential. It is also important to bear in mind that some shop areas tend to be very noisy. Thus, the woods, metals, and small engine shops should be placed at locations that are remote from the quieter parts of the building.

Figure 10.4 also shows other clusters of closely related spaces servicing specialized functions. The reader is invited to review an interesting progression of specialized spaces beginning with the computer labs located on the lower left section of the diagram. This lab is connected with the general mathematics room in which business mathematics is usually taught. The mathematics room is connected to the home economics room where measurements are an integral part of the course. The sequence continues to the art room and follows to the mechanical drawing room, which, in turn, is related to the shops.

The science cluster is a self-contained unit that may be placed in any of several locations within the building. Logically, the science room/lab could start the science sequence by being positioned adjacent to the regular mathematics rooms. Or, the science cluster could be the link between the academic subject classrooms and the shop areas.

The auditorium and the music rooms are also closely related and form a self-contained, independent cluster. The placement of this cluster in relation to the rest of the building is very critical because of the high intensity of the sound generated within these spaces. If possible, this cluster should be acoustically isolated from the quieter areas of the building. The auditorium is also planned for community use. Thus, it should also be located close to the parking areas for the convenience of the public. (See figure 10.2.)

DISCUSSION QUESTIONS

1   How do school administrators determine and classify their sequence of grade levels at each of their schools?
2   Identify the formula for helping determine the size of an elementary school site. How would you ascertain the grade sequence for the district's schools?
3   Discuss seven examples of special design features that should be considered when designing an elementary school.
4   Define and explain the formula which is used to determine the number of periods per week that could be required in a middle school.

Chapter 11

Planning Secondary Schools

Because of the current state of flux in grade organizations, it is not always clear what grade levels are included in the secondary school grouping. For the purpose of this chapter discussion, secondary schools are facilities designed to house students from ages thirteen to eighteen years. Students in this age grouping may attend: middle schools, junior high schools, or senior high schools. The term used to designate a school is of little or no consequence in planning, but educational function and physical needs of students in this age group play an important role in the design, size, location, orientation, and interior treatment of school buildings.

In the absence of validated research regarding the design of secondary school buildings, the rationale underlying the various topics discussed in this chapter is based primarily on generally accepted practices in secondary school planning. Admittedly, it would be far better to rely on research findings, but they are not conclusive at this time. The Educational Facilities Laboratories in New York sponsored important projects in school-building research, which made a significant impact on the design of educational facilities in the United States and Canada (http://ncef.org/pubs/efl2.pdf).

Nevertheless, the quantity of validated research on school buildings from the standpoint of educational function is still disappointing. For this reason, it is necessary to rely primarily on professional judgments and opinions that may or may not be based on research findings. School planners confronted with the problem of planning school buildings for the thousands of students who need school facilities today, or perhaps even yesterday, cannot afford the luxury of waiting until research findings are available.

CONTEMPORARY EDUCATIONAL PRACTICES COMMON TO SECONDARY SCHOOLS

In planning secondary school facilities, it should be borne in mind that secondary school programs vary from district to district and sometimes even from school to school within the same school district. For this reason, there is no common or typical secondary school facility that can be described in definitive terms. Within these different facilities, however, there are a number of educational practices that are similar in most of them. The degree to which these practices are employed in each situation will vary somewhat from school to school, but they will generally appear in one form or another. The most prevalent version of each practice is described in the following paragraphs.

Complete Departmentalization

Under prevailing practice, the secondary school is fully departmentalized by subject-matter area. A department head is given the responsibility of determining the course content, selecting textbooks, and choosing the type of instructional materials to be used in a given area of learning. He or she is the instructional leader and supervises the teaching and methods followed in the department. If the leader is imaginative, forward-looking, and sensitive to good human relations, the instruction may be superior.

On the other hand, if the leader's appointment was not based on competence, the instructional effectiveness of the department may be disappointing, the methods obsolete, and teacher morale low. By and large, the department structure has operated at an acceptable level of efficiency for at least a half century. Conscientious department heads have made the system work from an administrative point of view. Psychologists, on the other hand, might question the wisdom of compartmentalizing learning.

The Teaching of Classes

In most situations, teachers instruct students in groups called classes. The usual class includes between 25 and 32 students for most courses. With good reason, teachers and administrators much prefer class size as close as possible to 25. The size of the group also depends upon the subject being taught. As a rule, most group sizes lie within the aforementioned limits, with the exception of classes in advanced sciences, art, and home economics, where the maximum may fall well below 25.

The class size in music may vary over a wide range. In some secondary schools, the group size for music instruction may range from 25 to 250, depending upon the type of musical activity. Industrial arts classes are often officially restricted to 20, but may actually reach 25–30 students. Physical education may be taught according to prevailing practice, in groups of 40 to 45, while keyboarding may be taught effectively to groups of about 35 under the guidance of a single teacher.

The teacher instructs a given class for a period ranging from 45 to 60 minutes four or five times per week for a total of about 250 contact minutes per week per class. Each teacher usually offers instruction four or five periods a day for a total of about 1,250 minutes per week. The time spent by students in formal classes of various types range from 1,200 to 1,500 minutes per week at the upper secondary level of instruction. At the lower secondary level, it is customary to reduce the length of class period and to increase the number of periods the student must attend each week.

For example, a thirteen-year-old student in grade 7 might enroll in seven courses for a total of thirty-five instructional periods per week. In this case, the length of the class period is usually reduced to about 40 minutes. A student in grade 12, on the other hand, may be assigned to twenty of the 60-minute periods of formal instruction per week, for a total of about 1,200 minutes in supervised classes.

Student Movement

In the contemporary school, teachers are usually assigned to a given classroom where students come to them period after period for instruction during the school day. Under this system, the students move from one room to another where the different courses are offered. At the end of each period, a complete reshuffle of students occurs within the school. This situation can create a real problem in circulation within a secondary school. Students move not only from class to class, but also from classroom to library, to cafeteria, to gymnasium, to auditorium and to other supplementary spaces.

Grouping

In the secondary school, students are grouped homogeneously, according to some predetermined criteria, or heterogeneously in random fashion. Oftentimes, they are grouped according to reading ability, aptitude, general intelligence, curricula, and the like. When two or more sections of the same course are taught, homogeneous grouping reduces the range of differences in learning ability among the class. There is still much controversy regarding the value of homogeneous grouping over heterogeneous grouping. Both are found in secondary schools, depending on the philosophy of the administration and the school board.

Once the group is formed, it remains intact during the entire semester or year. It is generally not combined with any other similar group. The teacher simply treats it as a class, introducing learning experiences appropriate to the group and subject matter being taught.

Teaching Aids

The instructional tools of the prevalent secondary school consist primarily of textbooks, whiteboard, and paper. Demonstrations are restricted primarily to the physical sciences, home economics, art, technology and industrial education. LCD projectors are used in many classrooms. Some teachers introduce PowerPoints into the curriculum at some point. While electronic teaching aids such as cable TV, computer instruction, and feedback systems could be effectively utilized in all schools, the orientation of some secondary schools does not place a very high value on such aids or assign them a very important role in the educational program.

Large-Group Activity

In the contemporary secondary school, the major large-group activity is the school assembly. Secondary school principals often insist on facilities that can accommodate the entire student body at a single sitting for assemblies, which may be called as often as once a week or as infrequently as ten times a school year.

Secondary school principals can make a very strong case for the inclusion of an auditorium that can seat a minimum of the largest single class—usually freshmen—plus about 50 percent of that class enrollment. Often an auditorium that can seat one-half of the student body is adequate. Under the contemporary concept of a secondary school, when the total enrollment exceeds 1,500 it is difficult to justify an auditorium capable of seating the total student body simultaneously for assembly and dramatics alone.

Student Detention

In-school student detention is being adopted by more and more school districts due to the changing character of the modern family. In the past, unruly and disruptive students, particularly at the secondary school level, were temporarily suspended from attending school. They were sent home and placed under the supervision and control of their parents. Today, there are often no parents at home to supervise them. This situation poses a real problem for school administrators. Suspension is no longer viewed as punishment by such students. Rather, some unruly students look forward to it as an opportunity to play video games or engage in whatever activity strikes their fancy. Thus, suspension simply reinforces their unruly behavior in school.

Educators are still searching for a constructive solution to this problem. Ideally, some method must be found to change the behavior of disruptive students, utilizing established principles of psychological therapy. In the meantime, school administrators have implemented a makeshift solution. Instead of suspending problem students from school, they are assigned to a student detention room, where they are supervised by school personnel.

Students assigned to the detention room are expected to do schoolwork in isolation. They are allowed to have whatever instructional materials are related to their course of study. They may not mingle with other students during school hours. Except for dining and meeting other bodily needs, they must remain in the detention room for the entire school day(s).

The planning of a student detention room must satisfy a number of crucial criteria. It should be located where it can be continually supervised by school personnel. It may be strategically placed in the administrative area or within the view of personnel working in the learning resources center. Its walls and doors must withstand abuse from students occupying the room. While conducting a school survey recently in a school system, the writer examined the student detention room, which was originally planned as the workroom for the librarian. It was observed that the lower part of the walls was severely damaged by students trying to kick in the walls. Large holes were made in the gypsum board by students giving vent to their frustrations.

While the detention room restricts student freedom, it should not be planned as a jail cell. The space should be pleasant and comfortable. It should be a small study cubicle for one person and be equipped with a desk and chair. There should be glass vision strips on one or two walls between 3 and 5 feet above the floor for student supervision.

THE RELATIONSHIP OF EDUCATIONAL FUNCTION
TO SECONDARY SCHOOL FACILITIES

A vital responsibility of educators involved in planning a school building is the translation of teaching and learning activities into the physical features of a building. The accent at this point is on activities, actions, and direct experiences of both students and teachers. We are more concerned at this juncture with the curriculum than with the broad educational program, although both ultimately play a crucial part in the planning of a secondary school.

The architect is not expected to be familiar with the curriculum of a given secondary school unless they are given a clear picture of it by school officials. He or she should be presented with a document that translates curriculum into suggested space requirements, commonly called educational specifications (see chapter 5) by educators and simply "a program" by architects. In any event, the architect is entitled to a fairly detailed set of educational specifications. They should be free from ambiguities and restrict the architect's work as little as possible.

It should be borne in mind that the creative talents of the architect cannot be released if educators insist on making quasi-architectural sketches of the various spaces in a proposed school. It is far better to inform the architect about the activities and functions to be housed in a given space and to provide an estimate of the number of net square footage of educational spaces that are required. Sometimes special features such as orientation, ceiling height, or length of a space are necessary to accommodate unusual equipment or instructional practice. In these instances, the architect would welcome specific information, but generally educational specifications should be prepared to give the architect as much freedom as possible.

METHODS AND FUNCTIONS ASSOCIATED WITH SECONDARY SCHOOLS

One or more of the following methods is employed in teaching both small and large groups of students. Some of them are easily recognized, and others are not.

Presentation Method

The most common method of instruction is one in which the teacher presents ideas to a group of students. The students receive instructional stimuli via sight and hearing. The learner, in this situation, is passive. The teacher transmits ideas by a number of means; books, e-books, locally prepared materials, the whiteboard, smartboard, LCD projector, computer, iPad, netbook, and the like. In all of these situations, however, the process is directive. The presentation is made by the teacher or with the aid of technology.

Demonstration Method

This method of instruction is somewhat similar to the presentation method. The major difference is in the matter in which the student receives the stimuli. In demonstrations, sight plays a major part in the transfer of ideas. In general, the teacher sets up an experiment to demonstrate a basic principle or phenomenon. Demonstration is a direct experience by the student as opposed to the vicarious experiences conveyed by the teacher using the above presentation methods.

Diagnostic and Evaluation Function

The diagnostic aspect of the instructional function is frequently overlooked by school planners. The testing, evaluation, and analysis of student progress are of paramount importance in any educative process. School facilities do not generally lend themselves to testing and diagnosing student work. In fact, cheating is made easy in the typical classroom by the proximity of one student to the other. Admittedly, the cost of providing individual cubicles in a room that is scanned by a 360-degree security camera might be difficult to justify solely on the basis of the need to reduce cheating.

On the other hand, it is possible to introduce features that are likely to minimize the temptation for students to copy one another. Flexible seating arrangements, and electronic devices that provide immediate feedback from student to teacher, should be considered in planning a school. The function of testing, evaluating, and diagnosing a student's work should be borne clearly in mind when schools are being planned.

COMMON ELEMENTS OF SECONDARY SCHOOL PLANNING

The Secondary School Site

The requirements of the school site have already been discussed in chapter 5. The rule of thumb regarding optimum size of a secondary school site varies considerably from source to source, but in practice a site of 25 acres (junior high school level) or 40 acres (high school) plus one acre for each 100 students of ultimate enrollment is generally accepted as a minimum (see table 4.2).

There appears to be no validated research thus far that indicates the optimum size of a secondary school site with respect to educational returns. The increasing cost of land and the accelerated urbanization and suburbanization of the population reduce the availability of desirable land, and prices for school sites are rising rapidly. It is conceivable that the size of school sites may have to be drastically reduced in some areas. In open country, every effort should be made to meet or surpass the practical standard stated above.

Translating Program Requirements into Instructional Spaces

After the educational program has been fully worked out by the school staff and approved by the school board, the number of students that will probably be enrolled in each course should be estimated. The number of periods per week that each course will be offered to a given number of students should also be noted. Two techniques may be employed in arriving at the required number of spaces.

The Conrad Method

Conrad has developed a very accurate technique that indicates either capacity or number of needed teaching stations for a given student enrollment (see chapter 10).[1]

The Castaldi Nomogram[2]

The nomogram consists of a chart that the required number of spaces can be read directly for high schools organized on a 25-, 30-, or a 35-period school week. For other administrative organizations of the school week, the Castaldi formula shown here can be used directly. The formula takes into account that every student station (seat) in every classroom in a secondary school cannot be scheduled for occupancy 100 percent of the time. Thus, it provides for a student utilization factor of 80 percent in order to compensate for scheduling difficulties, teachers keeping their classroom unoccupied for their prep period, and variations in class sizes.

$$T.S. = 1.25 \frac{E}{C} \times \frac{n}{N}$$

Where:

T.S. = Required number of teaching stations
E = Number of students enrolled in a given course
C = Desired class size
n = Number of periods per week student attends a given class
N = Number of periods in the school week.

The formula may be used to answer questions such as:

How many rooms are needed if 300 students are to be enrolled in art, which meets twice a week? The desired maximum class size is 25 and there are 40 periods in the school week.

$$T.S. = (1.25) \frac{300}{25} \times \frac{2}{40} = 0.75$$

In this case, one art room is needed. The 0.75 teaching station obtained by applying the Castaldi formula is rounded off to the next highest integer.

Determining the Size of Various Spaces

The Functional Analysis Approach

The most satisfactory way to determine the size of an instructional space is to list all the major activities expected to occur in it together with the type of equipment and number of students involved in each activity. A layout designating the space needed for the equipment and for each student or group of students will yield the approximate area needed for the activity in question.

The total area included in a teaching space is the sum of the combination of activities carried on simultaneously that requires the greatest floor space. It is presumed that other teaching experiences can be conducted effectively within the given space, even though the room is larger than it actually needs to be for the activity under consideration.

The Rule-of-Thumb Approach

As mentioned earlier, validated research indicating optimum sizes or capacities of various types of instructional spaces is practically nonexistent. Since the need for school facilities is urgent, and the construction of school buildings cannot be postponed until such research findings become available, school planners have resorted to a rule-of-thumb approach. Although there is no proof that the specific figures in the rule of thumb apply to minimum, maximum, or optimum conditions or otherwise, there seems to be general agreement that spaces planned according to the rules of thumb function satisfactorily, at least when judged on a subjective basis.

In the absence of other more specific data, the rule-of-thumb approach seems acceptable, and no apologies should be made for its use now in planning of school buildings. It is important that school planners be aware of the subjective origin of the rules applied in the design of school buildings.

SPECIFIC GUIDELINES FOR PLANNING SECONDARY SCHOOLS

Suggested Space Allocations

The specific sizes and comments presented in table 11.1 through table 11.4 are not the product of research, nor are they attributable to any one person or group. They reflect the current thinking of both educators and school planners. Admittedly, the quantities listed in tables 11.1–11.4 are likely to change from time to time as research becomes available or as educational practices undergo certain transformations. It is felt, however, that school planners will deviate from the figures presented in tables 11.1 to 11.4, of course, when the educational and service functions demand more or less space in certain situations.

Relationship of Clusters of Spaces to Each Other

Figure 11.1 shows the arrangement of groups of spaces in a traditional secondary school building. Essentially, the groupings are divided between quiet and noisy areas. They are also arranged with regard to the need for proximity to the service drive, outdoor grass field areas, or main entrance.

It should be reemphasized that the space arrangements shown in figure 11.1 conform to current accepted practice. For example, it is generally agreed that all science rooms should be clustered together, that locker and shower rooms and PE grass areas should be adjacent to the gymnasium, and so forth. The degree of relationship is indicated on the diagrams by the number of lines drawn between each element. Three lines denote a very close relationship, in which case one space should adjoin the other. Two lines mean the two spaces should be in the same general area, perhaps no farther apart than a corridor's width. One line between two spaces for clusters indicates that it is desirable but not essential that the two spaces be located in the same general area. An absence of lines between any two spaces or groups of elements means that no

Table 11.1. Specialized Instructional Spaces in Secondary Schools

Type of Space	Suggested Max. Class Size	Suggested Area of Each Space	Suggested Area of Adj. Store Rm.	Comments
A. Art				
1. General art	25	1,000–1,200	100–150	North orientation not mandatory if adequate lighting is provided.
2. Arts and crafts	25	1,100–1,400	175–225	
B. Commercial Education				
1. Office machines	25	800–900	20–40*	Special attention should be given to sound transmission problems.
2. Office practice	25	800–900	20–40*	Electrical outlets should be available at every student station and at the teacher's desk.
3. Keyboarding	35	850–950	20–40*	
C. Homemaking				
1. General	24	1,200–1,400	50–75	It would be desirable to design this space so that by opening or closing partitions it could become part of either room adjacent to it.
2. Multipurpose area (living center)	4–8	400–500	50–75	
3. Clothing	24	900–1,000	50–75*	
4. Foods	24	1,000–1,200		
D. Music				
1. Band-orchestra	Varies	1,200–1,600	Cabinets	Music practice rooms should be slightly over-acousticized to prevent the blending of sounds.
2. Instrument storage	Varies	250–300	Cabinets	
3. Chorus	1–6	1,200–1,400		High-grade stereophonic equipment should be installed in band and chorus rooms. One amplifier can serve more than one space.
4. Practice room	1–4	100–125		
5. Practice room	1–2	75–100		
6. Practice room	30	50–75		One office per instructor needed.
7. Theory	6–10	700–850		
8. Office		150–200		
9. Listening/recording room and music library		350–450		
E. Physical Education				
1. Gymnasium (one teaching station for PE only)	40	3,700–4,400	300–400	The size of the gymnasium varies with bleacher seating capacity. Standard-size basketball court requires a gymnasium with an area of approx. 5,600 sq.ft.
	40	5,600–7,000	250–350	
	20	600–900	250–300	

(Continued)

Table 11.1. (Continued)

Type of Space	Suggested Max. Class Size	Suggested Area of Each Space	Suggested Area of Adj. Store Rm.	Comments
2. Gymnasium (two teaching stations w/ folding partition)	40 40	250–300 See comment	250–300 w/ 14–16 ft. ceiling	Add 3 sq.ft. per person for bleacher seating capacity. Where more than two teaching stations are required, balcony area spaces should be considered for both movable seating and teaching space.
3. Corrective room		700–900		Adjoining gymnasium area.
4. Coach office		3,000–4,000		The total of areas 3–7 inclusive should be approx. 0.7–1.0 × total area of gym. Number of shower heads: 1:4 boys, 1:3 girls
5. Toilets (including public)		2,000–2,400		
6. Showers and locker rooms		800–1,000		
7. Team room				Provision should be made for ticket office, checking, public toilets, and display.
8. Other standard girls gym				
9. Auxiliary gym—one teaching station				
10. Lobby				
11. Visiting team room				
F. Physical Sciences				
1. Biology	25	900–1,000	150–175	Science rooms should be "squarish" to permit use of the peripheral laboratory units. Network connectivity should be installed in all science spaces.
2. Chemistry	25	1,000–1,100	200–250	
3. General Science	30	900–1,000	125–150	
4. Physics	25	900–1,100	200–250	Need not be exposed to the out-of-doors if appropriate lighting provided.
5. Growing room		200–300		May be related to either the art room or science area.
6. Darkroom		60–100		
G. Industrial Arts (nonvocational)				
1. General (composite) shop	20 25	1,500–2,000 850–950	150–200 50–75	One locker, dressing-washing room per two shops, if possible. Avoid the use of loft storage areas in all shops.
2. Mechanical drawing	20	1,700–2,000	150–200	Provide high ceilings only in metals and wood shops
3. General metals	20	1,500–1,800	150–200	Planned as a single large space.
4. General woods	20	900–1,200	100–150	
	20	1,600–2,200	150–200	

Item				
5. Electrical shop	20	1,600–2,000	150–200	
6. Power mechanics	20	1,400–1,600	150–200	
7. Metal shop	20	1,000–1,100	150–200	
8. Wood shop		400–450	100–125 per shop	
9. Graphic arts		100–300		
10. Planning room				
11. Other finishing room				
12. General storage space				
H. Occupational Education				
1. Agriculture shop plus	20	2,400–2,600	500	Storage area fireproof.
agriculture greenhouse	20	1,400–1,600	500	Dust-free and well ventilated.
2. Auto repair	20	5,000–5,400	300	Storage for unfinished work.
3. Auto body shop plus	20	5,000–5,400	400	Storage for unfinished work.
Frame straightener	20	450–500	300	Storage for specific clothing.
spray booth	20	450–500	400	Storage—fireproof.
4. Baking	20	2,400–2,600	400	
5. Boat building	20	2,800–3,200	200	
6. Cabinet making	20	3,000–3,400	150	
Finishing room	15	300	200	
7. Carpentry	20	3,000–3,400	150	
8. Commercial art	25	1,400–1,600	100	
9. Cosmetology	20	1,400–1,600	150	
10. Data processing	20	1,100–1,300	100	
11. Dental lab	20	1,600–1,800	100	
12. Distributive Ed. rm plus	20	1,000–1,200	400	
store	20	500	20	
13. Drafting	20	1,500–2,000	400	
14. Electronics	20	1,200–1,500	150	
15. Electrical shop plus	20	1,800–2,000	200	
electrical lab—	20	800	400	
machinery electrical	20	500–600	200	
lab—appliances	20	2,000–2,400	200	

(Continued)

Table 11.1. (Continued)

Type of Space	Suggested Max. Class Size	Suggested Area of Each Space	Suggested Area of Adj. Store Rm.	Comments
16. Food trade areas plus dining and sales	20	800	200	
2 dressing rooms		50 each	250	
17. Machine shop plus inspection room	20	3,000–3,200	300	
		300–400	350	
18. Medical Assistant	20	1,100–1,300	300	
19. Medical lab	20	1,200–1,400	300	
20. Metal fabrication	20	2,800–3,200	200	
21. Optical tech.	20	1,400–1,600	350	
22. Painting and decorating	20	1,500–1,700	200	
23. Pattern making	20	1,900–2,100	300	
24. Plant maintenance	20	2,800–3,000	300	
25. Plumbing	20	2,000–2,400	300	
26. Practical nursing	20	1,800–2,200		
27. Printing	20	3,600–3,800		
28. Sheet metal	20	2,000–2,400		
29. Upholstery	20	1,500–1,700		
30. Welding	20	2,400–2,600		
31. Clothing textiles		1,600–1,800		
32. Consumer economics		800–900		
33. Dietician's assistant		800–900		
34. Family living		800–900		
35. Fashion design and merchandising		1,000–1,200		
		1,500–1,800		
36. Foods and nutrition		1,000–1,200		
37. Home aides		1,000–1,200		
a) Geriatric aides		1,200–1,400		
b) Pediatric training		1,000–1,400		
38. Nursery school aides		800–900		
39. Kindergarten aides				
40. Related classrooms				

I. Other Specialized Spaces			
1. Mathematics lab	25	850–900	100–125	Located near similar rooms.
2. Language arts lab	30	900–1,000	75–100	Located near similar rooms.
3. Social studies lab	30	900–1,000	75–100	Located near similar rooms.
4. Other				
J. Nonspecialized				
Instructional Spaces				
1. Large classrooms	35	800–850	20–40*	About one-third of the nonspecialized classrooms should
2. Medium classrooms	30	750–800	20–40*	be grouped in pairs separated by a movable partition
3. Small classrooms	25	650–700	20–40*	having a noise reduction coefficient in excess of 38
4. Core curriculum	30	850–900	75–100*	decibels.
5. Commercial	30	750–800	20–40*	Internet connectivity should be installed in these rooms.

* Optional

Table 11.2. Supplementary Instructional Spaces in Secondary Schools

Type of Space	Suggested Area of Each Space	Comments
A. Auditorium		
1. Stage	1,800–2,200	An auditorium that seats 350 persons is needed for any secondary school.
2. Audience space	7–8 sq.ft. per student	For larger schools, the absolute minimum should be an auditorium seating the largest single grade plus 50. But it is recommended the auditorium seat at least one-half the ultimate capacity of the building.
3. Check room	200–300	Maximum capacity—seating the whole student body at one time, provided its seating capacity is not greater than 1,200–1,500.
4. Lobby	1,500–2,000	
5. Public toilets	250–300	
6. Storage space (as near stage as possible)		
B. Audiovisual (related to the library)		
1. Workroom—preview room	250–300	Adjoining workroom
2. Storage space	350–450	
C. Library (Instructional Material Center)		
1. Reading room (40–75 capacity)	1,200–2,000	Reading space should accommodate about 10% of the enrollment, plus carrels (3–5% of enrollment).
2. Office (librarian)	125–150	Minimum capacity—about 40, and maximum about 75 students.
3. Book processing room	150–200	For larger schools, plan 2 or more reading rooms.
4. Conference room(s)	150–300	Space for receiving, recording and cataloguing new books and for repairing worn or damaged books.
5. Storage space	175–240	1 per 300 students of enrollment.
6. Carrels for self-instruction. Provide carrels for 3–5% of school enrollment.		Approximate—25 sq.ft. per carrel.
		Allocate about one square foot per student based on total school enrollment.
D. Cafeteria		
1. Kitchen	2 sq.ft. per meal, minimum	Plan to feed the ultimate anticipated enrollment in not more than three shifts.
2. Dining area	12–15 sq.ft. per diner	The capacity of the dining area of the cafeteria should not be less than 1/3 of the ultimate anticipated enrollment plus 50. Consider continuous feeding, which can add up to 20 percent of the capacity of the cafeteria.
3. Serving space	0.5–0.8 sq.ft. capacity of dining area	For secondary schools whose enrollments are less than 300, plan to seat at least 1/2 of the ultimate anticipated enrollment. (This allows more
4. Storage space and can wash area	Approx. 09.8 sq.ft. per meal	time for the use of this area for other activities such as music, study, and assembly.) Locate one or two handwashing areas adjacent to the cafeteria.
5. Toilets	12 sq.ft. per pupil	
6. Handwashing area		
7. Teachers' dining area		

		Plan one serving line for every 200–250 students dining in each shift.
		Kitchen area—allow at least 2 sq.ft. per meal to be served.
		Dietitians office—one per cafeteria
		Lavatory and dressing room facilities—one per cafeteria.
		Easily accessible from service drives.
		Located near, but separate from, student cafeteria.
E. Remedial Instructional Spaces		
1. Reading	400–500	Remedial rooms may be located in library area and planned for supervision by the librarian through the use of vision strips. Privacy gained by closing draw curtains when needed.
2. Speech	400–500	
3. General	400–500	
4. Computer lab	See chapter 2	
F. Student Activity		
1. Activity room	450–600	Size depends upon the nature of its uses.
2. Storage space	80–100	Location within view of main office.
G. Study Hall		
1. Study room	15–20 sq.ft. per pupil	Storage is needed if study hall is used as a multipurpose room.
2. Storage space		

Table 11.3. Administrative and Related Areas

Type of Space	Suggested Area of Each Space	Comments
A. Administration		
1. Principal	200–250	One principal's office per school.
2. Assistant Principal	150–200	One assistant principal's office for every 500
3. Clerk—waiting area	300–350	students in excess of 400.
4. Storage (office supplies)	100 per clerk 75–100	One general office per school.
a) Vault	50–75	
5. Toilet	40–50	
6. Conference rooms	250–300	
B. Guidance		
1. Guidance counseling office(s)	120–150 150–200	This suite should possess a pleasant and informal atmosphere with drapes, carpets,
2. Guidance director's office	200–250 125–150	and easy chairs. One guidance counselor's office for every 300
3. Guidance library and waiting room	40–50 30–40	students of ultimate anticipated enrollment. One guidance counselor library-waiting-
4. Space for guidance small groups		browsing room per guidance suite. One testing cubicle for every 3 guidance
5. Space for individual testing		counselors.
6. Storage space		
C. Health		
1. Office (nurse)	150–175	Should be located adjacent to guidance suite
2. Exam room	275–300	on the opposite side of administrative suite.
3. Waiting space	100–150	One exam room.
4. Restrooms (2 cots)	100–125	At least one waiting room per suite.
5. Toilets	30–40	One nurse's room.
		At least two dressing-restrooms.
		One dental room, if the community has a school dental program.
D. Teachers' Rooms		
1. Common lounge	700–800	The size of this space depends upon the
2. Toilets—restrooms (one or more) for each sex	250–300 300–350	number of teachers to be served. The suggested size would be adequate for a
3. Workrooms	30–40	faculty of 30 teachers.
4. Storage	450–500	At least one common teachers' lounge and
5. Faculty library	100–120	workroom per school.
6. Faculty office		At least one teachers' restroom per school for each sex.
		A small teachers' lavatory related to each gang student toilet is desirable.
		This function could be housed in the faculty dining room if it is properly designed for a dual function.
		Simple movable partitions could be used to screen one or two work alcoves.
		Located within the library complex.
		One office for each three teachers.

Table 11.4. Service Areas

Type of Space	Suggested Area of Each Space	Comments
A. Custodian		
1. Office	100–150	Located near the general receiving
a) Storage	50–75	room and boiler area. At least one
2. Toilet and shower	100–125	office per building.
3. Workshop	250–300	Shower and locker facilities.
4. Storage of custodial	150–200	At least one workshop per school.
supplies	20–25	Storage space for custodial supplies and
5. Service Closets (with slop	150–200	cleaning agents.
sinks)	100–150	These closets should be located
6. Receiving room		adjacent to each gang toilet and
7. Storage of outdoor		near each of the large spaces, such
equipment		as auditorium, gymnasium, and
		cafeteria.
		Adjoining storage spaces.
		Should be at grade level so wheeled
		equipment can be driven or pushed
		into the storage area.
B. Other Service Spaces		
1. Book storage at various	40–50	One serving each wing and floor of the
locations	1/2 sq.ft. per	building.
2. General storage of	pupil in school	One or two per school depending upon
instructional supplies		the size and plan of the building.
3. Toilets		See chapter 9.

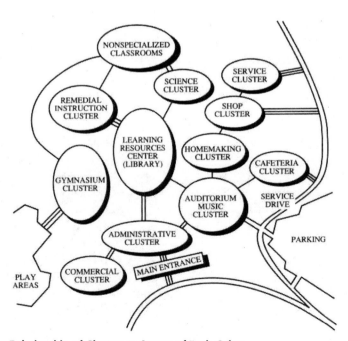

Figure 11.1. Relationship of Clusters to Spaces of Each Other

relationship exists between them. In this case, the architect may locate the space wherever he or she believes it will best fit into the architectural scheme of the building.

The art cluster is sometimes related to the stage rather than to the industrial arts cluster or home-economics cluster on the premise the art room is used in relation to the painting of scenery. While this argument has some merit, the functional relationship between art and mechanical drawing, between art and interior decoration, and between art and clothing design is more obvious. In some plans, the fine arts areas are completely divorced from related instructional areas, but such an arrangement is perhaps more a matter of architectural convenience than it is of educational function.

The Administrative Cluster

The administrative cluster is made up of three distinct but functionally interrelated parts, as indicated in figure 11.2. The location of the guidance suite is crucial in this cluster. It should be between the general office and the health suite. If possible, the student entrance to the general office should be completely divorced from the entrance to the guidance waiting area. It is often possible to locate the entrance to the general office around the corner from the entrance to the guidance room.

This arrangement keeps the disciplinary function of the principal's office completely dissociated from the guidance function. Internally, however, these two activities are closely related. Records kept in the general office are of basic concern to the guidance counselor. Conversations between the principal and the guidance people are also part of an effective guidance program.

The health and guidance functions are closely related. Many times, guidance counselors find that student difficulties arise from health problems. In such instances, the nurse and the guidance counselor work as a team in seeking to help the student. The nurse's office and health records should be easily accessible to the guidance counselors, and these two spaces can be closely related externally, as well as internally, since the functions involved are psychologically compatible.

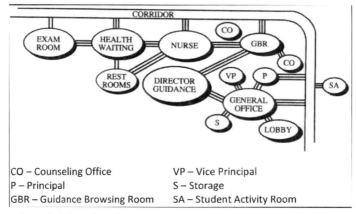

CO – Counseling Office	VP – Vice Principal
P – Principal	S – Storage
GBR – Guidance Browsing Room	SA – Student Activity Room

Figure 11.2.   The Administrative Cluster

The Commercial Cluster

It is desirable, but not essential, to locate the commercial cluster near the general office. Those who advocate relating this cluster (figure 11.3) to the office do so based on the premise some of the students may get actual office experience in the school office. Also, it is argued that where school funds are restricted, some of the office machines in the classroom may also be used by regular office employees. These reasons have merit, but if the architectural scheme does not permit the location of commercial classrooms near the office, no serious educational handicap is likely to result.

The Library Cluster

The library itself is surrounded by a large number of spaces occupying a first order of importance. In figure 11.4 these spaces are connected to the library by three lines. It is essential that these spaces be arranged in the library area so that they can be easily supervised by the librarian. This can sometimes be achieved by installing vision strips in certain spaces and by locating others for direct supervision. Regular English or reading classrooms should be located in the general library area if such

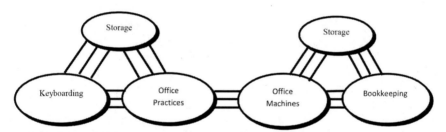

Figure 11.3.   The Commercial Cluster

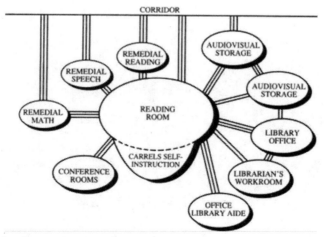

Figure 11.4.   The Library Cluster

an arrangement is feasible. Sometimes the library is isolated when it serves both the school and the community.

School planners do not generally view the isolation of the library from nonspecialized classrooms with any degree of alarm, although it would be convenient to place regular classrooms in the library area.

The Science Cluster

If the architectural scheme permits it, the science cluster might well adjoin the rooms in which mathematics is taught. While the specific location of the science cluster (figure 11.5) itself is not critical, the clustering of the individual science rooms in one area is essential, partly to facilitate the movement of costly equipment used for demonstration purposes from one laboratory to another. It is also important that the science teachers be able to work as a team and exchange ideas freely.

The Shop Cluster

This group of related instructional areas may be located wherever the architect feels it best fits into his or her total concept, provided it is at ground level near a service drive and that it is far enough away from quiet instructional areas not to disturb them. The progression shown in figure 11.6 starts with the heavy industrial shops and culminates with arts and crafts shops. Existing shop clusters suffer most from a lack of sufficient storage.

The need for storage in shop areas is threefold. Space is needed for the storage of large tools, unfinished student projects, and materials and supplies. Small tools are often stored in the shop itself in lockable wall cabinets. The storage room for materials and supplies should be easily accessible to the service drive for unloading lumber, steel, and sheet material. It should also be convenient to students in the adjoining shops.

Planning rooms, one serving two shops, are essential in shop areas. Some educators feel that it is just as important for students to learn how to plan and detail projects on the drawing board as it is to learn how to use tools to construct the project itself. Planning rooms can also be used by teachers giving special instruction to individuals or groups of students working on a given project.

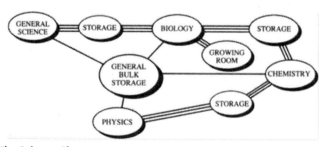

Figure 11.5. The Science Cluster

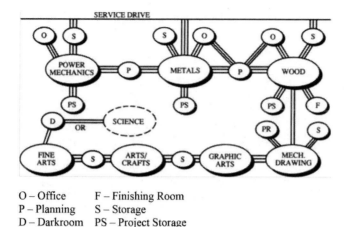

O – Office   F – Finishing Room
P – Planning   S – Storage
D – Darkroom   PS – Project Storage
                  PR – Print Room

Figure 11.6. The Shop Cluster

The Auditorium-Music Cluster

The auditorium and music areas are closely related. Dual-purpose use of dressing rooms is necessary to justify such spaces, for they will be required very few times during the school year. The author has seen a number of dressing rooms near auditorium stages filled with broken chairs, desks, and other school equipment. Instead of being used for junk storage when not used for dressing, these spaces can be utilized efficiently at all times as combination music practice-dressing rooms. Figure 11.7 is self-explanatory. The music areas shown in this cluster should be designed and located so that the sounds emanating from them do not interfere with quiet activities in the auditorium or in other instructional areas.

The Gymnasium Cluster

In addition to what is shown in figure 11.8, it should be pointed out that no driveways should be interposed between the gymnasium and the PE areas of the school. Also, students should be able to travel directly from the locker and shower area to the out-of-doors without walking through the gymnasium.

A few special requirements of this area are worth noting. Each teaching area of the gymnasium should be provided with a storage room and instructor's office. At least two health classrooms should be included directly off the floor of the main gymnasium, one for the girls and one for the boys. Drinking fountains should not be installed in the main gymnasium area (to avoid any possible overflow of water on the wooden floor), but in an alcove of the gymnasium or in a corridor. Architects can ingeniously provide additional teaching stations by locating supplementary spaces on balconies that are also used as seating capacity when folding bleachers are open. In the closed position, the bleachers form a partial wall between the upper main gymnasium and the auxiliary balcony gymnasium.

Music Appreciation Room

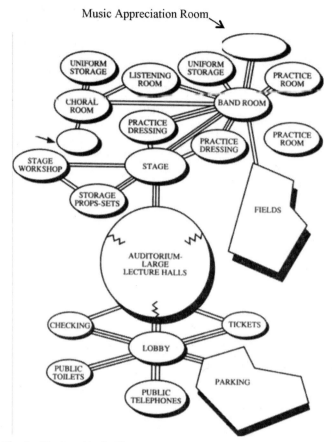

Figure 11.7. The Auditorium-Music Cluster

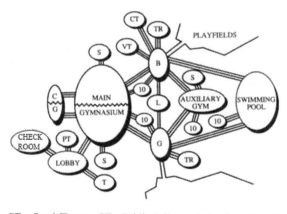

CT – Coach/Team   PT – Public Toilets   CG – Corrective Gym   G – Girls' Locker/Showers
TR – Towel Room   L – Laundry   VT – Visiting Team   B – Boys' Locker/Showers
S – Storage   C - Check   IO – Instructor's
                                            Office

Figure 11.8. The Gymnasium Cluster

The Home Economics Cluster

The specific location of this cluster (figure 11.9) is not very critical. However, if a nursery program is to be served by this cluster, it is essential that it be located at ground level adjacent to a play area for the four-year-old children who participate in the program.

In the past, some school planners insisted that the home economics cluster be located next to the cafeteria. There is little basis for this. The home economics suite serves an instructional function, while the cafeteria is a service. Some school people argue that the home economics cluster teacher should be near the cafeteria to supervise the cafeteria personnel. Such an added duty overburdens these teachers and short-changes students. To avoid this questionable practice, it might be desirable to remove the home economics cluster from the vicinity of the cafeteria, as is customary in many conventional secondary schools.

The Cafeteria Cluster

The individual elements in the cafeteria cluster are shown in figure 11.10. Of primary importance is the strategic location of the kitchen, dishwashing area, and storage room. Two flow charts should be prepared when this cluster is being planned. One chart should show the student circulation from the point where they enter the cafeteria to the point where they leave the area after dining. The other chart should indicate the flow of food from the storage room to the food preparation and cooking area, and to the serving counter. The chart should also show the movement of dishes from the clean-dish storage to the serving areas, to the dishwashing machine, and back to the point of origin.

The location of the service drive is critical to the kitchen function. The delivery zone should be designed so that bulk foods may be easily unloaded at the storage areas. And there should be provision for the storage dumpsters and removal of trash from this area, a feature that is usually overlooked in planning a kitchen area. Empty

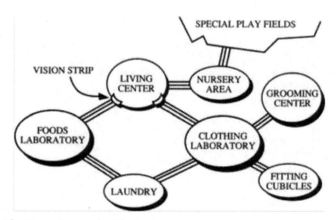

Figure 11.9.   The Home Economics Cluster

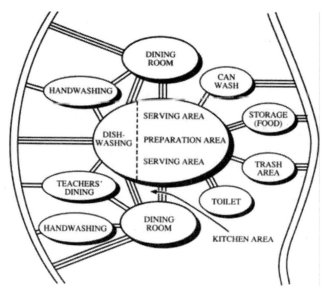

Figure 11.10.   The Cafeteria Cluster

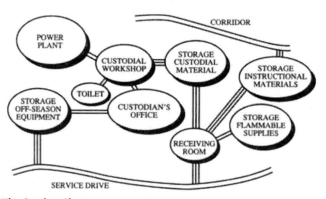

Figure 11.11.   The Service Cluster

food cans are unsightly and usually attract flies. It is suggested that a special screened-in can wash and storage area be provided in a location convenient to the service drive.

The Service Cluster

The basic feature of this cluster of spaces is its location next to the service drive. Very few schools provide adequately for receiving and storage of supplies and for maintenance facilities. Storage often seems to end up being located wherever the architect has excess space rather than where it is needed. It is true, of course, that a few odd spaces cannot be avoided in any school plan. The use of such spaces for storage is most acceptable. In addition to these spaces, however, special-purpose storage spaces are needed in specific areas properly related to other spaces. Figure 11.11 indicates the type of spaces that should be located in the service cluster.

DISCUSSION QUESTIONS

1   How do school planners and architects prepare for the task of avoiding student flow problems between classes?
2   Show and explain the "Castaldi Nomogram formula" for computing the number of instructional spaces.
3   Discuss the three administrative clusters and why they are functionally interrelated.
4   What is the best way to design the service cluster? Why is it important to plan for these spaces early on in the site design concept?

NOTES

1. Marion J. Conrad, "A Technique for Determining Operating Capacity of Secondary School Buildings," *Doctoral dissertation*, Ohio State University, 1952.

2. Basil Castaldi, *The Castaldi Nomogram* (Cambridge, MA: New England School Development Council, 1953).

Chapter 12

Post-Planning Procedures and Construction Costs

After architectural plans have been developed to the satisfaction of the planning team and the school board, they must be translated into a school building by the cooperative efforts of the architect and the builder. The conversion from plans to building is a crucial part of school planning. It includes bidding, supervision, and a good working relationship between architect and general contractor or construction manager.

PRUDENTIAL CONTRACT STIPULATIONS

Construction Time

It is generally agreed that the number of months allowed for construction should be stated in the contract. If the expected completion date of the project is clearly specified, the contractor will not be tempted to shift his workforce from one project to another of higher priority and thus postpone the completion of the respective school building(s).

In specifying a completion date, however, both parties should agree that the length of time allowed for construction is reasonable, whether or not penalties are involved.

Penalty Clauses in the Contract

The insertion of penalty clauses in a construction contract is not an unmixed blessing to the owner. Generally, where penalties are imposed upon the contractor on a per diem basis for exceeding the stipulated construction time, he/she also be allowed a stated bonus for each day in advance of the specified completion date that he/she completes his/her work. Unless the allocated construction time length is reasonable, a penalty clause in the contract is likely to cause a significant increase in the contract price of the job.

Even where a penalty clause exists, there is really no positive assurance that the contractor will be legally penalized for not completing the project on time. In most situations, district-initiated change orders of one form or another are bound to be made. If penalties are involved, the contractor will always seek a time extension whenever a district-initiated change order is requested. In one instance, a contractor requested a ten-day extension of time to move two electrical outlets from one part of a wall to another (at the request of the school district).

The owner has little choice under such circumstances. If he/she wants his requested change, he must accept the extension of time. In a state project having an area of about 120,000 square feet, the contractor requested and received a total time extension of 240 calendar days as a result of numerous change orders (both contractor- and district-initiated). The penalty clause in the contract was never invoked, although about 1,000 students were deprived of the use of that school facility for an additional academic year.

The Liquidated Damage Clause

Under this clause, the builder agrees to complete the project on a given date, but the owner does not automatically receive payment in the event that he/she fails to do so. The owner must prove damages directly resulting from the delay in completion of the project in order to collect any damages. As a rule, it is rather difficult to prove that damages are directly traceable to the builder's failure to comply with the contract. For this reason, the liquidated damage clause is not always effective in assuring completion of educational facilities on time.

Insurance

In any contract between a school district and the builder, provisions should be made for various types of insurance. The liability insurance is usually carried by the contractor and the fire insurance by the owner. One school district found that it was less expensive for the district to carry both the liability and fire insurance. As a result, it requested the contractor not to include the cost of liability insurance in his/her bid price. It is suggested the board explore these alternatives and select the option that provides adequate insurance coverage at the least cost.

Performance Bond

According to Strevell and Burke, "The performance bond is an assurance that the person or firm to whom the contract(s) is awarded will faithfully perform the contract including all provisions of plans and specifications."[1] The performance bond should not be executed prior to signing of the construction contract. The terms of the performance bond must meet with approval of the owner. The premium for this bond may be paid by either the owner or the contractor. It is important, therefore, the owner specifies who will pay the premium for this bond at the time the construction bids are being requested by the school district.

BIDDING PROCEDURES

The accepted method for selecting a contractor is competitive bidding. This procedure, generally followed by private enterprise, is almost always required by state and local statutes for the construction of public school buildings. Bids are not always required to be awarded to the lowest bidder. Many state laws simply require that contracts be awarded to the lowest responsible bidder.

The usual procedure is to invite bidders to submit a proposal and then for the architect or construction manager to supply them with plans and specifications to use in preparing cost estimates. Invitations are usually announced through the press and construction publications. Such invitations include the name of the project and the time and source from which plans and specifications may be obtained.

The announcement must also state when and where the bids must be filed and the documents returned, and whether or not a deposit is required for the drawings. Very frequently the bidders must give some assurance that they will accept the bid if it is offered. This assurance usually takes the form of a deposit of a certified check or the filing of a bid bond. The amount of the deposit allowed is usually specified in the state statutes.

Time for Preparing the Bid

The contractor should be allowed ample time to make cost determinations and prepare their bid. Usually a period of about four weeks is allowed, but in less complicated projects two weeks is generally sufficient. Sometimes, extension of bidding time is necessary. In such cases, all bidders would be notified of the extension at least forty-eight hours before the original opening time. At times, the architect may be required to issue explanations and clarifications during the bidding period. When such action is necessary, he/she should be sure to issue the entire supplementary information to all the bidders.

Opening of Bids

In general, bids are opened at the appointed time in public and are tabulated by the architect or construction manager. After prices and alternatives are carefully weighed and compared, the successful bidder(s) is selected. Before receiving the contract for the project, however, the successful bidder is usually required to post a performance bond for the full amount of the contract. This bond serves as a guarantee that should the contractor fail to complete his work satisfactorily the bonding company will assume the financial obligation for the completion of the building.

Awarding of the Contract[2]

The contract for the construction of the school is signed by both the awarding school district and the contractor. It is strongly suggested that legal advice be sought at this point to make certain that the documents are properly prepared and fully protects all concerned, and the persons signing the contract are legally authorized to do so. The school board may have a policy that requires them to approve of the contractor and the board chairperson will sign on their behalf.

Upon signing the contract, the builder is customarily required to submit to the architect a breakdown of the estimates concerning items set forth for the work of the various building trades as listed in the specifications. He/she also submits a detailed schedule of dates for the completion of the various aspects of the construction projects, such as footings, foundations, electrical roughing, plumbing, and heating.

BUILDING THE EDUCATIONAL FACILITY

Once the contract is let, the builder must commence construction within the time specified in the contract. The building of a school, as mentioned earlier, is basically a cooperative effort on the part of both the contractor and the architect. In order to be sure that work is performed in accordance with specifications, continuous supervision should be provided. Unless the project is fairly large, in excess of, let us say, $500,000 it is difficult to justify the employment of a full-time clerk-of-the-works, even though the employment of such a person is highly desirable in any project. If the school district selects a construction manager and a general contractor then they will have the 24/7 oversight of the project and a clerk-of-the-works will not be necessary.

The Supervisory Responsibility of the Architect[3]

Contrary to popular belief, the architect is *not* responsible for continuous supervision on the job, unless this is specifically stated in their contract. On the other hand, the supervision provided by the architect should be sufficient to ensure that the building is constructed according to specifications. On small projects, the architect may supervise the work as infrequently as one afternoon per week, while on a multimillion dollar project he or she might provide a full-time on-site architect or engineer.

The builder cannot deviate from the plans and specifications without the approval of the architect. Neither can the builder devise his/her own method of construction unless it is approved by the architect. Oftentimes, the architect is called upon to verify shop drawings produced by fabricators of the several components of construction. Also, the owner makes no payments to the builder without the authorization of the architect. A construction manager (CM) will pay all of the subs directly, while the school district makes one monthly check to the CM.

The Clerk-of-the-Works

In fairly large projects, a clerk-of-the-works is employed by the owner to supervise and inspect every detail of the construction on a full-time basis. He/she reports any irregularities to the architect, who then takes the necessary corrective action.

The clerk-of-the-works is often worth many times his/her salary. He/she makes certain the contractor delivers a full measure in materials and workmanship. While visiting a school building under construction, the superintendent was conversing briefly with the clerk-of-the-works. In the middle of the conversation, the clerk-of-the-works departed abruptly and climbed a ladder leading to the roof where a workman was installing a flashing around the chimney. Upon his/her return, he/she stated, "Just as I thought, they were using 3/4 inch copper nails instead of the required inch and a half." When he was asked how he/she had detected this deficiency at a distance of 300 feet, he/she answered, "Whoever heard of driving a one-and-one- half-inch roofing nail with a single blow of the hammer which is possible with the smaller 3/4 inch nails?"

Change Orders

A change order is defined as a change made in the plans of a building while construction is in progress. These can either be district or contractor initiated. The number of change orders should be kept to a minimum, but where the function of a school building can be substantially improved, or serious deficiencies corrected, change orders should be made.

In general, change orders are more costly than the same changes would have been if they had been included in the original working drawings. They need not be so costly, but because of the very nature of competitive bidding, the contractor's profit is often not included in a deductive change order. On the other hand, an additive change order is often treated as a single project without competitive bidding. Thus, the amount that is added to the contract is ordinarily greater than it would be if competitive bidding initially was entered into the cost estimate.

For example, one school district had awarded a substantial contract to a builder for pointing the mortar joints in the exterior of a fairly large junior high school. While work was in progress, it was discovered the parapet was loose and constituted a safety hazard. The school board voted to remove it from the building. The contractor was asked to quote a price on a "district initiated change order" basis for the removal of the parapet, on the assumption that he/she was already on the job and his her price would probably be lower than others. As a matter of academic interest, one of the board members suggested that several other quotations be sought. To the surprise of all concerned, the price of the contractor on the job was about 25 percent higher than that supplied by others! Needless to say, no district-initiated change order was issued.

Relationship between the Contractor and School Officials

Generally speaking, there is no direct relationship between the owner and the contractor. The owner deals with the contractor through the architect. It is true, of course, that the owner retains the right to inspect the work during construction, but the builder is usually not required to take any orders directly from the owner. It should be pointed out, however, that the builder generally has complete jurisdiction within the contract limits of the project during construction. He/she almost always has the authority to prevent anyone from trespassing within the contract limits. Builders are reluctant to permit any person (including school administration) not having official business in the construction zone because of legal liability in case of accidents.

Manual for Administration and Staff

The normal procedure after the school facility is ready for occupancy is relatively simple. The school boards are the ones to legally accept the building. The contractor turns the keys of the building over to school officials and, at some early future date, an open house (ribbon-cutting event) is held for the public under the auspices of the school board. Speeches are made, the taxpayers are congratulated, and the school band plays on. This marks the end of the major construction works, on the part of the contractor, the architect, and educational consultants. Of course, all parties may be called in to correct problems that may arise during the "shake down" period (one year warranty) of the building operations.

Eventually, all parties responsible for the planning and construction of a building will become disassociated with the occupied school facility. After a decade or so, very few people will know who these parties were, without reading the bronze plaque that is usually affixed to one of the walls in the lobby area of the building. There is nothing improper or unusual about this sequence of events.

However, the administration and staff assigned to the building inherit a complicated educational facility that they are required to operate for many years in the future. In some instances, no one will remember or know the intended function for each space (unless an education specification sheet was produced and duplicated for the school administrators/maintenance) in the building or how the mechanical and electrical equipment should be maintained, inspected, or operated.

In order to avoid this situation, it is suggested that the architect be required to prepare a manual and video recording regarding the maintenance and operation of the school building. The manual and video recording should describe:

1   How each space was intended to be used when the building was planned.
2   All of the lighting, heating, and ventilating switches, where they are located, and what they control.
3   How each critical building or working surface and each piece of mechanical equipment should be maintained, including cautionary statements as to "what not to do."
4   How the building is planned for expansion and the specific points in the electrical, mechanical, and architectural systems where extensions can be made.
5   Where all the shut-offs are for water, gas, electrical, etc.

This manual should also show the "as built" plans in logical segments on several pages of the booklet, so future modifications of the building can be made economically and intelligently.

COMPARISONS OF CONSTRUCTION COSTS

As many architects and educators readily admit, comparing the unit cost of one school with that of another is meaningless and often misleading. Costs simply indicate the number of dollars that are spent for a unit area, volume, or student. This much of the comparison is quite specific and definite. On the other hand, there are several aspects of a school building that are not revealed in unit cost figures.

In computing any type of unit cost, there is only one figure that is certain, namely, the total cost. For this reason, unit costs in school construction are really quite vague. Unit costs are determined by dividing the cost by another item, usually the number of students, the number of square feet, the number of cubic feet, or the number of classrooms. Since only the numerator or cost figure is definite, the unit cost loses much of its significance.

Inadequacy of Unit Cost Comparisons

Unit cost figures alone are quite meaningless in making cost comparisons. There are several shortcomings inherent in all unit cost figures applicable to school buildings.

Inadequacies Common to All Unit Cost Figures

A cost of a school building per square foot, per cubic foot, per classroom, or per student cannot be used by itself in comparing school building costs sensibly for the reasons listed below:

1 It does not indicate what is actually included in the building in terms of unusual spaces, laboratory units, and special built-in equipment.
2 It does not reveal the quality of the construction materials selected by the architect and school boards.
3 It does not tell anything about extraordinary site conditions.
4 It fails to indicate the type, extent, or quality of mechanical equipment used in the building.
5 It neglects to provide an index of economy regarding the cost of operation and maintenance of the building after it is completed.
6 It omits any information regarding the educational efficiency of the structure.
7 It does not reveal the extent to which the building may be over-planned for future expansion.
8 It fails to indicate how much site development and educational equipment are included in the cost figure.
9 It does not reveal how efficiently the space within the building can be utilized.
10 It does not specify if soft costs are included or excluded.

*Additional Shortcomings Peculiar to the Use of Cost per Square
Foot in School Buildings*

Such a unit cost is also deficient due to the following reasons:

1 It fails to indicate what areas are included in obtaining the total areas. For example, is attic space included? Are pipe trenches counted?
2 It does not reveal how overhangs, enclosed walkways, and covered walks have been treated in the computation.
3 It does not specify if third-floor mechanical rooms are included.

Shortcomings of the Use of Cost per Classroom or per Student

These unit costs are even less reliable than those listed above, for several obvious reasons:

1   The capacity of a school building is not fixed or uniform for every school of the same type. There is no standard of measuring building capacity. In most cases, it is simply an "educated guess."
2   The cost figures do not reveal the number of square feet in a school building per student or per classroom. Clearly, a building with inadequate instructional spaces costs less to construct than one with adequate spaces.
3   It does not account for the program offerings that require large amount of square feet such as wood shops, practice gyms, and robotic labs.

How to Make Reliable and Meaningful Unit Cost Comparisons

The view of unit cost comparisons expressed in the previous paragraphs is not altogether dismal. Up to this point, it has been assumed that a school board seeks to compare simply by reviewing unit costs supplied by architects, school personnel, or educational consultants. Such figures, as indicated earlier, are quite meaningless, except in making crude estimates of school building costs. Unit costs can be extremely valuable, however, when they are compiled by a central statistical agency.

Which Is the Most Reliable Unit Cost Figure?

A study of two of the unit costs in common use; 129 elementary units were included in the study. Costs were derived from the official records of the Massachusetts School Building Assistance Commission. A coefficient of correlation was computed between the construction cost of a school and

(a) the cost per square foot and
(b) the cost per student.

It was found that the coefficient of correlation between cost per square foot and total construction cost was 0.92, and the coefficient of correlation between cost per student and total construction cost was 0.71. Obviously, the cost per square foot is a more *accurate predictor* of the total cost of a building. This fact is not surprising. Architects have used this method since the beginning of architectural costs analysis.

Obtaining Reliable Cost Figures

Sensible cost comparison using cost per square foot can be made if the following instructions are followed carefully.

1 Start with the basic data. Use working drawings of the various buildings and request a breakdown of all of the costs involved

2 In measuring the areas, observe the following rules:

   a Use all outside dimensions of the buildings (not net sq.ft.).
   b Include only usable floor spaces. For example, storage rooms in the basement would be considered part of the area of the building, while unfinished spaces and pipe trenches would not.
   c Divide the areas of all covered walks and overhangs by 3 before adding them to the area of the rest of the building.
   d Divide enclosed corridors by 2 before adding them to the area of the rest of the building.
   e Staircases should be included at each level at full value for each level.
   f The area of elevator shafts should be included only once, but the wall thickness at all levels should be included in the spaces surrounding the elevator shaft.

3 Costs should be treated as follows:

   a Construction costs should include the cost of the structure, all equipment attached to the building, and the cost of site development for about 25 feet around the building. Care should be taken in comparing costs of buildings in which expensive laboratory equipment or air conditioning is installed. In these cases, be sure that buildings compared are similar. Otherwise, the cost of the highly specialized equipment must be omitted from the total cost.
   b Exclude architectural, legal, permits, classroom furniture, and other fees.
   c Exclude the cost of the site development and site acquisition.

If these guides are observed, a central office can accumulate a reliable set of cost figures for both predicting and comparing school building costs. This service can best be rendered to school districts by the various State Departments of Education and by the statistical branch of the U.S. Department of Education.

DISCUSSION QUESTIONS

1 How do school planners and architects know what a reasonable amount of time is for the construction of a school(s)?
2 Define "change orders." What are the two types and when should they be allowed?
3 Discuss five examples of using sensible cost comparisons when dealing with square footage.
4 How can a school district prepare to operate a new school once it is turned over by the contractors? What steps are needed to be put in place to avoid any problems with this challenge?

NOTES

1. Wallace H. Strevell and Arvid J. Burke, *Administration of the School Building Program* (New York: McGraw-Hill, 1959), p. 411.

2. Harold W. Boles, *Step by Step to Better School Facilities* (New York: Holt, Rinehart and Winston, 1965), p. 151.

3. *Guide for Planning Educational Facilities* (Columbus, OH: Council of Educational Facility Planners International, 1976), p. M-8.

Chapter 13

Modernization of Educational Facilities

The terms *rehabilitation, remodeling,* and *modernization* are common in the parlance of school people, but they often have different meanings to a variety of people. As used in this textbook, *rehabilitation* is a form of deferred maintenance. The school building is simply restored to the same condition it was in when it was built. Old equipment and worn parts are replaced. Interior walls, floors, and ceilings are repainted and refurnished, and the exterior of the building is painted and reconstructed wherever needed to make it weather-proof again. These changes are essentially cosmetic.

Remodeling goes one step beyond rehabilitation. It also includes additions in the square footage and shape of any space within the building. To this extent, a remodeled school facility could improve its function and suitability as an education tool.

The term *modernization,* as defined in this textbook, is a process whereby an existing school facility is brought up-to-date structurally, technologically, educationally, and environmentally. In this process, certain spaces within the school building may be reshaped to accommodate modern educational practices. Worn or outdated mechanical equipment, weathered parts of the structure, and unsightly/unsafe interior surfaces may be restored to their original state.

Modernization also includes the installation of new technology equipment, efficient mechanical equipment, electrical equipment, and the addition of energy-efficient materials on the exterior walls and roof. Finally, modernization accommodates a forward-looking educational program, improving the health and safety of the students occupying the building, and provides for special education services.

AN OVERVIEW OF SCHOOL FACILITY MODERNIZATION

School facility modernization is a more complex and time-consuming task than planning of a new facility. It is much easier to change lines on a computerized drawing than it is to move partitions, reroute electric wires, cut and rejoin pipes, and redesign the structural members of an existing school building.

On the other hand, educational facility planners and architects are presented with both a challenge and an opportunity to transform an obsolete school building into one that is educationally efficient, structurally safe, and environmentally healthful. Several aspects of school facility modernization are outlined in the following sections of this chapter.

Improvements in Educational Function, Energy Conservation, and Environmental Quality

The interrelated improvements in a school facility can be illustrated best by introducing a hypothetical situation involving the Smith Elementary School, typical of those built in 1923. It is a two-story building with a flat roof and parapet. It contains eight classrooms, and features a principal's office on the second floor over the main entrance. It has a brick exterior, wooden sash, wooden frames, and two basement play areas with toilets adjoining each room.

The classrooms are fairly large, each containing slightly over 900 square feet. A coatroom is about 10 feet wide and 22 feet long that adjoins each classroom. The central corridors and lobbies are constructed of fire-resistant materials. The ceilings and walls are plaster on wooden lath, except in the corridors and exterior walls, where plaster is applied directly to the brick walls. The lighting system in each room consists of four suspended globe-type fixtures furnished with 200-watt incandescent bulbs. The heating system consists of a coal-fired steam boiler and cast-iron radiators in the classrooms and corridors. The ventilating system is capable of providing about 25 cubic feet of fresh air per student per minute.

After a review of the findings of this respective school survey completed by a team of educational consultants, the school board decided to follow the recommendation in the long-range plan calling for modernization of Smith Elementary School. The study described some of the school's shortcomings as follows:

> The wooden floors in the corridors and classrooms are dark, warped, and creaky. The window sashes are loose and in need of repair. There is no suitable place for physical education and assembly.
>
> There is also no health room or workroom for the teachers. There is neither technology equipment nor internet in any part of the school. The building, as a whole, is in excellent structural condition but the atmosphere found in the classrooms is not conducive to effective learning.

On the basis of this report and a study of the curriculum, educational specifications were developed and the following were accomplished.

In addition to a face-lifting around the front entrance and main lobby, the Smith Elementary School was modernized as follows:

1   The foundation was examined, repaired wherever necessary, and insulated with panels of Styrofoam or equivalent structural insulating materials.
2   A gas hot water heater was installed and piped through insulated pipes to the cafeteria, adjoining lavatories, and to the multipurpose room. A small, self-contained electric hot water heater was installed near the principal's office and teachers'

lounge. (This eliminated long hot water pipe lines from the central hot water heater.)

3 A gas hot water heater was installed and hot water piped to all lavatories.

4 The old boiler was replaced with eight rooftop energy-efficient heating units that each have an A/C condenser located at the main exterior level.

5 Two coat rooms on each floor were converted to modern toilet rooms, one for boys and one for girls. Ceramic tile was installed on the floor and walls, and new LED lighting and improved ventilation were provided. Wall-hung fixtures were used throughout, and spring-loaded spigot faucets with tempered water were introduced.

6 A new base was installed on all of the wooden floors in the corridors and class-rooms, and light-colored vinyl asbestos tile was laid over it.

7 The upper part of all classroom and corridor walls was repainted in pastel colors. A warm wood-toned Formica-type material was installed on the lower walls of the classrooms.

8 The ceilings in all of the classrooms and corridors were lowered to a height of about 10 feet, using a mechanical steel grid system. Acoustical tile was installed on all ceilings.

9 The lighting in corridor and classroom areas was replaced with LED fixtures. The school was completely rewired.

10 The wooden window sashes and frames were replaced with modern anodized aluminum units with insulating mirror glass.

11 The parapet was removed and new flashing was installed to give the building a modern, sleek appearance and to correct a leaking roof.

12 The three outside doors were replaced with modern glass doors.

13 All stairs were resurfaced using abrasive, nonslip materials.

14 The single wooden handrail was replaced by a modern, double stainless steel handrail set at two heights.

15 Coat closets with vertically sliding panel doors were built in the classrooms along the corridor walls.

16 The gray slate whiteboards were removed and the walls beneath were sheet rocked, refinished, and painted. Vertical standards 4 feet apart were installed in all areas where whiteboards and tack boards were needed.

17 Standards were installed in the main lobby to support display cabinets and shelves.

18 The lower walls in all corridors were sprayed with plastic-type paint to a height of about 4 feet.

19 At least two duplex electrical outlets were installed on the opposite walls of each classroom and in strategic locations in the corridors.

20 The old shades in the classrooms were replaced by vertical-type wooden slat blinds for improved light control.

21 Eight solar heating panels, each having an area of about 40 square feet, were installed on the roof facing south and tilted at an angle from the horizontal, approximating the latitude on which the Smith Elementary School was located. This unit was tied into the new gas hot water heater.

22 One coatroom on each floor was converted to a remedial room for speech therapy, reading, and arithmetic.

23 The remaining coatroom on the first floor was used for storage of instructional and custodial materials. Locks were installed on the doors.

24 The principal's office on the second floor was enlarged, refinished, relighted, paneled in birch, and converted into a teacher's lounge. The entire floor was carpeted except the area surrounding the work space and the sink-refrigerator-range combination, where vinyl tile was used. This space was enlarged by removing the wall between the principal's office and the adjoining cloakroom.

25 The two basement playrooms with relatively high ceilings were converted into a kitchen and cafeteria for the hot-lunch program. The ceiling was dropped about 6 inches below the former ceiling and covered with acoustical tile. Surface-type, plastic-covered fluorescent strips were attached to the ceiling. Wooden paneling was used on the walls and colored vinyl tile was installed on the floor. A movable raised platform was placed at one end of this space.

26 Modern, movable, colorful plastic chairs and white marker top tables were provided.

27 Lounge furniture and a comfortable work table were provided in the teachers' room.

28 The two large toilet areas in the basement were reduced in size and completely restyled with new electronic fixtures, ceramic tile floors and walls, LED lighting, and improved ventilation.

29 A general storage area for instructional materials was developed in the basement of the building.

30 A fire-resistant area for storage of cleaning agents was built in the basement area.

31 New partitions were installed in the basement areas to separate the kitchen from the dining area.

32 The walls between four pairs of classrooms were replaced with movable partitions having a rated sound transmission loss of about 40 decibels.

33 The bricks on the exterior walls were steam-cleaned and repainted. The outside walls and the roof were insulated and basement walls were repaired and waterproofed.

34 An addition to the Smith Elementary School was also built. The new section was connected to the side entrance by an attractive carpeted corridor. The addition was designed so that it could stand by itself architecturally and structurally if the main building were to be demolished at a later date.

35 The new addition contained the following spaces:

   a One 1,200-square-foot kindergarten room of modern design with wall-to-wall carpeting, except in the dressing space and in the wet work areas.

   b One library room having an area of about 1,500 square feet, plus space for storing movable technology equipment.

   c Four regular classrooms, each about 950 square feet in net area. Wall-to-wall carpeting was installed in all except for the wet work areas.

   d A multipurpose room having an area of about 2,500 square feet, plus space for a portable stage and chair storage room.

e A clerk, principal's office, health suite with an office and examination room. A toilet and hospital-type sink were also located in this area. These areas also had wall-to-wall carpeting.

36 The four regular classrooms mentioned in item 35 were located in a circular cluster so that movable partitions between them could be opened to produce a single unified space for about 120 pupils.

37 WiFi and power outlets were installed in both the new and original classrooms of the Smith Elementary School.

38 A special conference room was located adjacent to the library. It was directly connected to the library for the convenience of team teachers using this space in the preparation of their work. It was furnished with WiFi, comfortable chairs, and trapezoidal tables.

Thus, Smith Elementary School was extensively modernized. The cost? Close to a million dollars. Was it worth it? Probably not from a sound expenditure basis. A formula will be presented in the latter part of this chapter to assist school planners in making this crucial decision.

HEALTH-RELATED IMPROVEMENTS

The modernization process demands that educational facility planners concentrate heavily on matters related to the safety and health of the occupants of a building. Lighting, temperature, humidity control, sound pollution, water quality, ventilation, fire protection, and potentially dangerous situations should be improved to the maximum possible degree. Any flaw in the design of the building or construction material that may have a deleterious effect on the health of the occupants must be corrected in its entirety, notwithstanding economic considerations. One example of this type of health hazard is cited in the next paragraph.

Medical research scientists have discovered that asbestos is a cancer-producing agent. Immediately following World War II, asbestos was widely used in the construction industry because of its excellent thermal properties. It was fireproof and a good heat insulator. It appeared in several forms. It was pulverized and made into a cement-like substance that was plastered around boilers or steam pipes.

Often, the asbestos insulating tubes were covered with a fabric. During this period, the walls and ceilings were constructed of materials containing asbestos. Sometimes, asbestos and other sound-absorbing materials were sprayed on ceilings for acoustical and insulating purposes. School administrators should not wait until a school building suspected of containing asbestos is modernized.

All asbestos materials should be replaced immediately with non-carcinogenic materials. In situations where asbestos materials cannot be removed, another solution may be considered once the mechanics of the asbestos danger are understood. As long as the asbestos remains where it was installed and it is not disturbed by staff or students, there is no real danger from it. But, since it is a cement-like substance, it ultimately pulverizes and becomes airborne. When such air is inhaled, the danger of developing cancer is real and imminent. There are resinous sprays that can be applied to the surface of the materials containing asbestos. This treatment seals/encapsulates the asbestos-laden material temporarily and prevents the asbestos powder from becoming airborne.

TO MODERNIZE OR TO REPLACE SCHOOLS

One of the most perplexing questions confronting citizens within a school district is whether the existing school facility should be modernized or replaced. Many approaches are possible, but there seems to be no single line of reasoning that will satisfy everyone.

Paradox and Controversy

For various reasons, the issue of modernization or replacement is often fraught with paradox and controversy. There seems to be a natural tendency among many citizens to favor modernization over replacement for two reasons:

(1) They may feel a sense of loyalty to the grand old school that served them and their predecessors well in the past.
(2) There seems to be a common belief that modernization automatically means greater economy because part of the old structure is preserved.

Unfortunately, the average citizen sees only a part of the picture, unaware school buildings, like automobiles, become functionally obsolete. Too few citizens realize that the educational process today is considerably different from what it was when they attended school. Consequently, when citizens' committees examine today's school buildings, they often fail to perceive the presence of educational obsolescence.

Under these circumstances, they cannot be expected to make valid judgments of the educational worth of an existing school building. Nonetheless, citizens are currently making judgments about their schools, arriving at conclusions, true or false, and acting accordingly. Having convinced themselves, with or without a valid basis for judgment, that a building is educationally useful, citizens frequently presume that it is more economical to modernize it than to replace it.

This line of reasoning is perfectly understandable from the standpoint of the taxpayer, who, after all, sees only the outside walls of an apparently useful educational structure that represents a real value in dollars and cents. Why abandon it only to replace it with another structure? During a recent controversy regarding the question of modernization or replacement, the mayor of a large, conservative city said, "Our city has no use whatsoever for that (high school) building except as an educational facility. There's been talk of turning it into a new City Hall, but it would cost millions to turn classrooms into office space. Abandoning that building as a school would be abandoning a facility valued at some $6,000,000 private assessors have told me."

This statement or one similar to it is quite familiar to educators in all parts of the country. Whenever the question of modernization versus replacement arises, someone is almost always certain to remind the voters of the replacement value of that wonderful old, sound school building in the middle of town. This subtle emotional appeal and the desire for economy lend considerable power to such statements. This argument places economy and sentiments above educational values, and it is very difficult to combat it with reason, logic, common sense, or a promise of a better educational program for all of the children.

Modernization is both a blessing and a curse. When modernization is warranted in terms of the criteria presented in this chapter, it is usually easier to "sell" it to the public than other proposals. On the other hand, when new construction is preferable to modernization, the issue may become highly emotional and controversial. The resistance to new construction seems to stem from the feeling of some citizens that a perfectly *good* building is being abandoned only to be replaced by a new one on the same or on another site (at a considerable wasteful cost).

Modernization or New Construction

The decision whether or not to modernize a given school building(s) requires time, study, vision, and courage. A comprehensive study of all aspects of the problem is a necessary first step. Time and imagination are needed to identify and explore alternatives and to study and evaluate the consequences and educational returns associated with them. A hasty and ill-conceived decision to modernize a school may penalize the education of children yet unborn. School officials and members of school boards should identify the real issues and act in the best interest of the public and the school district.

The Generalized Formula for School Modernization

A thorough search of the literature of school modernization uncovered virtually no information about what defensive factors should determine whether or not a school should be modernized. The authors asked the question which at some time or other has confronted all school planners, "When should or should not a school be modernized?" Only two rules of thumb were discovered and they are as follows:

1   According to Linn, the decision to modernize a building is questionable to consider if the cost to modernize it exceeds 50 percent of the cost for a similar new project. He suggests a 40 percent figure would be more realistic to use as the gauge to give the school further review to be modernized.[1]

2   The second rule of thumb was proposed by construction experts who believe that when any two of the following five items are required, modernization should be strongly questioned. The items include:

   a)   major replacement of plumbing and/or heating;
   b)   total replacement of electrical wiring;
   c)   basic structural changes involving removing load-bearing walls;
   d)   complete replacement of roofing; or
   e)   complete revamping of the fenestration (windows, doors, etc.) pattern.

There is, to be sure, much merit in these two guidelines to modernization. Both statements focus upon economic considerations, but the Linn statement is more precisely related to the actual expenditure that may be required for modernization. The rule of the building construction experts, on the other hand, does not require that the cost of modernization be estimated into dollars before a decision is made.

Also, since the decision whether or not to modernize is based upon the need for any two of the major projects noted above, the actual cost that serves as the determinant in making the decision may vary over fairly wide limits. This does not mean the second rule of thumb is of little value. The rule of the building construction experts serves a most important function in alerting superintendents, school boards, and school planners to take a second and then a third look at the advisability of modernizing one of these existing schools that would require two or more of the five problem areas.

Another approach to the financial aspect of modernization is proposed here. In developing a generalized formula for school modernization presented in this textbook, the authors have sought to set forth a mathematical expression that;

1   Separates, insofar as possible, the total cost of modernization into its major component parts: cost for educational improvements, cost for improvements in healthfulness, and cost for improvements in safety.
2   Takes into account the educational adequacy of the modernized school, which also includes the school site.
3   Clearly indicates whether or not modernization would be of financial advantage to the school district over an extended period of time.
4   Places the replacement cost and the modernization cost on a comparable basis.

This formula is based upon a rate-of-depreciation concept and contains both a determinant and a hypothesis (underlying the formula).

The fundamental determinant in the proposed formula for school modernization is the annual rate of depreciation of the school facilities. It is hypothesized that the lower the effective rate of depreciation[2]—represented primarily by the amount of capital required to provide a school that is adequate in every respect—the sounder and more justifiable are the expenditure of public funds.

It is postulated, therefore, that the determinant of financial advantage on the part of a school district is not the initial cost, but the *rate* at which the initial cost is likely to depreciate over a period of years.

The general formula is stated as follows: Modernization is justifiable if:

$$\frac{C_E + C_H + C_S}{(L_M)(I_A)} < \frac{R}{L_R}$$

where:

C_E = Total cost of educational improvements
C_H = Total cost for improvements in healthfulness (physical, aesthetic, and psychological)
C_S = Total cost for improvements in safety

I_A = Estimated index of educational adequacy (0–1)
L_M = Estimated useful life of the modernized school
R = Cost of replacement of school considered for modernization
L_E = Estimated life of new building

Discussion of the General Formula

The three terms in the parentheses include many items that are not readily apparent. For example, C_E may include, in addition to remodeling, the expansion of the site, new wiring for educational television, and accommodating new teaching practices. C_H may involve an improved heating system, improved lighting, redecoration, refenestration, resurfaced floors and ceilings, and better ventilation. Finally, C_S may cover items such as structural repairs, fireproofing corridors and stairways, elimination of plaster, repairing loose shingles or the entire roof.

I_A is an index of educational adequacy ranging in value from 0 to 1 that is applied to the school for which modernization is being proposed. The value of the index is determined in relation to the educational adequacy of a replacement for the school in question. Often, when a school is modernized, compromises must be accepted. They may appear in the form of inconveniences to students and teachers or as restrictions of the educational function of the school. The school site is a case in point.

The authors do not believe that an inadequate site, per se, is sufficient reason for arbitrarily deciding that a school can be neither replaced nor modernized at a given location. The size of a school site is an important factor, but it is only one of many that must be considered in deciding where a school should be located. In situations where school sites do not meet desired standards, the site deficiency should be reflected in the index of educational adequacy unless the replacement school would also be located on an inadequate site.

It is important to bear in mind, however, that the index of educational adequacy applies to the entire school, of which the site is only one element. Since the index of educational adequacy is determined subjectively and represents a professional judgment, it might be desirable to obtain an evaluation of educational adequacy both from professional persons within the school system and from one or two qualified professionals outside of the school district.

L_R refers to the estimated number of years of useful life remaining in the school (in question) after it is modernized. It is quite possible that under certain circumstances, the expected life of the modernized building can be extended through various structural improvements.

R and L_R represent the cost of a school that would replace the building under consideration and the number of years it is likely to remain in operation, respectively. Admittedly, both the modernized school and a new building would require maintenance over an extended period of time. It might even be argued that the average annual cost of maintenance could differ considerably between the modernized school and its replacement.

For the purpose of the generalized formula, it is assumed that the average annual cost of maintenance for the modernized building is the same as that for its replacement.

It should be pointed out, however, that a well-designed modern school should have a greater life expectancy than the building designed in the past.

Application of the Formula

The figures required in the formula should be determined as accurately as possible and entered in their proper places in the formula. If the left side of the formula is numerically smaller than the right, modernization would be financially advantageous to the school district. The smaller the numerical value of the left side in comparison with the value of the right, the greater would be the financial advantage of modernization to the school district.

If both sides are approximately equal, the authors would use the 50% formula and favor replacement over modernization. A word of caution is in order, however. The formula should be the determining factor *only* if the prerequisites mentioned later are met.

Comparison of the Linn Rule with Results from the Generalized Formula

It should be remembered that Linn suggested that modernization may be justified if the cost of modernization is about 40 percent of the cost of new replacement. It will also be recalled that, in the life cycle of a building, forty seems to be the age at which most schools are considered for modernization. Let us assume that a school building is forty years old and is estimated to have a remaining life of thirty years after modernization. Let us further assume that the modernized school would contain a few unavoidable compromises so that its educational adequacy is judged to be about 90 percent of that expected for its replacement. It is also assumed that the replacement would have an expected life of sixty-five years.

$$\frac{(\text{cost of modernization})}{(30)(0.90)} < ? \frac{(\text{cost of replacement})}{65}$$

But according to the Linn hypothesis, if cost of modernization equals 0.40 (cost of replacement), modernization is justifiable. Let us test the Linn hypothesis in the general formula for the situation in this example. Substituting 0.4 (cost of replacement) for the cost of modernization in the general formula, we have:

$$\frac{0.4(\text{cost of replacement})}{(30)(0.90)} < ? \frac{(cost\ of\ replacement)}{65}$$

$$\frac{0.4}{(30)(0.90)} < \frac{1}{65}$$

$$0.0148 < 0.0154$$

Since the left side of the expression is less than the right, modernization is justifiable according to the generalized formula. It can be concluded, therefore, that the Linn hypothesis is a special case of the general formula presented in this report, and is valid for schools similar to the example described above. It should be noted, however, that the Linn hypothesis would not agree with the generalized formula when the school considered for modernization is more than forty-five years old.

REQUISITE CONDITIONS FOR MODERNIZATION

Before modernization can be justified as the best expenditure of public funds in any school district, the answer to *every* question listed below must be *in the affirmative*. It cannot be overemphasized that a negative response to any *one* of the criteria listed below is a sufficient reason for rejecting a proposal to modernize a given building unless a blue ribbon committee mentioned under question 7 deems that there are extenuating circumstances. These statements may appear to be exacting and uncompromising. They are meant to be just that. School officials and school boards cannot afford to yield to selfish pressures when the welfare and education of students are at stake and if tax funds were to be used inefficiently.

1   *Is the school building under consideration needed in its present location for at least 75 percent of its remaining useful life after modernization is completed?* Stated differently, the question might be, "Why spend money to modernize a building that will be phased out of operation in the very near future?"

2   *Is it impractical to distribute the student load of the school considered for modernization among other nearby adequate schools?* In some instances in large cities, it is possible to abandon an obsolete school building after reassigning students to other schools. This alternative, when feasible, should take precedence over modernization.

3   *Does the school structure lend itself to improvement, alteration, remodeling, and expansion?* If the answer is "no," the cost of remodeling or expanding such a building could be unreasonably high and/or the educational function could be restricted because of the technical impracticability of accomplishing certain necessary structural changes.

4   *Does the modernized building fit into the respective district's well-conceived long-range plan?* There are situations in which a modernized building can be justified on all other counts. On a short-range basis does it provide for an immediate and predictable need? But a short-term perspective is sometimes costly where modernization is concerned.

Let us illustrate this point. A school district was operating a single, centrally located high school (9–12 grades) enrolling about 1,000 students. The building was about thirty years old and it was in fairly good repair, but it was situated in the middle of the city on a site of about 4 acres. The site was hemmed in by business enterprises on three sides and was bounded by homes in the rear. The school district was confronted with the problem of providing space for an anticipated increase in enrollment of approximately 1,100 students within the next three years.

The district had several alternatives: (1) it could change the grade organization so that it could house the lower level (9–10 grades) of the high school in the existing building with only a few modifications and construct a new building for the upper level (11–12 grades) on an adequate site; (2) it could sell the school for use as an office building and construct a single large high school on a site of about 30 acres located less than one-half mile, from the existing school; or (3) it could modernize and expand the existing (9–12 grade) school.

After a great deal of controversy, the school district chose to modernize and expand the existing building. Although this action satisfied a number of criteria favoring modernization, it failed to pass the test of fitting into a plan designed to meet the long-range needs of the school district. Nevertheless, the adjoining block of houses was acquired by the school board for the expansion of the school. This addition pushed the rear boundary of the site back to a railroad track that served as a major railroad trunk line.

Two years after the project was completed, it became obvious that the expanded school lacked sufficient capacity to house an additional 400 students. The school board found itself in a dilemma. It did not feel that it could justify construction of a separate high school for this enrollment, but there was no free space on the already crowded 7½-acre site to construct the needed facility. Furthermore, the school board realized the present site was already severely overloaded. It recognized, too, that it would be folly to add student capacity to an already inadequate site and simultaneously reduce its land area still further by placing another structure on it.

This unwelcome situation could have been avoided if the electorate had been better informed when the decision to modernize was made. At least *two* of the criteria for modernization discussed here were not met. Indeed, the site could not be expanded to the minimum size needed for the ultimate enrollment, and the modernized building did not fit into a long-range plan for this school district. Nonetheless, in this particular instance, the school board recommended—and the electorate blindly supported—the modernization and expansion of the original high school building.

5   *Can the site of the school considered for modernization be expanded to meet minimum standards for the ultimate enrollment envisioned on the site?* In the example cited in the previous section, it was clear that the school district had not developed a long-range plan to guide its action. But the modernization proposal would have alone been indefensible on the basis of its site size considerations. The original building housing about 1,000 students was situated on a 4-acre site. A 3½-acre block was added to the original site taking out many homes that were sure to have caused owners heartaches. Consequently, the board recommended that a 2,100-student high school be situated on this 7½-acre site. When it was determined the school board could have purchased about 30 acres of open farmland less than half a mile from the existing high school, the case for modernization considerably weakened.

6   *In accordance with the generalized formula, is the annual cost of capital outlay for modernization less than it would be for a replacement building?* Regardless of the purported value of an existing building or the initial cost of new construction, it is the rate of consumption of capital outlay funds that is significant in the

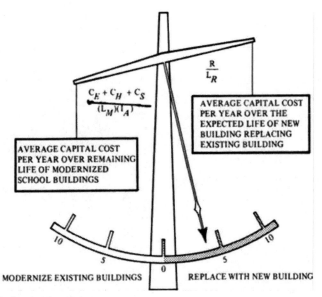

$$\frac{R}{L_R}$$

AVERAGE CAPITAL COST PER YEAR OVER THE EXPECTED LIFE OF NEW BUILDING REPLACING EXISTING BUILDING

$$\frac{C_E + C_H + C_S}{(L_M)(I_A)}$$

AVERAGE CAPITAL COST PER YEAR OVER REMAINING LIFE OF MODERNIZED SCHOOL BUILDINGS

MODERNIZE EXISTING BUILDINGS | REPLACE WITH NEW BUILDING

Figure 13.1.   Modernization Balance

choice between modernization and new construction. Figure 13.1 illustrates the application of balance to modernization.

7   *Has a blue-ribbon committee concluded that educational obsolescence of a given building can be substantially eliminated through the process of modernization?* A team consisting of the superintendent of schools, a member of the school board, a qualified educational consultant, an architect, and a citizen selected by a group or person (mayor) outside of the school should be organized and put together when a school building is being considered for modernization.

This group should review, study, and discuss all of the educational aspects of the building, particularly its limitations, and then decide whether or not it is *physically* possible to correct its educational shortcomings. The team should also make an estimate of the index of educational adequacy of a modernized building. This figure should then be substituted in the generalized formula.

SEQUENTIAL STEPS IN PLANNING FOR SCHOOL FACILITY MODERNIZATION

As school districts develop, expand, and reach maturity, the cumulative investment of public funds for educational facilities becomes progressively larger. It is not long before this total dollar investment in school buildings by a school district (over a period of years) represents an enormous accumulation of capital assets. The dollar and cents value of this investment may be quite impressive from the position of an economist, but may look quite different from the standpoint of an educator.

In a few cases, the educational value of this large capital investment may even be close to zero. This low educational assessment of capital expenditures occurs when the existing school and its site are no longer capable of sustaining, reinforcing, and promoting an effective program of instruction.

In many instances, school buildings become antiquated only after thirty to forty years of occupancy. A few become obsolete even sooner, particularly if they were not designed to accommodate foreseeable changes in future educational practices. In the natural course of events, however, obsolescence ultimately sets in. This phenomenon cannot be evaded or sidestepped in spite of the imaginative and advanced features that might have been built into a school building when it was conceived.

The reason for this unavoidable outcome is quite clear. The educative process is inherently dynamic and is in a continual state of flux. School facilities, on the other hand, are rigid, fixed, and quasi-permanent. Thus, educators find themselves constantly trying to fit a changing educational activity into a static and immutable structure. As the gap between the needs of the educational program and the original design function of the building widens, it becomes more and more difficult to house the desired educational program in a building that was not planned for it.

Consequently, in due time an existing school building becomes obsolete. Unfortunately, too many school buildings must be continued in operation even after they become obsolete because there is insufficient bonding capacity and taxpayer support to replace them. This situation exists in many of the fast-growing school districts throughout the country. Hopefully, some of the suggestions presented in this chapter can help to remedy this situation at a reasonable cost.

The modernization of obsolete school buildings is perhaps one of the most controversial and difficult decisions confronting a superintendent and school board. The *first* basic question that must be answered is whether or not a given obsolete school facility should be remodeled or replaced. This question has already been thoroughly discussed in this chapter. It must be stressed again that no decision should be made to modernize an obsolete school building *until* it has been demonstrated beyond any doubt that such modernization is in the best interest of the school district. The criteria set forth in the preceding section were developed to assist school planners and school boards in arriving at a sound, defensible decision regarding this issue.

This discussion is intended primarily for those school districts that have come to a well-reasoned conclusion that the modernization of an obsolete school building is clearly warranted. In this context, it should be mentioned that, in most cases, modernization of obsolete school facilities is not a wise expenditure of public funds. This rule is especially true in situations where a school district has a choice between modernization and replacement.

A sound rule of thumb to bear in mind that should be considered is, "When in doubt, do not modernize." In some instances, however, modernization of obsolete school buildings is justifiable and appropriate. The suggestions and procedures described in this chapter are therefore dedicated to the sound planning and design of such obsolete school buildings. In presenting the practical aspects of modernization, it is presumed that an obsolete school is direly needed in its present location, fits into a valid long-range plan, and has the potential of being transformed into a facility that is educationally and economically equivalent to a new school building.

A Suggested Plan of Action

At the risk of being repetitious, it is strongly recommended that all persons involved in the consideration of whether or not to modernize an existing school facility concentrate heavily on Task Unit I, below. This is one task that deserves as much time as is required in order to arrive at the solution in the best interest of the school district. Take time, think clearly, objectively and act logically.

Task Unit I: Can the Obsolete School Building Being Considered for Modernization Be Fully Justified—Educationally, Structurally, Geographically, and Economically?

It is suggested that the section in this chapter entitled "Requisite Conditions for Modernization" be reviewed and studied carefully. It is further suggested that each question be listed on a blank piece of paper and that the answers to each item be unanimously committed to in writing by all persons contributing information related to the decision on whether or not to modernize a given school building. At some point in the decision-making process, such persons should meet as many times as needed to share and exchange views on the issue.

If the answer to any one of the first six questions is "no," the modernization issue requires further study and analysis. The findings of the "blue-ribbon" committee under question 7 should be given very serious consideration since this group recommendation is made by a majority of its members, representing citizens, school officials, experts, and the school board, which, of course, must make the official decision on this issue. It should be mentioned that it is the people, except in some cities that do not require levies, who really make the final choices by supporting or not supporting a bond referendum authorizing funds for the modernization project(s).

A word of explanation regarding the answers to the questions on the modernization issue is in order at this point. A "no" answer to any one of the first six questions does not necessarily kill the project, but certainly places it in serious jeopardy. For example, if the site is inadequate and cannot be improved at a reasonable cost, it may still be advantageous to modernize an existing school facility, provided the "yes" answers to the other questions are preponderantly positive.

Or, the modernization cost of an existing school may not be in the best financial interest of the school district according to the generalized formula, but the school district may find itself in such financial straits that its bonding capacity is not sufficient to replace the building. Although modernization is not the ideal solution in this instance, the decision to modernize would be more in line with the financial capability of the school district.

The modernization of a school facility should not be ruled out as *a priority*. It is well known among educators that modernization is often justifiable and in the best interest of the school district. On the other hand, a modernization project should not be undertaken until every facet of the problem is studied in depth.

Such a study is required under Task Unit I. In conducting this study, it is important that the first six questions mentioned earlier be fully addressed and that the recommendation made by the "blue-ribbon committee," described under question 7, be affirmative and supportive of the modernization proposal. If, upon completion of this full investigation, a final decision is made to modernize an existing school facility, then proceed to Task Unit II.

Task Unit II: Developing a Set of Ideal Educational Specifications

At this point in the planning process, it is assumed the decision has been made to modernize a given building for a specified capacity and a stated grade grouping. For example, "The Jones Elementary School shall be modernized to serve 750 pupils in grades 5 through 8." Once these two elements have been stipulated, educational planners should develop educational specifications for a school facility designed to house the desired educational program. Modernization should be temporarily set aside.

It should be stressed that one of the premises leading to a decision to modernize was that the school building would approximate the function of a new facility. In order to achieve this goal, it is essential the educational specifications be exactly the same as those prepared for a new school building. Obviously, compromise will need to be made in a later stage of the planning, but it is imperative that an ideal set of educational specifications be prepared at this stage.

It is suggested the procedures described in chapters 5, 10, 11, and 15 be reviewed and followed as much as possible. Information contained in these four chapters will have a direct bearing on the preparation of educational specifications.

Task Unit III: Fitting Available Spaces Contained in the Existing Building into the Ideal Educational Specifications

This is one of the most difficult and crucial steps in modernizing an existing school building. Obviously, the present structure may not contain very many spaces that conform to the educational specifications. If it did, the existing structure would not be considered obsolete. The major objective at this point in the planning is to search for the most effective use of existing spaces in relation to the spaces specified in the educational specifications prepared under Task Unit II.

Before attempting to develop a variety of options designed to satisfy the educational specifications—more or less—it is suggested that the next section of this chapter, entitled "Practical Considerations in School Modernization," be reviewed very carefully. This section provides helpful approaches designed to assist school planners in developing a multitude of options for consideration by the superintendent and the school board.

Task Unit IV: Preparing a Revised Set of Educational Specifications

After completing the time-consuming procedure suggested under Task Unit II, the school board is in a position to approve the combination of options making the most effective use of existing spaces. Once these options are defined, the educational consultant and the designated school official should revise the original specifications and rewrite them in relation to the building to be modernized.

Let us cite an example illustrating the nature and type of revision.

The ideal educational specifications for the media center calls for a total area of 7,000 square feet distributed as follows:

Reading area	3,500 sq.ft.
Librarian's office	250 sq.ft.
Librarian's workroom	300 sq.ft.
Audiovisual storage	500 sq.ft.
Audiovisual workroom	350 sq.ft.
Computer workroom	350 sq.ft.
Media studio	750 sq.ft.
Self-instructional area	500 sq.ft.
Conference Room	500 sq.ft.

The present mini-auditorium containing 5,000 square feet will be converted as part of the learning resources center. The three regular classrooms across the corridor from the present auditorium, together with the intervening corridor, will become part of the learning resources center. The architect will develop various schemes of this area incorporating the space relationships described in the ideal educational specifications. Existing walls may remain.

Vision strips should be installed in all walls separating operational units in the learning resources center. Such vision strips shall be approximately 3 feet high. The bottom edge of the strip should be about 3 feet above the floor. Where vision strips cannot be installed, supervision will be conducted using video cameras.

The instructions to the architect should be as flexible as possible. Specifics should be included only when they have educational significance. Otherwise, the architect should be given as much freedom as possible. For example, in the above illustration, the upper edge of the vision strip is specified at a level about 6 feet above the floor. There is a specific functional reason for this.

It is extremely annoying when an obstruction is located in a vision strip at eye level. One finds oneself subconsciously either standing on tiptoe trying to look over the obstruction or bending down to look under it. Such annoyance is not conducive to effective teaching or learning. The remedy is simple and not costly. Educationally important details should be clearly stated in these educational specifications. This is the only way the architect will understand what is desired.

Task Unit V: Architectural Planning of the Modernized Building

The revised educational specifications described in the previous section become the basic educational requirements that the architect will make every effort to satisfy. As plans develop, the architect will discover a large number of previously unknown obstacles. For example, he or she may find that a major waste line is imbedded in the wall that was scheduled for removal. As these problems arise, the consultant, school officials, and the architect will convene and discuss alternatives, arriving at the best resolution in each instance.

The general procedure from this stage to the awarding of the bids for a modernized building needs to be clearly delineated by the architects and construction management. It will be the responsibility of the facilities consultant to make certain that the plans conform to the requirements stated in the educational specifications. From this standpoint, the consultant will need to be devoting far more time to a modernized building than to a new one. Under new construction, lines can be electronically redrawn quickly and easily. In a modernized building, it is definitely more difficult to move or remove existing walls.

Task Unit VI: Generating Public Support

The importance of gaining public support for any school project has already been discussed in past chapters. There is no hard evidence showing it is easier to win a bond referendum for modernization than it is for a new school building. Whenever public funds are being expended, it can be anticipated that opposition to such expenditures will develop (refer to chapter 14 on this subject). The extent of such opposition, however, is unpredictable. It is therefore essential that early attention be given to the matter of public support in the respective community within the school district boundaries.

It might be helpful to review the section in chapter 14 dealing with public support and the ten strategies that might be used to develop a favorable attitude toward the project(s) among the registered voters residing in the school district boundaries. Unless this support can be identified and generated prior to the referendum, the project may be doomed to failure.

PRACTICAL CONSIDERATIONS IN SCHOOL MODERNIZATION

The modernization of an existing school is far more complex and time-consuming than the planning of a new school building for the same educational program and capacity. The design, construction, and structural system of an existing school facility often impose serious physical constraints upon the architect. Some of these obstacles are frequently difficult, if not impossible, to overcome. To say that school modernization is a challenge to ingenuity of school planners is an understatement of high order.

The best that can be expected in the modernization of a school building is finding a solution that contains the lowest number of least harmful compromises. For this reason, school planners often develop several options that are designed to satisfy the educational specifications. In most cases, none of the options completely meet the requirements of the educational program. Consequently, choices are usually made so that each compromise solution has the smallest negative effect upon the educational program. A number of guidelines are presented in this section to assist planners in the search for solutions that are the least harmful to the overall educational functions.

1   *The modernized school facility should be equivalent to a new building housing the same educational programs.* When a decision is made by school officials to

modernize an existing school building instead of replacing it with a new one, the implied assumption is that the modernized facility is equivalent to a new building that would be constructed to replace it. Very rarely do school officials think this equivalency cannot be achieved when the decision is made. The decision to modernize is usually made in good faith with the full expectation that such equivalency is possible (when most times that is not true).

In the real world of planning, however, it is almost impossible to modernize an existing school building without making a number of significant compromises. The validity of this premise is well recognized by most school planners. Thus, the architect often presents several options to the superintendent and school board. It is suggested that the principle of "least educational compromise" be kept clearly in mind when choices are being made among a number of reasonable solutions to the many modernization problems.

2   *The least costly conversion from one space use to another is one that requires only a change in a room label.* In the interest of economy, school planners should actively seek out spaces that can be used effectively almost as they are, for one or more instructional purposes. There are frequently many spaces in an existing building that can be well utilized for functions different from those currently housed in them. For example, a large regular classroom could possibly be used as a CAD drafting room. A large computer room can be utilized for large-group instruction. A shop planning room can be converted to a room for small-group discussion. The educational specifications should be scanned to identify existing spaces that meet the physical requirements of the desired educational programs.

Decisions of how to best utilize existing spaces, however, require extreme care and sound educational judgment. When the educational specifications are compared with the physical features of existing spaces, it is often quite possible to find a number of existing spaces that satisfy the size requirement as are stated in the specifications. Many of these properly sized spaces, however, cannot be used effectively in a modernized building, because they may not be well related to other spaces functionally associated with them.

For example, the small-group discussion room mentioned in the preceding paragraph may be isolated at the end of a wing of a building. Thus, even though it meets all other criteria for a small-group discussion room, it lacks the proper functional relationship to other associated instructional activities.

On the other hand, it is frequently quite surprising to discover how many of the existing spaces can be utilized for other uses without making any major changes in the spaces. Oftentimes, when two or three spaces in a given area of an existing building are remodeled and converted to specialized uses, they may be surrounded by a cluster of spaces that could be adapted for functions associated within the remodeled area.

In some instances, these related spaces may be adequate and suitable as they are. Consequently, the decision of which rooms to remodel in an existing building becomes quite crucial. It is important, therefore, to look for clusters of spaces that are logically associated with the rooms considered for major modernization. This precaution could result in substantial savings through a more efficient utilization of existing spaces.

3   *The conversion of existing large spaces into smaller ones can be financially rewarding.* It is frequently advantageous to subdivide a large space in an existing building into smaller ones. Obviously, any space, large or small, that can be utilized effectively in its original location and design should be continued in operation with minimal changes. There are many instances, however, when existing large spaces are no longer adequate, suitable, or needed in their present form. Oftentimes, such spaces are replaced by new additions to the modernized structure. Consequently, there are situations when a large existing space should be considered for new educational uses.

The subdivision of large spaces into effective smaller instructional areas is an important aspect of school modernization. The multitude of potential uses of large spaces presents a wide variety of exciting options in the redesigned version of a modernized school building. In order to explore a large number of possibilities, it is suggested that the total usable area of each existing large space destined for conversion be determined and recorded, and that the total area included in each cluster of related spaces be computed from an analysis of the educational specifications.

All clusters that contain areas approximating the areas of the various large spaces should be given further study. School planners should prepare several options in which combinations of related functions can be housed in existing large spaces. Each combination should then be evaluated in terms of educational effectiveness, considering both the advantages and disadvantages of each proposed use of available space.

There are a few common uses of large spaces worthy of note. They are mentioned only as ideas that will hopefully suggest many other possible solutions to local school planners. An obsolete assembly hall, for example, has a number of possible uses. It can be converted into a library on two levels. The lower level might contain bookshelves, together with carrels, a librarian's office and workroom, a computer center, and an audiovisual center. The second level could be designed as a mezzanine for expanded library services.

It may be possible to include remedial rooms for speech, reading, and mathematics on the mezzanine level, with direct entry to such spaces from the second-floor level in a two-story building. This same large space could be converted into a two-story classroom area. A 6,000-square-foot assembly hall, for example, could be converted into approximately ten classrooms, five rooms on each floor. It may be possible to use certain large spaces for one or more clusters of related specialized rooms, such as science, home-economics, art, and business programs. Large spaces can also be subdivided into offices for administration, health, guidance, and faculty work stations (offices).

Sometimes one large space function can be substituted for another. For example, an outmoded gymnasium with a relatively high ceiling (20′–22′) could easily be converted to a sloping floor auditorium, particularly if it was originally designed as a gymnasium-auditorium with a stage and proscenium opening. Cafeterias can frequently be converted into multisized teaching areas for large-group–small-group instruction through the ingenious use of interlocking movable partitions.

Shop areas are usually large, single-story, high-ceiling enclosures. If these areas become available, it is often advantageous to consider using these spaces for specialized classrooms that require water, gas, and electricity. The functions that might be most appropriate for these areas are home-economics, art, drafting, business programs, and science. In school districts that provide student-activity-type facilities, a properly located large space can often be converted into spaces for a student lounge, quiet study areas, announcement viewing areas, and small computer rooms.

These facilities are essential in secondary schools where the open-campus concept is embraced by the school philosophy. Under this concept, students are free to leave the campus whenever they are not in scheduled class activities. In some instances, students do not leave the campus but congregate in the corridors and lobbies when no other facilities are available. Under these circumstances, the corridors become sources of distracting noise and teachers have found it difficult to conduct classes in adjoining classrooms. Consequently, when the open-campus concept is adopted, student activity centers are basic to the success of the plan.

4   *Housing large-space functions in a cluster of small spaces.* Although it is much simpler to convert a large space into a number of smaller ones, it is sometimes possible to house large-space functions within a constellation of smaller spaces. The media center function is one that can often be accommodated in a cluster of smaller spaces. Let us illustrate the application of this concept by citing an example.

In this illustration, it is assumed the educational specifications call for 5,000 square feet of space for the media center. What is needed in this instance is essentially a 5,000-square-foot block of spaces that can become a self-contained operational unit of the school. This large block of space might be located at the end of a wing or it might occupy a major part of one floor level in an existing building. If such an isolated area cannot be found, it may be possible to remodel the existing building slightly to create this condition.

Normally, a 5,000-square-foot block of space in an existing school building contains several classrooms, a small storage room or two, a main corridor, and possibly toilet areas. The boundaries of this block of spaces should be clearly outlined on the electronic drawings of the existing building. Hopefully, in designing the media area, this main corridor can be "dead-ended" and become an integral part of this center. Entrance to one end of this center can be gained from the terminus of the remaining corridors through a set of doors at that point.

In this situation, it is not necessary to remove entire load bearing walls to create the feeling of a library. It may be advantageous to simply install vision strips in the intervening walls so that the bottom of the vision strip is about 3 feet above the floor. The height of the top of the vision strip should be not less than 6 feet above the floor. Such vision strips provide visual coherence to the area and simplify supervision of the area. Obviously, it may not be possible to install such strips in all walls because of the location of utility pipes and wires in some partitions. Video cameras could be utilized for supervision in these instances.

In spaces where privacy is needed at certain times, it is a simple and inexpensive matter to install draw curtains across the vision strips. If double glazing is used on the vision strips, each cubicle or room can be acoustically insulated from adjoining spaces, thus making it possible to use different audiovisual materials for group viewing in adjoining rooms.

In some existing buildings it might be possible to convert classrooms, corridors, and small storage spaces into a cafeteria. If a sufficiently large block of space could be found with one end of it easily accessible to the service drive of the school, it might be feasible to convert this block of space to cafeteria uses. The cafeteria effect can also be created through the judicious use of windows.

There may be some decided aesthetic and functional advantage in using a series of smaller spaces in contrast to the usual institutional-type cafeteria. Special attention should be given to the circulation patterns established under this concept. Generally, classrooms already have two means of egress. These can be incorporated into the traffic flow pattern of the cafeteria function, which would be housed in a series of adjoining spaces.

5 *From the standpoint of cost and structural considerations, the removal of load-bearing partitions should be kept to the absolute minimum.* In school buildings constructed prior to World War II, most of the interior walls of the building are load-bearing. This was particularly true of the walls on both sides of the main corridor. In addition to being load-bearing, these corridor walls were also constructed of fire-resistant materials.

The question is frequently asked as to whether or not a load-bearing wall can be removed. In some instances, it can be removed entirely; in others, it can be eliminated only partially. Technically, walls can be removed and a new structural system can be substituted for the original wall in most situations. Indeed, all this can be accomplished, but usually at an enormous cost to the owner. Is such a tremendous cost justifiable? Not very often. These high costs can be supported only in rare cases where no other alternative is possible.

As a practical matter, therefore, it is suggested the removal of load-bearing interior partitions be avoided as much as possible. Windows or video cameras, as described in the preceding section, often solve the problem of visual contact very inexpensively. Nonbearing partitions, of course, do not present serious structural problems, except when utility pipes are located within them. The cost of removing nonbearing walls is often quite reasonable and justifiable. When vision strips do not serve an educational function, the cost of removing a non-loadbearing partition should be compared with the cost of installing a window.

6 *If the modernized building is to be expanded, it might be advantageous to plan large and specialized spaces under the new construction.* There are many reasons why existing school buildings become obsolete. The rooms may be too small for modern educational practices. There may be no provision for water, electricity, or gas in certain areas. The space for physical education may be too small. There may be no suitable space or power in which to install technology equipment.

Most often, however, the reason that school buildings are considered obsolete stems from the absence of adequate and suitable specialized classrooms and the lack of sufficiently large spaces for large-group activities such as assembly and physical education. Frequently, spaces originally designed for specialized uses can no longer support the more sophisticated teaching practices that require more space and more advanced equipment. These deficiencies must be taken into account during this modernization process. Consequently, the plans of the modernized facility must contain design elements that correct such deficiencies.

When modernization also includes new construction, it is often financially rewarding to locate specialized classrooms and large-space functions within the new addition. The benefits resulting from this suggestion are twofold. Since many of the specialized spaces in the original building are usually nothing more than oversized classrooms, it is educationally sound to use these existing spaces as regular classrooms. Also, most of these spaces can be used without any appreciable expenditure of capital outlay.

In many instances, the conversion of a former specialized space to a regular classroom requires simply changing the label on the door. This type of modernization is inexpensive and educationally sound. The reason for including large-space activities under the new construction, however, is usually more a matter of necessity than choice. Generally speaking, there are usually no spaces within an obsolete building that can be expanded or converted into suitable large-space use. For this reason, many additions to school buildings frequently include a gymnasium, an auditorium, and a cafeteria. Of these three, the gymnasium is the space that is most often included in new construction.

7   *Rehabilitation of obsolete school buildings.* It is important to bear in mind that obsolete school buildings have been occupied for several decades. After this long period of time, it is highly probable that the electrical, mechanical, plumbing, technology and heating systems in the building will require special attention when the building is modernized. It is also anticipated there will be a certain amount of deferred annual maintenance that can be dealt with at the same time.

As mentioned earlier in this chapter, modernization is very comprehensive in the respective scope. It includes both remodeling and rehabilitation. Several aspects of remodeling have already been discussed in the preceding six sections. Rehabilitation alone does not produce a modernized building. It simply brings the physical plant to the same level of appearance and function it possessed when the building was occupied for the first time. Thus, when a building constructed in 1940–1950 is rehabilitated today, it improves physically but not educationally. It is the combination of remodeling and rehabilitation that transforms an obsolete school building to one that is aesthetically pleasing, mechanically functional, technologically updated, and educationally effective.

Rehabilitation is primarily concerned with the restoration of the physical plant to its original condition. Consequently, all spaces and equipment within a school building should be subject to rehabilitation, regardless of whether or not it was remodeled. Ceilings and walls may need to be repaired or replaced. Floors may require resurfacing. Lighting fixtures may need to be replaced with more efficient LED units. Interior surfaces will undoubtedly need to be cleaned and redecorated. Masonry must be examined for evidence of deterioration, and corrective measures must be taken.

Plumbing fixtures may be in need of repair or replacement and valves converted to automatic shut-off or flushers. The heating system may be obsolete, inefficient, and needs to be replaced. There may be a need to change from one form of heating energy to another because of changes in the cost of various sources of energy, such as gas and electricity. Ventilation equipment may require new motors and control systems.

These are only a few of the many items to be included under rehabilitation. In rare cases, the total cost of rehabilitation may well exceed that of remodeling. The authors have observed on several occasions involving modernization that members of school boards were routinely surprised to learn that the cost of rehabilitation was sometimes as high as 40+ percent over the cost of modernization. This is especially true when the architect is trying to bring the level of the modernized building up to the code standards of a new building.

Remodeling without rehabilitation leaves much to be desired. Although the educational function of certain spaces will be improved, the general atmosphere within the school may not be conducive to effective learning. The cost of rehabilitation varies over a wide range. In school districts where there is an annual systematic program to fund school maintenance and upgrading, the cost of rehabilitating an obsolete school building is relatively small.

Unfortunately, when a school district must operate within budgetary cutbacks, funds for maintenance are among the first to be deleted from the budget. As a result, the cost of rehabilitation rises in direct proportion to the amount of deferred maintenance accumulated over a number of years. In spite of these situations, every effort should be made to fully rehabilitate a building scheduler for modernization. To do less means the modernized building is not equivalent to a new structure that could have replaced it.

DISCUSSION QUESTIONS

1   How do school planners and architects determine whether to modernize an existing old school(s) or to construct new?
2   Define "rehabilitation, remodeling, and modernization." Give an example of how each term applies to an educational setting.
3   Discuss five of the seven questions that help determine whether modernization should be justifiable.
4   When would a "blue-ribbon" committee be needed to be formed? Who are the members of this committee? What is their purpose during this process of improving an educational facility?

NOTES

1. Henry Linn, "Modernizing School Building," *American School and University*, v. 24 (1952), p. 401.
2. Effective depreciation includes both educational adequacy and capital outlay.

Chapter 14

School Bond Referendums

School bond referendums are no longer considered an easy task to get approved. They are becoming more difficult with many states only getting one in three (or 33 percent) of them passed on any given election date. School bond referendums are one of the few ways where the citizens can directly express their "anti" sentiment at the ballot box.

Two states currently (2017) require the super majority of two-thirds to get a school bond referendum passed. This allows one No vote to offset two Yes votes. School districts in those two states—Idaho and Kentucky—have an incredibly difficult task of achieving a 66 2/3 percent rate of approval.

A dramatic, carefully planned, and well-timed campaign using proven steps/techniques (see figure 14.1) are needed to convince the patrons of the respective school districts to vote YES on any given election day. The designed program outlined in this chapter has been successful in sixty of sixty-six school levies (90.9 percent) with an average 73.8 percent YES vote. These ten steps will now be reviewed more fully in this chapter.

(1) DEVELOPING A STRONG PUBLIC RELATIONS PROGRAM

Most school districts have already developed a clear mission and vision statement. This is an important prelude to also having a district-wide public relations plan. Building a successful school bond campaign needs to start with consistent communications on several levels with the patrons of the school district. Each month information should be disseminated about all upcoming calendar events, school programs, instructional offerings, positive activities in the schools/district, testing schedules and results, and an analysis of the school facilities. There should also be routine correspondence from teachers, principals, superintendents, and others to parents and other patron groups.

Patrons of the school district do not like receiving materials and correspondence *only* during the time just prior to a school bond election. Annual patron engagement with two-way communications with school personnel helps to develop trust and relationships that are long lasting. Research reveals parent numbers as a portion of all school district patrons are decreasing. Therefore, the public relations plan for the

School Bond Election
10 Steps for Winning at the Polls

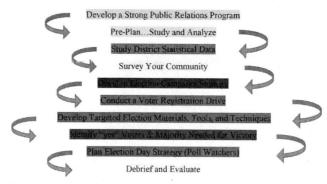

Figure 14.1. Winning at the Polls

school district needs to be comprehensive to ensure communication with all patrons residing within the district boundaries.

(2) PRE-PLAN—STUDY AND ANALYZE

It is recommended to start a year in advance of the bond referendum to conduct an in-depth study of the respective community(s). The final report should have discussions of: (1) collecting the necessary data and resources, (2) gathering the information through a variety of sources and interviews, and (3) preparing the report in a meaningful way to assist in the election endeavor by the school district.
   Prepare and collect the following information:

- A needs analysis of all facilities (have architect and construction manager (CM) assist in this task)
- Enrollment projections (past five years and future five to ten years)
- Bonding capacity (from fiscal adviser)
- Possible bond timeline (select advantageous dates)
- Bond scope (items that need to be done and are affordable)
- Bond cost estimates (from architect and CM)
- Tax implications (when recommended bond scope is agreed upon by a citizens task force)

(3) STUDY DISTRICT HISTORICAL DATA

It is recommended that each of the following tasks be accomplished within the year-in-advance time period:

- Collect three previous bond levy results (# of votes cast both yes and no, # registered voters, percentage of registered voters casting ballots)
- Calculate what percentage of voters were made up of parents

- Calculate what percentage of parents are currently registered
- Get a list of bond strategies utilized in past levies
- Get a list of who promoted the bond issue and frequency of their meetings, etc.
- If a levy(s) failed, try to find out what caused it to do so
- Collect demographics on population living within the school district boundaries (number by age group, number of renters versus home owners, and the number of new residents each year)

(4) SURVEY THE COMMUNITY

It is also recommended that within the year-in-advance time period each of the following tasks also be accomplished:

Conduct surveys of the community by telephone, e-mail, mailings, and/or person to person to determine these answers:

(1) What do they like about their schools?
(2) What would they like to see changed in their schools?
(3) As a voter do they tend to support their schools? (why or why not?)
(4) How do they feel about the current property taxes? (Are they appropriate or too high and, if too high, is the school levy the source?)
(5) Try to ascertain their overall attitude (likes and dislikes).
(6) Find out how they voted in the last school bond election (were there any hot buttons or negative things that could come up again with a possible school election?).

(5) DEVELOP ELECTION CAMPAIGN STRATEGIES

It is imperative to have the unanimous support of the school board. One member (of a five-person board) voting NO on a bond resolution may cause 20 percent of the registered voters to follow their lead.

The recommended strategy steps need to be approved by the school superintendent and board chair. They need to be discussed and incorporated into a timeline that provides ample time for implementation before the day of the bond election. A few examples of these might be: the role of an ad hoc committee, the tasks that are informative versus promotional, what funds can be spent on informative versus promotional materials, use of media and timing, use of yard signs, billboards, fliers, door knockers, use of a speaker's bureau, and use of school data (test scores, awards, overcrowded schools, growth, etc.).

It is recommended that the entire staff of the school district be fully informed so they each have a full grasp of the scope of the bond proposal. The staff all have numerous friends/family who live in the district and depend on the staff member to keep them apprised of what is happening in the district. They should also be armed with bond brochures to share with others as questions are asked of them.

Forming an ad hoc committee is a needed task. They should be organized with officers, each with specific roles. See figure 14.2 for the Committee Officer Table for examples of the officers utilized when implementing these bond strategies.

_____ **SCHOOL   DISTRICT**
[Nov. 8–28, 201_]

AD-HOC SCHOOL BOND COMMITTEE OFFICERS	
Tri-Chairperson	
Tri-Chairperson	
Tri-Chairperson	
Secretary	
Treasurer	
Promotions	
New Voter Registration	
Door-to-Door Canvassing	
Reminder Card Mailing	
Bird Dogger	
Election Day Phone Calls	

STEERING COMMITTEE MEMBERS

CONSULTANTS

Facility
Planner....................

Architects...........................

Financial Advisor.....................

Attorney...................................

Figure 14.2.   Officers, Members and Consultants

Each bond election committee will need to customize these strategies for their respective community. What works in one school district may not be successful in another. Success at the polls is a challenge and requires all "i's" to be dotted and "t's" to be crossed, leaving nothing to chance.

An intensive campaign must be run consistently for two months and has to be timed to not start too early. Too early of a start will give the opposition (CONS) a chance to take over the momentum in the weeks immediately preceding the election. Those in opposition (usually representing 20 percent of the voting population) can be very organized and often have a great deal of time on their hands to run a very negative campaign. They will utilize social media as well as other types of electronic correspondence to defeat the levies. Many referendums today are often won or lost by less than a dozen votes. This requires the PRO campaign to be well planned out and carefully executed to avoid being defeated.

Positive school data, test scores, awards, new programs, and athletic team success should all be utilized in news releases that fit within the public relations program.

A grassroots movement made up of parents, grandparents, and patrons of the district is effective in helping get the word out about the importance of their schools and how improvement of the facilities is important for their children/grandchildren's education. The above Committee Officer sheet (see figure 14.2) should be made up primarily of non-employees to avoid any conflict with their jobs or promotion during the school hours.

A levy timeline should be constructed nine months prior to the election date so that all of the tasks and legal requirements are spelled out in advance. See appendix I for an example of a timeline for an Idaho School District running a bond in August of 2017.

(6) CONDUCT SPECIAL VOTER REGISTRATION DRIVES

With over thirty years of experience as a consultant and a school superintendent it has been revealed (time after time) that the majority of school districts have only one-half of their eligible parents registered to vote. This creates a distinct disadvantage when it comes to having an ample number of registered voters who are supportive of their schools and facility improvements.

Therefore, one of the ten (10) strategies is to have the New Voter Registration Officer (NVRO) (see figure 14.2) be in charge of coding the parents regarding their registration status—R (registered) or NR (non-registered)—on the current county voter registration list for the people living within the school district's boundaries.

Once the list of NRs is sorted, the results will probably reveal that between 30 and 50 percent of them are not registered to vote. Then the NVRO is in charge of getting volunteers to conduct voter registration drives to get parents registered to vote. Care should be taken to determine the deadline date your local county has set to have voter registrations returned (see appendix I) as this task will be time-sensitive.

After a parent voter registration drive has been completed and the percent is raised up to 70–80 percent, it is recommended that the individual schools then continue this task with every new student's parents as they enroll their child(ren) for school. This will save a lot of time for future levy elections and keep the percent of R parents high.

(7) DEVELOP TARGETED ELECTION MATERIALS, TOOLS, AND TECHNIQUES

In many states funding of school facilities has not always been one of the higher-priorities items in public finance. Many school superintendents are not experienced in the running of bonds, nor have they ever created the needed election materials. Patrons today need to be shown specific benefit(s) affecting them before they will consider supporting the school district levies. To run a successful campaign it must be crafted with great precision as many more levies fail than are passed, reinforcing that a critical balance of materials and techniques is imperative.

The ten-step process reveals the importance of each task. When one or more tasks are omitted, the domino effect can cause the remaining tasks to fail. The developed plan will be your written roadmap to get the committee from point A to B without being distracted away from the target. It is recommended that you identify various constituents within the district boundaries. These include senior citizens, parents, business people, baby boomers, and so on. Develop information that appeals to each of those constituent groups and make sure they receive the information.

Prepare an easy to read bond brochure with graphs and charts. Remember, "Pictures are worth a 1,000 words." Avoid expensive brochures with flashy color pictures since many will see that as a sign money is readily available within the current budget and the district really does not need the money that is being requested.

Preparing the bond budget is another tool that needs to be completed early in the process with ALL the line items included. Many bonds get passed and then it is discovered some of the items (furniture, fees, athletic fields, etc.) were not included in the bond budget. This budget can kill the election if it is discovered errors were made prior to the vote. Having the bond budget in a spreadsheet to review at public meetings is a valuable means of public disclosure.

Create a Question and Answer (Q&A) sheet for use during the eight weeks of the campaign. Every time a patron asks a question put it on the sheet with the appropriate response. Continue to add to the spreadsheet throughout the campaign until all of the questions have responses and then disperse the Q&A out for patrons to read. This will enable the patrons to get answers to their questions and avoid negative rumors concerning "what if" scenarios.

Utilize the architects, fiscal advisers, and construction managers in helping to answer the above questions on the Q&A. These firms can also assist in providing the graphs and charts for the bond brochure. See appendix II for an example of a bond brochure that has been customized for an Idaho School District (as an example) in some forty different bond elections.

(8) IDENTIFY "YES" VOTERS AND THE MAJORITY NEEDED FOR A VICTORY

Early in the campaign, a valid and reliable number of those predicted to vote in the election should be developed. Strategically, the data from the three previous district levy elections will need to be evaluated to develop a hard data file. The latest voter record can be obtained to determine who has participated in the majority of the community elections. Campaigns should never be run by "shooting from the hip." There must be a target, or goal, as to how many YES votes will be needed to make the election successful.

Many superintendents and school boards have the false assumption that all parents will vote yes. Leaving these elections to chance will usually end up in a lost election. The inaccurate reasons provided by many superintendents and school boards for not preparing adequately for bond elections include:

- Parents are all registered (only half will be)
- Parents will all vote (of the half who are registered to vote, only one-quarter of them will cast a ballot unless they are personally contacted by a committee member)

- Parents will all vote YES (this does not happen automatically and voters need written details or personal conversations from committee members in order for this to happen)
- Patrons not supporting the schools will not vote (20 percent of them cast NO votes on all elections and they are the active and consistent voters in most elections)
- Turnout is not known (using past elections as a guide a reasonable prediction the total # of votes to be cast can be made)

Once the number of YES votes has been determined and accepted, then the campaign has a target and goal to reach during the eight weeks prior to election day. See figure 14.3 for an example of a YES Calculation Sheet used in past school district elections. Included is the county voter turnout percentage for that date which is used to determine the goal which needs to be reached on election day.

(9) PLAN ELECTION DAY STRATEGIES

Once the number of YES votes has been calculated, the goal of the ad hoc committee will be to identify (in writing) at least that number of projected YES votes. Some of the officers (see figure 14.2) will have as a role to get each of the committee members to identify twenty YES voters who are registered and get them to cast a ballot in the election. Several of those subcommittees will have numerous members with the responsibility of developing even more subcommittees for their area. Remember, this all happens in approximately an eight-week time period.

Each list of twenty names will need to be tracked by the originator of that list. This can be done through a request to see the absentee ballot list or for them to physically go to their polling location during the hours they are open. All of the committee members need to follow through with this task in order to meet the goal of the number of Yes votes needed to carry the election.

A reminder card, text, or personal call to these twenty names needs to be made on election day to ascertain each one submits his or her ballot. All registered voters should not be contacted on election day. Only those identified personally as YES votes by the committee members (in advance) should be contacted. Remember that in two states, one No vote equals two Yes votes since the state has the requirement of 66.67 percentage YES to pass an election.

(10) DEBRIEF AND EVALUATE THE END OF THE BEGINNING

Once the election has concluded, the committee should meet with the school superintendent to thoroughly summarize the election, whether it is won or lost. Hopefully all of the tasks and the ten strategies will have been followed and the election will have been a success. If the levy is lost, it will be imperative to identify the tasks that were not accomplished in order to help build the plan if the bond is to be run again in the future. If the election was passed the tasks need to each be reviewed and the validity of

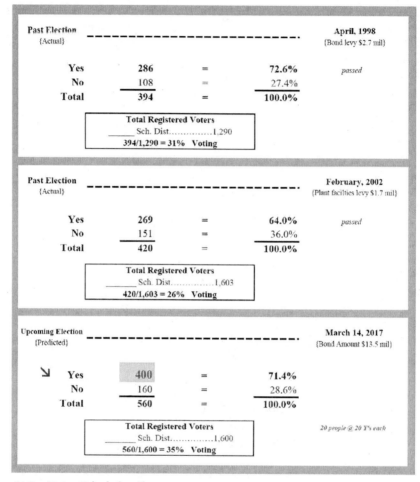

Figure 14.3.   Voter Calculation Sheet

each one determined, with notes for the future. If an educational consultant was used during this campaign they should be involved in this meeting to help collect data, take notes, and formulate plans to be used in a future bond referendum.

DISCUSSION QUESTIONS

1   There are ten steps that the author recommends you follow to win at the polls. Briefly review each of these.

2   Define an "ad hoc committee." What relationship does the superintendent have with this committee?

3   Discuss the five false assumptions that are associated with passage of a bond referendum.

4   Review the ad hoc committee officer setup. Outline the roles of each of the officers and the respective timeline for doing these tasks.

Part V

MODERNIZING, MAINTAINING, AND OPERATING AN EXISTING FACILITY

Chapter 15

Maintenance and Operation

School officials and school boards have realized for a long time that the construction and operation of school buildings involve a substantial expenditure of public funds. The investment for construction represents only the initial cost of a school facility. Operational costs for power, maintenance, and custodial staff become important items in the annual budget. The sequence of events is quite familiar to all educators.

Once the building is completed, the keys are turned over to school officials. Power and fuel are supplied to the building and, for the first time, are charged directly to the school district as school utility expenses. The switches are activated, and the building—hopefully—provides a comfortable and inspiring environment for learning. Ideally, once energized, all systems and equipment should operate flawlessly.

In practice, this situation almost never occurs. In most cases, there is a one-year warranty "shake-down" period when all equipment and controls are adjusted, rebalanced, or replaced if faulty. In the second year, the new or modernized building then becomes fully operative and begins to fulfill its intended purpose with any repairs (that are not found during the year warranty period) then costing the school district. The authors recommend that during this first year of operation ALL staff who occupy the new or remodeled school be on the lookout for "punch list items" that need to be repaired or replaced so the contractor is still responsible for both the labor and parts.

After five to ten years of use in a school the building will begin the aging process. The materials and surfaces of the structure begin to show some wear, and each piece of mechanical equipment starts to age at its own predictable rate. This process is natural, universal, and inevitable. It cannot be eliminated. For this reason, a well-conceived program of maintenance is an integral part of the daily operation of a school building. The details concerning the development of such a program are presented in this chapter. A number of promising practices dealing with the periodic care and maintenance of school buildings are also included.

Several publications have been prepared on the routine maintenance of school buildings. They contain a large number of details pertaining to a wide variety of daily housekeeping duties normally performed in a school building. A discussion of these specific matters is not within the scope of this book. Consequently, this chapter will deal primarily with the major concepts of school building maintenance covered in such texts.

There is no scarcity of custodial handbooks. Many of the larger school districts and most departments of education publish handbooks for custodians for the purpose of prolonging the life of a building and improving the environment for learning. Several custodial handbooks describe the work of the custodian in meticulous detail. As indicated earlier, a discussion of such details does not fall within the scope of this text. However, the availability of such practical information fulfills a basic need for the custodial workforce. With such information in hand, the custodian is well armed to cope with extraordinary janitorial situations or unforeseen building emergencies.

Dr. O. Barker Harrison prepared a comprehensive handbook (a little aged but still pertinent) for custodians who deal with both building maintenance and the care of mechanical controls and devices in a school building. According to Harrison,

> The school custodian is co-responsible with the principal for a building worth millions of dollars, its care and operation, and are indirectly responsible for the priceless lives of hundreds of children and their teachers, as their lives relate to the proper operation of the school plant.[1]

The great contribution made by physical plant personnel in maintaining a comfortable and healthful environment in a school building is rarely recognized by school officials, school boards, and the general public. Admittedly, the work of the school custodian is physical, time-consuming, and not particularly glamorous.

Nevertheless, an alert and knowledgeable custodian can save the school district thousands of dollars in future maintenance costs by paying attention to the "little things," such as water leaks, lubrication of equipment, erosion of soils adjacent to the building, excessive condensation of humidity around cold pipes, windows/doors with air infiltration, and replacement of defective temperature controls.

The men and women in the physical plant workforce also play an important part in the educational function of the school. It is these men and women who provide and maintain an environment that is conducive to effective learning. They do all this without interfering with the educational process. These dedicated people do most of their work after the teachers and students have left the building for the day or before they return to it in the morning. This often unseen workforce performs an indispensable service that benefits the students, teachers, administrators, clerical personnel, and the taxpayers. It is this group of people that improves learning by providing a proper environment by giving immediate and prompt attention to the little things before they become big and costly problems.

THE ROLE OF THE CENTRAL ADMINISTRATION IN THE OPERATION AND MAINTENANCE OF SCHOOLS

The central administration of a school district has an important part to play in the operation and maintenance of all of the school buildings within its jurisdiction. It develops district-wide policies concerning the working conditions of physical plant personnel, their rate of pay, fringe benefits, and other forms of compensation. It sets work standards and procedures that are implemented by the individual school principals. It develops procedures designed to help the entire physical plant staff better preserve and maintain the school buildings to which they are assigned.

But, according to Glass, one more ingredient should be added to the maintenance menu, commitment. He points out, "A good facility maintenance program *requires* commitment from board, administration, staff and the community. The maintenance of district facilities is a high priority and must annually be provided with adequate funding."[2]

DETERMINING THE SIZE OF THE WORKFORCE

The central administration of a school district has the basic responsibility of making certain that custodial personnel are not being overworked. It also has an obligation to the taxpayers of the school district to keep the number of personnel at a minimum. There are currently several rules of thumb that can be used to compute the number of custodians normally required in a given school building. Any one of them could be used to determine the theoretical custodial staffing number that is required in a school.

One of the nationally accepted methods, known as the "factoring formula," is presented in this section of this chapter. Although this rule of thumb is completely empirical, it does give the superintendent of schools or his or her assistants a valuable point of departure. In applying this formula, one should bear in mind that there may indeed be situations where the conditions within a particular school building make it necessary to assign more personnel to it than the formula would indicate.

For example, the building may be old and hard to keep clean and maintain, or it may be a new building that is severely overcrowded and used more hours per day than is customary. On the other hand, any staffing in existing school buildings that deviates substantially—too high or too low—from the theoretical staffing computation described previously should be studied and justified by the central administration. If the present staffing is too low compared to the theoretical result, the custodial staff are probably overloaded and relief for them should be sought.

On the other hand, if the present staffing exceeds the theoretical need, such additional personnel should be justified on the basis of each respective extenuating circumstance(s). If this cannot be done, the excessive staff should be reassigned to school buildings where staff deficiencies may exist. A worksheet for implementing the factoring formula is presented in table 15.1.

Divide the area of the gymnasium by 1,000 to determine the number of teaching stations for it.

There is another rule of thumb for determining the number of needed cleaning personnel, which is simpler and not as analytical, as the factoring formula. According to this unsophisticated approach, the number of cleaning personnel needed is simply one cleaning person for each eight or nine teachers assigned to the school building. The weaknesses inherent in this formula are obvious.

Table 15.1.   Worksheet for Estimating Custodial Staffing Using the Factoring Formula

Factor 1	Number of teaching stations (NTS)* divided by 11		
	$$\frac{(NTS)(\ \ )}{11}$$	=	Line 1
Factor 2	Number of teachers (NT) divided by 8		
	$$\frac{(NT)(\ \ )}{8}$$	=	Line 2
Factor 3	Building Capacity (BC) divided by 25		
	$$\frac{(BC)(\ \ )}{25}$$	=	Line 3
Factor 4	Gross area of building (BA) divided by 15,000		
	$$\frac{(BA)(\ \ )}{15,000}$$	=	Line 4
Factor 5	Area of site in acres (SA) divided by 2		
	$$\frac{(SA)(\ \ )}{2}$$	=	Line 5
Factorial Sum	Add lines 1–5		Line 6
Final Computation of Staff Need	Divide Factorial Sum by 5		
	$$\frac{(Enter\ Line\ 6)(\ \ )}{5}$$	=	Custodians Needed
			Round off to next higher whole number

* A teaching station is equivalent to about 900 square feet in which teaching is conducted.

It disregards student load, which contributes directly to the work of the custodian. It ignores the condition, number, and size of teaching areas in the school. It does not take into account the size of the school site nor the sidewalks to keep clean. It also makes no provision for the amount of custodial work required due to the overall size of the building. In spite of these shortcomings, this formula does offer a simple first estimation to the staffing needs in a given school building.

In addition to adjusting the custodial staff load for each school building, the central administration can also utilize this information regarding the number of custodians needed in each building for purposes of planning, budgeting, and assignments within the school district. If a study of custodial needs within the total school district reveals the number of existing staff is too small, the central administration has two options. (1) It may choose to employ additional custodians to correct the overloaded conditions. Or (2) if funds are not available for additional staff, it can reassign personnel among the various schools in order to distribute the overload equitably among all of the custodians on the workforce.

SELECTION OF CUSTODIAL PERSONNEL

The central administration establishes the qualifications for hiring custodial personnel. It conducts the search for qualified candidates for existing vacancies, and sets up a screening procedure to identify the best candidates. In many school districts the final selection is made jointly by the central administration and the principal where the vacancy in a school exists.

Qualifications

School districts should develop a set of job qualifications tailored for their particular situation. Some districts may have special needs, such as the requirement of custodians to be bilingual. There are, however, a number of qualifications that would apply to most school districts. These are presented below in outline form for the purpose of assisting local school districts in preparing their own job specifications for custodial positions. The set of qualifications given below contains items that would apply to most school districts. This list should be revised, expanded, or shortened according to the specific requirements of a given school district.[3]

The candidate:

1 Should be physically capable of performing duties required by the position.
2 Should be of good moral character, safe habits, and clean speech.
3 Should possess sufficient ability to carry out duties in an intelligent manner.
4 Should have a minimum of a high school diploma.
5 Must be free from communicable diseases and should be free from chronic disturbances that could cause him or her to be absent from the job excessively.
6 Shall present a neat, clean, and a well-kept appearance.
7 Should be dependable, and able to get along with people—teachers, principal, and patrons.
8 Should be orderly and willing to learn new techniques for housekeeping.
9 Must be able to plan and organize his or her work and (if asked) to supervise the efforts of other staff as to the proper housekeeping of the school.
10 Should be even-tempered and possess a good disposition.
11 Should be drug-tested and finger-printed to be clean in both areas.

MAINTENANCE AND BUDGETING

In addition to staffing, the central administration is responsible for providing funds for custodial supplies, cleaning and maintenance equipment, normal wear and tear of mechanical equipment, and preventive maintenance. Unfortunately, these are usually items of low priority in the overall school budget. It is true, of course, that when funds are limited, these expenditures can often be deferred without penalizing the instructional departments of the school. But this relief is only temporary.

Sometimes the cost of deferral is much greater than providing the funds where they can do the most good. For example, it may be possible to postpone the replacement of furnace filters for a year or two on the premise that "we'll just have to make do." In the meantime, the school district will be spending more money for utilities because the heating units are not as efficient when they have dirty or clogged filters in the transmitting of heat. Thus, in the long run, the school district is paying a penalty for such a postponement.

PROCUREMENT AND USE OF CUSTODIAL SUPPLIES

In this context, the central administration has two major responsibilities. The first one, obviously, is to include sufficient funds in the school budget to purchase custodial supplies. The second, and equally important obligation (on the part of central administration), is to make certain that the most efficient and least damaging cleaning agents are provided for each school building in the district. A person in the central staff should be charged with the responsibility of conducting the necessary study and research regarding the proper selection and appropriate use of various maintenance supplies and cleaning agents.

The importance of this task cannot be overstated. For example, one coat of ordinary paint over an acoustical plaster ceiling can destroy most of its sound-absorbing capability. The daily or prolonged use of abrasive powders on glazed materials, stainless steel, and chromium-plated fixtures can permanently damage their surfaces. The application of acid solutions on ceramic-tiled floors tends to weaken the mortar joints between each tile unless the floor is sealed perfectly. Consequently, the improper use of cleaning agents can be very costly to a school district over a period of time.

The selection and proper use of cleaning agents is usually the responsibility of the director of buildings or of plant operations in large school districts. In the smaller school districts, however, this function is often delegated to the head custodian of the building. Obviously, the superintendent of schools in these small school districts cannot be expected to conduct the necessary study and research pertaining to the selection and use of cleaning agents. The best protection may be for the school district, in these cases, to employ a high-level, well-trained, and well-paid head custodian with at least ten years of experience in a large school district working under the supervision of a director of physical plant.

Hiring a competent custodian, however, does not completely solve the maintenance problems of the small school district. The superintendent of schools in such districts cannot afford to give a low priority to the maintenance and care of school facilities on the grounds that he/she simply does not have time for it. Admittedly, time is limited and other duties are more pressing.

There are a few measures that the superintendent can take, however. He/she can make arrangements with counterparts in the larger school districts in the area to have the head custodian participate in training sessions held in the large school districts; purchase approved lists of cleaning agents researched and prepared by the larger school districts; and, finally, obtain a copy of a custodian's handbook from one or two of the larger school districts at a nominal cost. Armed with this material, the school superintendent in a small school district can feel fairly secure in the choice and proper use of cleaning agents, if he/she has selected an experienced and competent head custodian trained to use them appropriately.

Although it is simply good business to procure custodial supplies through a central purchasing office, care should be exercised to make certain that the needs of each building are reflected in the unified purchasing process. Centralization does not imply uniformity of need in each building in the school district. Each building should be considered unique regarding the type and amount of supplies. There are, to be sure, a wide variety of supplies common to all buildings. There are a few supplies that are needed in all buildings but in different quantities depending upon the age, size, and type of construction of the building, and there are certain supplies that may be peculiar to a given school building.

For example, a school building that uses energy pumps for heating and cooling may require a small supply of refrigerant to recharge the system, while other buildings may have no need for such materials.

NORMAL WEAR AND TEAR OF MECHANICAL EQUIPMENT

Seldom, if ever, does one find a school district that has been able to set aside funds in advance to replace all equipment that is in repair or completely worn out through normal use. The practice of establishing reserve funds for equipment depreciation is commonly found in business. It is a financially sound policy. In some states, however, school districts are prevented by law from establishing various reserve funds. This may be the reason why school districts have generally not become involved in reserve or sinking funds commonly found in business.

Nevertheless, it is both economically sound and financially wise to anticipate the replacement of sometimes costly equipment. If each piece of equipment were classified in terms of its normal life expectancy, it would be possible to determine its rate of depreciation in terms of dollars per year. Then, it would be relatively simple to determine the total cost of depreciation for mechanical equipment each year. If this amount of money, representing the total cost of depreciation, could be placed in a reserve fund, all of the mechanical equipment owned by the school district could be replaced when it was approaching the inoperable stage.

This practice would apply to items such as water circulators, motors in the ventilating system, motor vehicles, power equipment, mechanical units, electric resistance-type heaters, vacuum cleaners, machine scrubbers, computers, business equipment, and photocopiers. If this practice were instituted, the tax levy each year would include a proportional amount of money for equipment replacement. Thus, the cost of replacing mechanical equipment would be spread over the expected life of the item, rather than having the entire cost of such items fall upon the taxpayers in a single year.

If state laws prohibit the establishment of school reserve funds for equipment depreciation, every effort should be made to have them changed. If business finds this practice sound and in its own best long-range interest, it would seem reasonable and proper that public agencies be allowed to engage in the same healthy fiscal practice.

It might be possible, even under existing laws, to develop a program of planned replacement. It is suggested that the rate of depreciation be determined for each mechanical item and that the total annual cost of depreciation be computed for the entire school district. The next step in this suggested process is to examine the condition and life span of each piece of mechanical equipment and set forth the cost of equipment that needs to be replaced or will require replacement sometime during the next fiscal year.

The total cost of equipment that should be replaced could then be compared with the total annual cost of depreciation. If they are approximately equal, simply include the cost of equipment replacement in the school budget. If the cost of depreciation is greater than the total replacement cost, include at least the replacement cost in the budget. This type of imbalance occurs whenever replacement of worn equipment has been deferred in past years. Under the reserve plan practiced by business, this circumstance would never occur because the accumulated reserves would balance out the cases where the cost of replacement would exceed the total annual depreciation figure.

The above suggestion does not solve the depreciation problem. It simply eases it by focusing attention on the need for replacing mechanical equipment on an annual basis. Through this procedure, there would be an opportunity to include funds for equipment replacement each year on a systematic basis. Without this approach, or one like it, school districts would find themselves replacing worn crucial equipment from time to time on an emergency basis. Mechanical equipment of lower priority would probably be continued in use at a high maintenance cost to the school district. Such practice is certainly not prudent from the standpoint of economic efficiency. It represents an unnecessary waste of public funds. It can hopefully be corrected when educators make responsible legislators aware of the situation.

THE ROLE OF THE SCHOOL PRINCIPAL IN THE OPERATION AND MAINTENANCE OF SCHOOLS

The school principal is the key person in the school district responsible for the operation and maintenance of the school building to which he/she is assigned. The principal is the direct operational supervisor of all physical plant personnel assigned to the building. In some school districts, the custodian has a dual administrative responsibility. He/she reports to the school principal for all functional matters associated with the operation and maintenance of the assigned school building and is accountable to central administration for all technical matters related to his/her work.

For example, the custodian may be responsible to the principal for scrubbing a certain classroom floor at a given time on a specified day, but may be responsible to the central office staff for the number of hours worked, the type of cleaning agents used, and the procedures to be followed. Thus, he/she is functionally responsible to the principal and technically responsible to the central administration. These two responsibilities are normally compatible, easily differentiated, and administratively consistent.

CUSTODIAL OBLIGATIONS

In the daily operation of a school building, the principal can reasonably expect that the custodian will fulfill these requirements:[4]

1   Have knowledge of the principles of heating, ventilating, sanitation, and care of school buildings.
2   Have knowledge of the safest tools, materials, cleaning agents, and methods to use in various phases of custodial work.
3   Have knowledge of the correct use of mechanical equipment in school buildings.
4   Have skill in using proper tools, materials, cleaning agents, and the methods and procedures for handling different kinds of custodial jobs under various conditions.
5   Possess a scientific attitude toward the study of various phases of custodial services, in order to effect the greatest efficiency, economy of time, and energy conservation measures.
6   Possess an attitude that will lead to serious, wholehearted, and unselfish attention to custodial service duties.
7   Possess an attitude that makes for harmonious cooperation with students and with the administrative, educational, and custodial forces.
8   Have an idea of what constitutes good custodial service and of the importance of the service to both the educational work of the school and the protection of the school property.
9   Have an appreciation of beauty, harmony, and cleanliness throughout the school grounds.

MAINTENANCE AND OPERATIONAL RESPONSIBILITIES OF THE CUSTODIAL STAFF

The school principal has the right to expect his/her custodial force will perform the duties listed below. They are presented in two groups. The first category deals with tasks related to the maintenance of the school building. The second group includes routine operational responsibilities subdivided into three classifications—a) daily operations, b) weekly operations, and c) periodic operations. The principal should hold the custodian responsible for the performance of each of these tasks.

A. Maintenance responsibilities:[5]

1   Replace broken door and window glass.
2   Make minor repairs to locks, hinges, door closers, etc.
3   Repair and adjust faulty window shades.
4   Keep stair handrails tightly in place.
5   Make minor repairs to students' and teachers' lockers.
6   Replace faulty lamps, bulbs, light switches, etc.
7   Keep all firefighting equipment securely in place.
8   Maintain paper towels, soap dispensers, and toilet paper racks.

9   Maintain students and teachers furniture.
10 Report minor repairs needing to be performed on the various heating and plumbing equipment to the director of facilities or principal.
11 Make minor repairs to playground equipment.
12 Repair or replace pencil sharpeners as needed.
13 Lubricate heating and ventilating fixtures.
14 Paint rusting and corroding metal surfaces with inhibitors in small areas. Report large-scale rusting or corrosion to the principal.
15 Fix minor water leak problems and report major leaks to the principal or director of facilities.

B. Operational responsibilities

1   Daily operations

   a Display the flag as weather permits.
   b Clean and dust all classroom areas.
   c Clean and dust all administrative areas.
   d Clean and dust all stairway and corridor areas.
   e Clean and service all restroom areas.
   f Clean whiteboards.
   g Service all entrances, walks, and drives as weather permits.
   h Clean and service physical education and auditorium areas.
   i Inspect and service playground equipment.
   j Dispose of trash, waste, and recyclable items.
   k Clean and care for custodial rooms, supplies, etc.
   l Clean drinking fountains.

2   Weekly Operations

   a Clean or dust doors and window glass.
   b Spot clean soiled floor and wall areas.
   c Clean restroom walls, doors, and partitions.
   d Polish floor areas as assigned or scheduled.
   e Clean inside glass as assigned or scheduled.
   f Clean furniture as assigned or scheduled.

3   Periodic Operations

   a Clean, finish, and polish floor areas.
   b Clean window glass inside and outside.
   c Clean or dust window shades.
   d Clean ceilings, walls, bulletin boards, and trim.
   e Clean lighting and heating fixtures.
   f Care for yard and ground area.
   g Inspect and clean storage areas.
   h Replace furnace filters on a scheduled basis.
   i Attend to custodial maintenance functions listed under section A.

TIME STANDARDS, SCHEDULING, AND DESCRIPTION
OF THE CUSTODIAL DUTIES

The general duties of the custodial force were listed in outline form in the preceding section. No reference was made to the allocation of these tasks among the custodial workforce or to the operational features of a care and maintenance program for a given school building. In order to accomplish this task, it is necessary to make a job analysis of the individual custodial tasks together with the time required to complete each one of them.

Time Standards for Selected Custodial Tasks

It is helpful to both the principal and the head custodian to know how much time is routinely required to complete a number of specific custodial tasks. It is also important to establish the frequency with which these jobs must be repeated in maintaining a high level of custodial services. Table 15.2 contains a list of jobs normally performed by most custodians assigned to a school building. It also includes the frequency of each task and the time normally required to perform it.

Normal Custodial Work Load

The time standards and frequency with which each task is to be repeated form the basis for determining a reasonable work load for the custodian. In developing a custodial work schedule, it should be remembered that the time standards listed in table 15.2 do not include preparation time.

For example, the time required to mop and rinse a 900-square-foot classroom is 40 minutes. Additional task start-up time is required by the custodian to fill the water bucket, add detergent to it, place the container with the cleaning agent back on the shelf, locate the mop, and carry these materials from the custodial closet to the class-room. The time standard of 40 minutes does not include the time necessary for the custodian to return to the custodial closet, clean the mop(s), dispose of the dirty water, and rinse out the buckets. Depending upon the location of the custodial closet with respect to the classroom, the additional time required could easily be 10 percent higher than the standards would indicate.

It should also be borne in mind that it may take the custodian time to reach the cus-todial closet from some other part of the building. Thus, the time standards should be used judiciously. They serve only as the starting points. The other conditions related to each task should be taken into account and the time requirement should be adjusted accordingly.

Normal Custodial Work Schedule

The schedule of work for each custodian should be structured so that it interferes minimally with the educational function. Custodial tasks are dovetailed with the instructional uses of the building. For example, classrooms can be dusted and swept

Table 15.2.   Time Normally Required to Complete Selected Custodial Tasks

Task	Frequency	Time Required
Classroom (Assumed area of 900 square feet)		
a) Dusting	Daily	5 min. per rm.
b) Sweeping	Daily	12 min. per rm.
c) Damp mopping	As needed	23 min. per rm.
d) Wet mop and rinse	As needed	40 min. per rm.
e) Machine scrubbing	As needed	25 min. per rm.
f) Machine Polishing	As needed	15 min. per rm.
g) Wet vacuum pickup	As needed	14 min. per rm.
Servicing classroom	Daily	15 min. per rm.
a) Remove waste paper		
b) Sweeping floor with treated mop		
c) Dusting marker board rails, window sills, etc.		
d) Closing windows and adjusting shades		
e) Adjusting temperature controls		
f) Making note of needed repairs		
Servicing men's lavatory	Daily	35 min. per lav.
Servicing women's lavatory	Daily	38 min. per lav.
Lavatory area		
a) Cleaning lavatory	Daily	1 min. per fixture
b) Cleaning toilet bowl and seat	Daily	1 min. per fixture
c) Cleaning urinals	Daily	2 min. per fixture
d) Cleaning urinal trap	Weekly	2 min. per fixture
e) Cleaning wash sink	Daily	2 min. per fixture
f) Mopping toilet floors	Daily	2 min. per 100 sq.ft.
Stairways		
a) Damp mopping	Weekly	4 min. per flight
b) Sweeping	Twice daily	6 min. per flight
Other		
a) Cleaning drinking fountains	Daily	1 min. per fixture
b) Dusting fluorescent tubes	Twice Weekly	12 tubes per min.
c) Sweeping auditorium	Daily	15 min. per 1,000 sq.ft.
d) Sweeping corridors	Twice Daily	8 min. per 1,000 sq.ft.
e) Sweeping gymnasium floor	Daily	5 min. per 1,000 sq.ft.
f) Washing glass	As needed	1 min. per 10 sq.ft.
g) Buffing and reconditioning plastic-finished	As needed	50 min. per 1,000 sq.ft.
floors	6–9 months	90 min. per 1,000 sq.ft.
h) Machine scrubbing traffic areas	Every 6 months	100 min. per 1,000 sq.ft.
1. Light-soil areas	Every 3 months	110 min. per 1,000 sq.ft.
2. Medium-soil areas	As needed	20 min. per 1,000 sq.ft.
3. Heavy-soil areas		
i) Refinishing floors (waxless finish)		

before school, after school, and when they are not in use during the school day. For this reason, some school systems stagger the hours on which the custodians report for work. In general, most of the custodians are on duty at the close of the school day when the bulk of the cleaning tasks can be accomplished.

Barker Harrison has developed a sample daily schedule that could be adapted in many school buildings.[6] This applies to a school building employing a head custodian and two assistants. This building would house 20 to 25 secondary school teachers and serves between 550 and 600 students. The schedule also depends upon the grades housed in the building.

The sample schedule is presented in table 15.3. This schedule applies to a relatively small school building where all custodial staff are employed during the day. In some of the larger schools, this schedule might have to be changed substantially if night crews are hired to perform some of the work listed in the sample schedule. Regardless of the time when each member of the custodial staff reports for work, however, it is essential that each person be scheduled for his/her eight-hour shift.

Preventive Maintenance Program

School boards are often not aware of the potential savings that could accrue to a school district by instituting a well-defined plan of preventive maintenance. Over an extended period of time, it is economically advantageous to avoid the complete breakdown of mechanical equipment and the serious deterioration of the physical elements of a school building. It is far better, for example, to repair hairline cracks on the exterior surface of the roof when it is barely visible and is still harmless, than it would be to do it later.

In time, the extreme changes in temperature, and the repeated melting and freezing of ice, can enlarge the crack to such an extent that water can seep into the building and discolor ceiling tiles in a classroom directly below the deteriorated roof. Under these conditions, the lack of preventive maintenance could subject the school district to the cost of replacing a classroom ceiling at best, and the possible replacement of some of the sheet rock walls as well.

Developing a Preventive Maintenance Plan

The creation of an effective (five to ten year) plan of preventive maintenance is highly technical. It is not something that can be delegated to the school principal or head custodian. The central administrative staff should take an active role in the development of such a plan. Except in a very large school district, the necessary expertise will not be available to create a maintenance prevention plan. The accomplishment of this task requires the talents of an architect, a mechanical engineer, heating and plumbing engineer, an electrical engineer, and a structural engineer. These services should be secured by the school district on a per diem basis.

When a new building is being planned and constructed, the architectural firm can supply these services gratis or at a nominal fee because each expert has worked on this school and they are intimately familiar with all of the materials and systems included in the new building. Although the breadth of the talents required to produce a maintenance prevention plan is wide, the amount of time required by each expert is quite minimal.

Table 15.3.   A Sample Custodial Schedule

Time	Custodian	Helper	Maid
7:00–7:30	Raise flag Open building Checking heating/cooling systems Check fire bells Check building		
7:30–8:00	Dust all classrooms, principal's and secretary's offices, library, and any other room to be used during the day	Same	Same
8:00–10:00	Sweep sidewalks Check with office Install glass if needed Check heating/cooling systems Make minor repairs	Wash sweeping mops	Begin dusting corridors
10:00–10:30	High School Check all toilet rooms—see that all fixtures are flushed Ensure proper ventilation Pick up paper from floor Replenish towels, paper, and hand soap as needed Elementary School Same as High School but completed immediately following the morning recess	Same	Same
10:30–11:00	Check heating/cooling systems Check with office Walk building to check for needed repairs	Return to dusting and cleaning in halls	Same
11:00–12:00	Check toilet rooms Shake out doormats	Lunch	Check drinking fountains and wash sinks (clean and replenish soap and towels)
12:00–1:00	Lunch	Brush and pick up papers in corridors Clean sweeping brooms and mops	Lunch
1:00–1:30	All toilet rooms—same as 10:00–10:30	Same	Same
1:30–2:40	Check drinking fountains and wash sinks Dispose of paper and rubbish collected during the day Clean some inside door glass and any writing from walls (In High School, right after noon recess)		

(Continued)

Table 15.3.   (Continued)

Time	Custodian	Helper	Maid
2:40–3:00	Ready equipment and materials for afternoon cleaning	Same	Same
3:00–5:00	Sweep all classrooms and halls	Same	Same
	Clean all toilets	Classrooms ____,	Same
	Mop toilet floors	____, ____ (10 in	
	Carry out trash and paper	all) with halls and	
	Empty pencil sharpeners	other areas and	
	Head Custodian begin checking behind help so entire building is checked prior to day's end	two toilets	
	Secure building		
	Take down flag		

Each expert should be able to list the items requiring preventive maintenance in a given situation within a period of one or two days. The basic question to each one of these experts should be, "What should I do on a regularly scheduled program to extend the life of each piece of major mechanical equipment, and to preserve the physical properties and function of the building itself?"

Once the plan is developed, it is the responsibility of the building principal to implement it. The head custodian or their assistant(s) are required to perform all of the work called for in the preventive maintenance program. The principal should hold the head custodian accountable for the proper execution of the plan.

The success of this program depends largely upon the commitment of the building principal to it. If he/she carefully supervises the work of the custodians and maintains some form of check on whether or not certain work has been performed, the success of the plan is assured. And with such success, the school district can reap rich financial rewards in the form of reduced cost of school building maintenance.

Implementing the Preventive Maintenance Plan

In any prescribed maintenance program, the list of tasks to be performed is described in detail. The frequency and nature of the work are clearly stated. The materials to be used are specified in considerable depth. The manner in which the work is to be accomplished is expressed in simple language.

It is suggested that the head custodian develop a reliable system for accomplishing all of the required work (along with a check and balance sheet). He/she may wish to record each task to be performed on a card. This may include a description of the task and the tools and materials to be used. These cards may well serve as a "tickler file" or a reminder to the custodian as to when the task should be completed.

He/she should note on the card the date of the next time when the work is required and file all of the cards chronologically by date, starting with the current date. In this way, the custodian will know at a glance what needs to be completed within a given month, week, or day. Once the work is completed, he or she can record what was done on the back of the card. The principal should scan through these cards from time to time to assure that the preventive maintenance program in the building is effective and in full operation. He or she may also wish to compare the work described on the card with that stated in the preventive maintenance plan versus viewing the actual work as developed under the auspices of the central administration.

The maintenance plan described in the preceding paragraphs can be made more cost-effective through the use of a district-wide computerized database management system. In addition to providing a list of items needing preventive maintenance at certain specified times, a computerized building file can generate a wide variety of up-to-the-minute reports on matters related to the maintenance and operation of the building. A district-wide system can project maintenance costs within specified categories and allocate such costs to each educational facility in the school district.

The system could generate current information on the inventory and rate of consumption of supply items. It can provide an up-to-date list of student-station utilization factors for each instructional space in the school district. In view of these benefits, it is suggested that the implementation of a computerized database management system be considered for the maintenance and operation of educational facilities on a district-wide basis. According to Borowski, "The installation of a space and equipment inventory system improves the use of resources and offers a wealth of information for the management of these resources."[7]

DISCUSSION QUESTIONS

1   There are currently several rules of thumb for computing the number of custodians required in a given school. Briefly review each of these.
2   Define a "teaching station." What is the equivalent square footage for a regular classroom?
3   Discuss seven of the ten qualifications desired when hiring a school custodian.
4   Review the role of the principal in the operation and maintenance of the school building(s). Does the custodian report to more than the principal and, if so, who is that other person? Provide an example of when the shared responsibility could occur.

NOTES

1. O. Barker Harrison, *Suggested Methods for Custodians for the Routine Care of Schools* (Nashville, TN: Yearwood and Johnson, 1973).

2. Thomas E. Glass, "Planned Maintenance Programs: A Memorandum to Facility Officers," *CEFP Journal* (May–June 1984), p. 13.

3. Harrison, *Suggested Methods for Custodians*, p. 55.

4. Ibid., p. 56.

5. Ibid., p. 159.

6. Ibid., p. 131.

7. Paul D. Borowski, "Maintaining a Computerized Building File," *CEFP Journal* (September–October 1984), p. 18.

Appendix I

Bond Timeline Example

_____ SCHOOL DISTRICT #___
(_____ County)

Timeline for
August 29, 2017 Bond Levy Election

April 20, 2017   Regular school board meeting to receive recommendation from the Citizens' Taskforce Committee on a proposed bond scope

May 1–13, 2017   Random telephone survey conducted of 400 registered voters

June 15, 2017   Regular school board meeting to approve of a bond levy resolution for an Aug. 29, 2017, election, for Attorney and Fiscal Agent agreements

June–August 2017 Citizen's ad hoc committee meetings (*held off of the MSD grounds*)

July 7, 2017   Finalization of the bond election brochure (to mail out to box holders)

July 10, 2017   Last day to supply wording and a resolution to the county clerk for a bond election for the Aug. 29, 2017, election. (Sec. 34–106, Idaho Code)

July 28, 2017   County clerk to mail absentee ballots out for the Aug. 29, 2017, election to voters who have requested absentee ballots. (Sec. 34–308, Idaho Code)

July 30, 2017   Last day for county commissioners to designate polling places prior to Aug. 29, 2017, election. (Sec. 34–302, Idaho Code)

Aug. 4, 2017   Last day to pre-register to vote with the County Clerk until 5 p.m. for the Aug. 29, 2017, election. Election day registrations will still be available. (Sec. 34–408, Idaho Code)

Aug. 14, 2017   Last day to begin "Early Voting" for the Aug. 29, 2017, election for the county who conducts it. (Sec. 34 1012, Idaho Code)

Aug. 17, 2017   First notice of election is published for the Aug. 29, 2017, election by the county clerk in the official newspaper of the county. Published in at least two newspapers within that county. (Sec. 34–602 and 34–1406, Idaho Code)

Aug. 17, 2017   **Last day for the county clerk to receive written requests for the purpose of authorizing persons to act as challengers at the polling places for the Aug. 29, 2017, election.** (Sec. 34–304, Idaho Code)

Aug. 18, 2017   Last day for an application for a mail-in absentee ballot to be received by the county clerk (no later than 5 p.m.) for the Aug. 29, 2017, bond election. (Sec. 34–1002, Idaho Code)

Aug. 24, 2017   Second notice of election for the Aug. 29, 2017, election is published by the county clerk in the official newspaper(s) of the county. Facsimile sample ballot published at this time by the _____ **Sch. Dist.** (Sec. 34–602, 34–1406, and 34–2425, Idaho Code and Secretary of State)

Aug. 25, 2017   Last day for in-person absentee voting (until 5 p.m.) for the Aug. 29, 2017, bond election at the county election office. (Sec. 34–1002, Idaho Code)

Aug. 29, 2017   Last day to return absentee ballots to the county clerk's election office (by 8 p.m.) for the Aug. 29, 2017, election. (Sec. 34–1005, Idaho Code)

Aug. 29, 2017   Election day [8 a.m. to 8 p.m.] voting at all polling locations. (Sec. 34–106 and 34–1101, Idaho Code)

Sept. 8, 2017   **Last day for the Board of County Commissioners to meet and canvass the vote for the Aug. 29, 2017, election.** (Sec. 34–1410, Idaho Code)

Sept. 15, 2017   **County clerk to issue certificate of election to the school district for the Aug. 29, 2017, bond election.** (Sec. 34–1410, Idaho Code)

Sept. 21, 2017   Regular school board meeting to approve and accept election results from the Aug. 29, 2017, election (if bond levy is approved).

Sept. 28, 2017   Last day for an elector to contest the past August 29, 2017, bond election. (Sec. 34–2008 Idaho Code)

From the desk of Dr. R. H. Bauscher

Appendix II

Bond Brochure

ABOUT VOTING

WHO? All registered voters in the _____ School District. Anyone not registered may do so by completing the Idaho voter registration form -- on or before Feb. 17th. Or, you can still register at your polling place during election hours on March 14th. Bring your **ID** & a **proof of residence**.

WHEN? Tuesday - March 14, 2017
8 a.m. to 8 p.m.

WHERE? Vote at the *same* location where you have in the immediate past elections:

_____ *County Voters*
♦ American Legion Hall [126 S. 2[nd]_____]]
♦ County Extension Office [238 8th Av. _____]

_____ *County Voters*
♦ Lions Clubhouse

ABSENTEE VOTING? If you will be gone during voting hours on **Tuesday March 14th** and qualify as an elector, you may request to vote absentee (by mail) beginning **Friday, February 10th** and ending at 5 p.m. on **Friday, March 10th**.
To vote absentee -- complete the County application form and send it to the respective County Election's Clerk to receive your _____ SD ballot in the mail.

_____ SCHOOL DISTRICT #____

School Bond Election

273

FINANCIAL FACTS

This school bond proposal will pay for the design, construction labor, materials, permits, fees, equipment and all other necessary project costs. The total bond cost is $13.5 million and it will amortize over 25 years or less, which in today's bond market will ensure a very competitive interest rate at historically low interest rates.

Passage of this bond would add to the existing bonds -- yet it will **NOT increase our current levy rates**, rather we would continue the levy rates currently being paid. The _____ School District would also qualify to receive approximately $3.1 million of subsidy payments from the State of Idaho's School Bond Levy Equalization Program. These State payments will cover a significant portion of the interest cost for the local taxpayers.

If you are a senior citizen, disabled person or widow/widower with an adjusted gross income of $29,640 or less per year, you may file a circuit breaker property tax exemption with the county assessor's offices, which could reduce your property taxes by as much as $1,320 annually.

FURTHER TAX INFORMATION

Annual S.D. Levy Rates (per $1,000 assessed value):

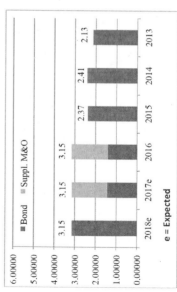

■ Bond	■ Suppl. M&O

2018e | 2017e | 2016 | 2015 | 2014 | 2013
3.15 | 3.15 | 3.15 | 2.37 | 2.41 | 2.13

e = Expected

BUILDING PROGRAM

The _____ School Board, District Admin. and various Staff members have studied the District's present and future facility needs. Currently many of the students are walking over to attend classes 6-7 times per day. This MS addition onto the end of the HS will improve student safety practices as well as adding to the instructional time for the MS students.

The School Board commissioned a random telephone survey consisting of a 13% sampling of the 1,600 registered voters.

The results revealed that the majority of the respondents favored:
- Adding a new middle school building attached to the current high school – with 13 new classrooms
- Adding a new library attached to the current high school
- Adding a new physical education/gym attached to the current HS
- Doing some minor renovations to improve the current HS
- Adding a covered walkway between the elementary and cafeteria
- Paving of various parking lots and associated school access roads

School Board Members:

Committee Chairs:

Comparable Total S.D. Tax Rates (per $1,000 assessed value):

	Estimated FY2017 w/new bond	Current FY2016	Past FY2015
S.D. #1	$5.91	$6.09	$4.46
S.D. #2	$5.82	$5.82	$5.82
S.D. #3	$4.95	$5.25	$4.94
S.D. #4	$4.72	$4.72	$2.49
S.D. #5	$4.48	$4.35	$4.23
S.D. #6	$4.18	$4.18	$4.60
S.D. #7	$3.20	$4.73	$5.26
S.D. #8	$3.16	$3.16	$2.37

Index

Page references for figures are *italicized*.

About the Authors

Dr. Richard Bauscher   has been a school superintendent for twenty-three years, as well as serving as an assistant superintendent in Washington, a principal and an athletic director in Idaho. He spent eight years as a full-time educational consultant working with architect firms, school districts, state departments, and other state agencies in the northwestern states of Idaho, Montana, Oregon, Utah, and Washington. Bauscher has currently assisted sixty-three school districts (1990–2017) in passing their levies with a 90 percent success rate (sixty-three of seventy levies have passed) with an average passage rate of 73.9 percent. He has been involved for fifteen years with the assessment of school facilities, as well as thirty years with many school construction projects including new buildings, remodels, additions, and their respective designs. Bauscher is currently an associate professor in the Educational Leadership Department for the University of Idaho, and he remains as an educational consultant with his Facility Planners firm.

Dr. E. Michael Poe   has been an administrator for thirty-five years in a variety of settings including middle school, high school, and university levels. He has been involved with numerous school construction projects, including new buildings, remodels, and additions. Poe is currently a professor and the program director for Educational Leadership at Northwest Nazarene University in Nampa, Idaho.